Activism and Digital Culture in Australia

Debbie Rodan is Associate Professor in Media & Cultural Studies at Edith Cowan University, Western Australia, and author of *Identity and Justice: Conflicts, Contradictions and Contingencies* (2004), and co-author of *Disability, Obesity and Ageing: Popular Media Identifications* (with Katie Ellis & Pia Lebeck, 2014). Her research interests include identity and attitude construction as well as the engagement of digital media for social change, and her work has been published in various national and international academic journals and book chapters both individually and in collaboration with Jane Mummery.

Jane Mummery is a Senior Lecturer in Philosophy at Federation University Australia. She is the author of *The Post to Come: An Outline of Post-Metaphysical Ethics* (2005), of *Understanding Feminism* (with Peta Bowden, 2009), and *Radicalizing Democracy for the Twenty-first Century* (2017). Her research interests include the ethical and political dimensions of everyday life, and her collaboration with Debbie Rodan has resulted in numerous journal articles and book chapters examining the possibilities for identity construction, deliberation and social change within participatory and social media.

Media, Culture and Communication in Asia-Pacific Societies

The Asia-Pacific region houses some of the richest and most diverse cultural, media and social practices in the world, with much of it yet to be analysed or uncovered. At the same time, there is a growing scholarly interest in understanding the breadth and depth of culture and media/communication practices in Asian societies. The aim of this series is to support this quest by enabling high-quality accessible and emergent scholarship on culture, media and communication in the Asia-Pacific to be published. It showcases innovative research produced in the region to a global readership with an eye to generating dialogue that will spark new ideas and enhance social and cultural understandings.

Series Editors:

Terence Lee, Associate Professor, Communication & Media Studies at Murdoch University, Australia

Susan Leong, Research Fellow, School of Media, Culture and Creative Arts, Curtin University, Australia

Titles in the Series:

Media Power in Indonesia: Oligarchs, Citizens and the Digital Revolution, by Ross Tapsell

Activism and Digital Culture in Australia, by Debbie Rodan and Jane Mummery

Willing Collaborators: Foreign Partners in Chinese Media, edited by Michael Keane, Brian Yecies and Terry Flew (forthcoming)

The Tastes and Politics of Inter-Cultural Food in Australia, by Sukhmani Khorana (forthcoming)

Activism and Digital Culture in Australia

Debbie Rodan and Jane Mummery

ROWMAN &
LITTLEFIELD
INTERNATIONAL
London • New York

Published by Rowman & Littlefield International Ltd
Unit A, Whitacre Mews, 26-34 Stannary Street, London SE11 4AB
www.rowmaninternational.com

Rowman & Littlefield International Ltd. is an affiliate of Rowman & Littlefield
4501 Forbes Boulevard, Suite 200, Lanham, Maryland 20706, USA
With additional offices in Boulder, New York, Toronto (Canada), and Plymouth (UK)
www.rowman.com

British Library Cataloguing in Publication Data
A catalogue record for this book is available from the British Library

ISBN: HB 978-1-7834-8944-2
PB 978-1-7834-8945-9

Library of Congress Cataloging-in-Publication Data
Names: Rodan, Debbie, 1956– author.
Title: Activism and digital culture in Australia / Debbie Rodan and Jane Mummery.
Description: Lanham : Rowman & Littlefield International, 2017. | Series: Media, culture, and communication in Asia-Pacific societies
Identifiers: LCCN 2017034726 (print) | LCCN 2017038176 (ebook) | ISBN 9781783489466 (electronic) | ISBN 9781783489442 (cloth : alk. paper)
Subjects: LCSH: Political participation—Technological innovations—Australia. | Blogs—Political aspects—Australia. | Social movements—Australia. | Digital media—Australia.
Classification: LCC JQ4029.A8 (ebook) | LCC JQ4029.A8 M86 2017 (print) | DDC 322.40285/4678—dc23
LC record available at https://lccn.loc.gov/2017034726

∞™ The paper used in this publication meets the minimum requirements of American National Standard for Information Sciences—Permanence of Paper for Printed Library Materials, ANSI/NISO Z39.48–1992.

Printed in the United States of America

Contents

Acknowledgements

As is the case for every author with every book, we are indebted to and thankful for the contributions and support offered us by colleagues, friends and family, as well as by our series' editors and Rowman & Littlefield's excellent staff. In particular, we would like to thank Terence Lee, Susan Leong, Marnie Nolton, Martina O'Sullivan, Kate Poynter, David Smyth, Holly Tyler and Michael Watson for all of their varied assistance in getting this book from a rather vague concept to reality. Without their help and support – and expectations that this project be finished in a timely manner – this book would still be in nascent form.

Chapter 1

Digital Culture, Activism and Social Movements in Australia

In 2010, protests and civil war broke out across the Middle East, and social media played a significant role in raising global awareness of the events dubbed the Arab Spring (Faris, 2011; Faris & Meier, 2013). The Paris terrorist attacks in 2015 saw social media used as a mechanism to show global support and empathy. For example, in the days following the January attack on the publication *Charlie Hebdo*, the hashtag #JeSuisCharlie spread across social media and at the time was named one of the most popular hashtags in Twitter history, with more than 5 million uses. The second incident, which took place in November – in this instance a coordinated attack by gunmen and suicide bombers – also saw social media users expressing their support and compassion for Parisians, this time with the hashtag #PrayForParis which was used more than 7 million times. In the United States, #BlackLivesMatter was tweeted 9 million times in just 2015, and over 30 million times by September 2016, with the hashtag becoming a social calling card for social justice and racial equality activists across not only the United States but globally. Taking a different form, the 'It Gets Better Project' – created by media personality Dan Savage and his husband, Terry Miller, in response to an increase in suicides in the United States by teens bullied because of their sexual orientation – is a video campaign to let LGBT youth know that life does indeed 'get better'. This project began when Savage and Miller uploaded the first 'It Gets Better' video on the campaign's official YouTube page on 21 September 2010. This video has since been viewed more than 2 million times. Since then, more than 50,000 video entries have been uploaded from around the world on the campaign's website, receiving more than 50 million views as of January 2017. The 'It Gets Better Project' continues to engage the community – both online and in person (via conferences, pride festivals and government outreach) – to rally for LGBT rights and equality on six continents.

In just the first weeks of January 2017, in Australia, we have between us received multiple digital updates from activist organisations we follow. We have also undertaken a range of actions using digital media tools, including donating to causes, signing campaign petitions, sending emails to politicians and other decision-making bodies, forwarding issue and campaign information through social media ourselves and using apps to support ethical consumption practices. For many of us, digital media is how we do activism in the everyday. We might not be carrying out distributed denial of service attacks – a tactic that involves sending so many requests to a target website that it crashes, described by some hacktivists as a kind of virtual 'sit-in' (see Sauter, 2014) – to draw attention to specific inequities, and we might not be physically chained to a tree or a bulldozer or holding a sign in a physical protest, but our 'clicktivism' is still activist action. Or is it? Has the ubiquity and convenience of digital technologies within the lives of many of us watered down our sense of what it means to take action? Is signing an online petition and sharing it with our friends in social media anything like the activism of earlier decades? Marching in a PRIDE protest in the 1980s and 1990s in Australia carried with it real physical dangers although it also gave rise to strong senses of solidarity; participating in the blockade protesting the proposed damming of the Franklin River in Tasmania carried with it a real chance of imprisonment (1,217 arrests were made, many simply for being present at the blockade, and nearly 500 people were imprisoned for breaking the terms of their bail) and again facilitated that strong sense of being part of a community. A similar situation prevailed during the 2016 and 2017 protests in Perth in Western Australia against the extending of a major highway through wetlands. Participating in a physical sense in any long-term protest also carries with it other material effects such as loss of income. Signing and sharing an online petition or carrying out other online actions rarely carries with it the same kinds of material effects as non-virtual activism. This is the sense in which Shonda Rhimes (2014) stated, in her invited 2014 Commencement Speech for Dartmouth College, that 'A hashtag is not helping', continuing with:

> Hashtags are very pretty on Twitter. I love them. I will hashtag myself into next week. But a hashtag is not a movement. A hashtag does not make you Dr. King. A hashtag does not change anything. It's a hashtag. It's you, sitting on your butt, typing on your computer and then going back to binge-watching your favorite show.

And yet, perhaps this is to forget that there always have been many components essential for an activist action to be successful, with two of these being communication and visibility. One person standing in protest simply does not have the same impact as 100, let alone 1,000. What about a 10,000- or 100,000-strong petition delivered to the relevant authority? In this context, international activist organisations such as AVAAZ – launched in 2007 – can work effectively on the global scale only due to digital media technologies. With 44,672,981 members spread throughout 194 countries (as of April 2017), it is only through the temporal and spatial compressions made possible by digital technologies that AVAAZ's (2016) online community has the capacity to

> act like a megaphone to call attention to new issues; a lightning rod to channel broad public concern into a specific, targeted campaign; a fire truck to rush an effective response to a sudden, urgent emergency; and a stem cell that grows into whatever form of advocacy or work is best suited to meet an urgent need.

In particular, AVAAZ operates according to a model of tipping point moments – what AVAAZ's founder, Ricken Patel, calls 'crisistunity' (as cited in Cadwalladr, 2013) – collecting public support of causes but only delivering it when a massive, global public outcry has the potential to make a significant difference. Digital media technologies make this work – and this timing – possible, as they did the coordination of the protests of the Arab Spring. They facilitate consciousness raising in a massively extended mode to that practised in earlier decades where you, in effect, had to be in the right place at the right time. Rather than needing to have your street and house leafletted – and reading the leaflet before it was thrown out – or passing a notice or being stopped on the street and invited to attend a meeting, the vast interconnected networks of digital media with their multiplicity of hubs and nodes through which information is circulated and recirculated mean that we can become aware of, give our support to and share causes with much less need of serendipity, and without the need to be physically present. In particular, they facilitate our engagement in issues we feel strongly about regardless of geographical distance.

This, then, is the context and focus of this book, to explore and examine – within the Australian context – the affordances of digital culture for activist organisations and advocates for social change. More specifically, this book introduces readers to the historical and theoretical framings and interconnections of activism, advocacy and digital cultures – and some of their points of tension – while illuminating these points with rich issues-based Australian case studies of activist take-ups of digital cultures, tools and platforms. Of particular interest is how digital cultures offer productive mechanisms and spaces for not only the reshaping of citizens into activists but also the achievement of progressive social change, through their explicit facilitation of both deliberative and affective models of popular citizen engagement. These possibilities and examples are pursued through chapters 2–6, with each one exploring a different facet of digital culture, action and activism, and examining it against the work of specific Australian activist organisations, collectives, causes and campaigns. The final chapter, chapter 7, then reframes these discussions in the broader context of digital activism, comparing and contrasting insights from the preceding chapters with regard to some of the main technological affordances and constraints that inform digital culture. This leaves the work of this current chapter, chapter 1. In the following pages, setting the scene for the rest of the book, we pursue three overlapping objectives. The first objective is to introduce readers to some of the key fields and debates informing the contexts and practices of digital activism, including ideas and (theoretical and practical) expectations regarding conventional models of activism and social movements. The second objective is to provide the reader with some background regarding the emergence, practice and make-up of digital culture and digital activism. The third objective in this chapter is to introduce a range of the productive tensions that we hope will resonate throughout the book: tensions between activism, participatory citizenship, consumerism, neoliberalism and tensions concerning the engagement of identities in activism. Understanding the operation of these tensions is, we suggest, imperative for understanding how digital culture can build a constructive nexus among (a) individual engagement, participation and deliberation; (b) collective action and effective activism; and (c) long-lasting social change.

ACTIVISM AND SOCIAL MOVEMENTS

Social movement theory defines a social movement as a sustained conscious effort to bring about social change through extra-institutional means (Goodwin & Jasper, 2003; Wrenn, 2012). A social movement is thus usually expected to be organised, to at least some extent, to possess change-oriented goals and some degree of continuity. Although social movements were once conventionally framed with regard to collective behaviour focusing more on what we typically consider to be Marxist concerns such as resource mobilisation, breakdowns in the social order mainly as a result of class differences, workers' rights and economic issues within organisations, as well as state and society (Buechler, 2011; Diani, 1992; Laclau & Mouffe, 2001; Touraine, 2002; Wieviorka, 2005), newer social movements tend to focus more on the production of collective identity, networks and the messy make-up of movements for social change (Melucci, 1980; Touraine, 2002). Newer ideas then have recognised that social movement activism should more generally be conceived of as encompassing those 'socially shared activities and beliefs' which can be 'directed toward the demand for change in some aspect of the social order' (Gusfield, 1970, p. 2). Such activism thus tends to be issues driven. This, of course, means that different social movements may diverge in their causes and tactics to the point that some movements arguably undercut the focus of others (e.g., the deliberate use of sexist promotional strategies by some animal rights organisations). Activism, in its turn, is generally understood as meaning the taking of action 'to effect social change' (Permanent Culture Now, 2013) – where this action may go beyond what is considered routine or conventional, and where this social change may or may not be framed by a recognised social movement – with activists being those committed to advancing a substantive political or social goal or outcome (Levine & Nierras, 2007). Of particular importance is that this work is usually understood to be a result of scarce or no funding in state-based institutional responses to identified systemic sociopolitical problems or inequities.

This aspect needs some clarification. Because activism is typically understood as action that goes beyond conventional politics, social movements and activists more generally exist in complex relationships with state-based political institutions (keeping in mind that the boundary between activism and conventional politics is always fuzzy and dependent on context). Extending the points made in the previous paragraph, this is to say, first, that activists are typically targeting issues that are either considered not recognised or being inadequately addressed by the state – climate change being one very topical example of such an issue. Second, activism is typically undertaken by those with less power, for the simple reason that those with positions of power and influence can usually accomplish their aims using conventional means. A third feature is that because activist action may take forms outside of state-recognised political processes, it may be framed by the state as disruptive of or threatening to state power. Here current state-based framings of some animal rights and environmental activist actions in the United States and Australia, for instance, as 'terrorist' are exemplary. The fourth feature is that social movements and activism, at least since the 1970s, tend to be oriented towards specific issues – themselves typically framed in terms of inequities and justice – rather than working to re-envisage (or take over) state power as such (Fuchs, 2006; Lummis, 1996). Certainly activists may be striving for change in certain state-based policies or practices, but this is a far cry from the aim of taking state power (as was arguably the case with early Marxist-inspired social movements). At the same time, however, and fifth, much of the social change–oriented work of social movements and activists – if, that is, framed by progressive goals informed by the principles of equality and justice – tends to be described as informed by ideals of democratisation (Martin, 2009; Mummery, 2017). More specifically, newer social movements and activists – through their calls for a collective challenging of inequities and better address of unmet needs (Piven, 2006; Reisch, 2005) – tend to present themselves as engaging democratic principles in their critique of sociopolitical society and can be understood furthermore as striving generally for the engagement 'of active citizens in a participatory politics' (Breines, 1982).

This latter principle is a central concept for examining the work of social movements and activism. Insofar as the work of social movements and activists falls outside of the usual frames for political action recognised by the state, it needs to be understood as voluntary in important ways. We suggest, in turn, that this voluntariness highlights the connections between the work of social movements and activists and what could be called participatory citizenship, which we would define – with the help of van Deth (2014) – as intentional and voluntary activity by citizens which is not limited to targeting government politics and is indeed more often directed at the sociopolitical system with the aim of 'solving collective or community problems' (van Deth, 2014, p. 358). In both cases what matters is active engagement in community issues, where this is based on the democratic belief that the involvement of citizens in the tackling of community issues makes for better citizens, better decisions and better government (Avritzer, 2002; Cohen & Sabel, 1997; Gaventa, 2004; Mansbridge, 1999). What is also important is that action is collective, in this instance meaning that it is undertaken by individuals or groups for a collective purpose, such as the challenging or addressing of a specific community issue or the advancement of a specific idea or ideology (Postmes & Brunsting, 2002). More specifically, this is the idea that individuals commit to coordinating their efforts to secure a common goal that would be impossible to obtain on an individual basis (Bimber, Flanagin & Stohl, 2005).

These are fundamental points insofar as the crucial test in the cases of both social movements and an activist cause more generally is always whether its ideological framing can successfully recruit and mobilise (potential) members to actually struggle for social change. Participation, in other words, matters; it is the overarching drive in all activism. This, however, is ideally a matter not just of a potential member taking up an activist role in the sense of performing a cause-inspired action but of coming to conceive of oneself in terms of the cause. This is the idea that 'individuals participate in protest because doing so stems from their understanding of who they are, both as individuals and as part of a collectivity' (Einwohner, 2002, p. 255). Activist participation, then, is about identification. So conceived, for an individual to identify as a member of a social movement, or an activist for a cause, he or she must have come to align his or her personal identity with the movement's collective identity (Snow & McAdam, 2000). In other words, the individual has to form 'a cognitive, moral, and emotional connection' with the movement's broader community (Poletta & Jasper, 2001, p. 285); it is only this identification that facilitates mobilisation and action (Hunt & Benford, 2004; Jasper & Poulsen, 1995; McAdam, 1994; Melucci, 1994, 2013). Collective action, in other words, represents both an enactment of identity and the strengthening of relationality, and it is on this basis Diani (1992, pp. 1–2) comes to define social movements as 'networks of informal interactions between a plurality of individuals, groups and/or organizations, engaged in political or cultural conflicts, on the basis of shared collective identities'.

The final issue we wish to consider here concerns typical assumptions concerning effective activist action. As has already been noted, it is clearly important that action be collective for it to have traction. This has been understood, as discussed earlier, as requiring individuals to identify with the causes for action, itself premised on the individual's recognition of connectedness with the cause community. Here the long-standing belief is not only that participants in the work of social movement and activist organisations are usually recruited through pre-existing social ties but that further mobilisation is more likely when members and potential members are linked by social ties – and shared world views – than when they are not (see, e.g., Diani, 1992; Oberschall, 1973; Tilly, 1978). In their discussion of social movements and networks, Krinsky and Crossley (2014) claim that the ways in which a network works and the effects it has depend on the strength of the interactions between members of the movement. This makes the development and maintenance of a sense of community between activists and potential activists – clearly also important for the effectiveness of the communications that are needed to facilitate any possible mobilisation – at least as important as the group's actual strategic planning of actions. In addition, activist action has long been framed as needing to be visible to be effective. These are all communicative problems, and, as Bimber, Flanagin and Stohl (2005) have stressed, collective action – although we might just as well say activist action – always includes (a) identifying and connecting people who share a common private interest(s) in a public good; (b) communicating messages to these people; and (c) coordinating, integrating or synchronising individuals' contributions. It is with these points in mind that we turn to consider the communicative and participatory vehicles provided to activists by the development of the Internet and the manifold digital technologies associated with Web 2.0.

THE RISE OF PARTICIPATORY DIGITAL CULTURES

The history of the development of the Internet has been traced elsewhere in detail (Clarke, 2004; Ryan, 2010); of significance here are only a few key points. First was the development of the World Wide Web, which connected multi-media sources with a single web interface. Second was its development as a 'networked environment' not only through communications between web browsers and web servers being always two way (Hinton & Hjorth,

2013, pp. 9, 10) but also with the development of hypertext. Hyperlinks were particularly significant for their capacity to interlink 'multiple digital media sources' – images, audio, video and other media – in an 'easy-to-use interface' (Hinton & Hjorth, 2013, p. 11; cf. Lievrouw, 2011). They thus allow users to follow an extensive and highly contingent path of successive linking. This architecture and its affordances were in turn key to the development of what has become known as Web 2.0, which prioritised – initially just from a commercial perspective – ideas of participation and collective intelligence through the facilitation and promotion of such methods as tagging, viral marketing and the peer to peer (p2p) mechanisms driving open source developments (O'Reilly, 2005).

Of the main features of Web 2.0, however, it has first and foremost been identified as a space in which all users have the capacity to produce and distribute content (Hinton & Hjorth, 2013). Although Internet content production was certainly possible prior to the roll-out of Web 2.0, users had to possess a relatively high level of skills. With Web 2.0 the technical aspects of content production and distribution began to be managed by software, thereby eliminating virtually all technical barriers to the creation, production and distribution of content. In addition, it is presented as being distinctive in its affordances of 'real-time' connectivity, interaction and social networking (Cammaerts, 2015; Fotopoulou, 2016). In many ways it is these features that have seen Web 2.0 framed as a new technical infrastructure, which has changed the way communicative networks are developed, populated and distributed (Munster & Murphie, 2009). In other words, Web 2.0 can be primarily framed in terms of *doing* words: users app, blog, map, mash, geocache, tag, wiki, search, share, shop and socialise. This last set of features is seen as particularly significant. Hinton and Hjorth (2013, p. 19) contend that Web 2.0 affordances allow users to experience 'new forms of affective sharing' and of community construction and belonging. John (2012) further suggests that even the concept of 'sharing' takes on new meanings through Internet services (such as Facebook and Flickr) founded on user-generated content. Most broadly the idea is that because Web 2.0 applications enable users to participate, post and share user-generated content easily, they, as a consequence, network and build communities with each other.

Manuel Castells's (2012) ideas regarding what he calls horizontal networks provide a toolbox with which to unpack Web 2.0 practices of increased participation. As he has stated,

> In our time, multimodal, digital networks of horizontal communication are the fastest and most autonomous, interactive, reprogrammable and self-expanding means of communication in history. (2012, p. 15)

These means of communication, as he and others have explained – drawing specific attention to the convergence of the Internet with the development of wireless networks and mobile technologies – enable a many-to-many model of communication. Previously individuals were most likely to be subjected to institutions transmitting in a vertical one-to-many style. This new communication model has in turn been understood as facilitating the emergence of new kinds of highly fluid communities and networks that themselves tend to low levels of vertical and hierarchical structuration, remaining, as such, open and participatory (Mercea, 2012). This is Castells's global 'web of horizontal communication networks' (2007, p. 246). Castells (2007, pp. 246–247) also notes two innovations that have enabled the development and growing interaction of multiple horizontal networks: (a) low-powered FM radio stations, and decreasing costs for the production and distribution of video, vlogs, podcasts, wikis and blogging; and (b) the low technical requirements and costs of sharing through p2p, as well as the associated ongoing developments in social media software programs. These are issues that will be shown to hold particular importance as we discuss activists' resource development (see chapter 4 in particular).

All of this has built what can arguably be called a culture of participation. Indeed Web 2.0 is seen as the quintessential online space harnessing participation (O'Reilly, 2005; Wu Song, 2010) insofar as all participants are not just users but also producers of information and knowledge, now talked about as 'produsers' (Bruns, 2005). Produsers, as Axel Bruns further describes them, are not to be framed by the traditional forms and practices of content production, being instead involved in 'produsage – the collaborative and continuous building and extending of existing content in pursuit of further improvement' (2006, p. 2). As he goes on to explain these practices (see pp. 3–4), what matters is that content production is user-led, the result of not just a collaborative process but one that is iterative, palimpsestic and evolutionary, facilitated by what he has called 'heterarchical' (as in operating neither as a leaderless anarchy nor via strongly hierarchical organisational traits; see p. 4) and permeable community structures, and requisite of a rethinking of the norms of intellectual property. This, then, is content that rather than being created and published – and owned – by individuals is continuously modified by all users in a participatory and collaborative fashion (a useful example here would be the development of Wikipedia entries). Developments in social media platforms – including applications such as blogging, Facebook, LinkedIn, Twitter, YouTube, Flickr and Instagram – have also facilitated this growth of produsage. Typified, as Castells had also noted, by 'many-to-many information sharing', social media should themselves be conceived of as 'network media' insofar as they enable material to be instantly created, uploaded and shared through the Internet (Poore, 2014, pp. 3–4). Social media platforms, in other words, need to be understood in three distinct ways: as a 'technical system', a 'system of opportunity' and a 'system of empowerment for its users' (Gillespie, as cited in Meikle, 2016).

It is certainly the case that with its applications having been expanded in such a way as to explicitly facilitate online creation and participation as well as collaboration – making all easy for everyday (prod)users (Tatarchevskiy, 2011) – the rise of social media in particular has seen increased participation in blogging and online communities and forums, as well as social networking. Indeed a social media–informed culture is fundamentally horizontally connected, comprised of a broad range of 'participatory practices', which include creating, appropriating, remixing and recirculating content (Jenkins, Ford & Green, 2013, p. 71). Also of particular interest, as Meikle (2016) has stressed, is the capacity of social media – also explicable via its commitment to produsage – to connect the private with the public, as he puts it, drawing attention to four main elements of social media: (1) personal communication is key; (2) users have profile accounts (and are called to update them regularly); (3) public media communications converge with personalised messages; and (4) sharing is both fundamental and ubiquitous. This is to see social media platforms such as Facebook, YouTube and Twitter as databases that are not only 'networked' but as such intermix '*public with personal communication*' (Meikle, 2016, p. 6). This, as Papacharissi (2010) has argued, means that such platforms have introduced and normalised a space in which the boundaries between the public and the private have become fuzzy, claiming that this imprecision opens up new possibilities for community and identity construction. Or, in Gregg's terms, such platforms have facilitated what she calls a 'presence bleed', where 'boundaries between personal and professional identities' and practices 'no longer apply' (2011, p. 2).

SOCIAL MEDIA AND ACTIVISM

Although, as noted previously, Web 2.0 development was initially framed as a commercial enterprise, and still operates as such in a multiplicity of ways (an issue whose impacts for activism towards social change will be considered throughout this book), the kinds of participatory cultures it has generated are not constitutively 'synonymous' with these business practices (Jenkins et al., 2013, p. 36). Indeed, as Castells has pointed out, the kinds of horizontal networks constitutive of a participatory networked culture show the capacity for 'counterpower' (2007, p. 258, 2012). This is to say that these networks can provide 'the essential platform for debate' for what may be called counterpublics (see Warner, 2002); they provide an effective 'means of acting on people's minds', ultimately serving as a potent political weapon (Castells, 2007, p. 250). Developments in social media have, in other words, also facilitated the growth of social networks especially for activist movements and organisations, allowing them to serve their own 'constituencies' (Rucht,

2013, p. 255) as well as extend their reach beyond their 'already consolidated support base' (Akin, Encina, Restivo, Schwartz & Tyagi, 2012, p. 94). Clay Shirky (2011), in particular, has argued that social media need to be understood as a crucial tool for the effective coordination of political movements: enabling low-cost coordination of actions and the sharing of information both within and across publics, while also facilitating ongoing dialogue through which participants can further develop their own political views. This is to say that because content can be shared across multiple networks – and easily shared again by any single network participant – activist activities in social media sites are constitutively generative, feeding and stimulating engagements well beyond the networks directly connected with the organisation. Indeed the global reach of such networks noticeably increases the amount of publicity received by an activist campaign (Youmans & York, 2012). More specifically, social media platforms – operating in such multiple roles as a 'high-volume website', 'broadcast platform', 'media archive' and a 'social network' (Burgess & Green, 2009, p. 5) – enable activists to carry out a range of actions. They can use them to promote campaigns, provide a feedback loop for campaigns, find out who is identifying with their messages, identify new campaign message recipients and build a content database. This last point is worth stressing given that both Internet web pages and social media platforms can operate as archival spaces in which activists can store campaign videos, multimedia testimonials, celebrity endorsements, hyperlinks, achievements and media releases, as well as records of public–private sentiments about campaign issues. Supporters and potential new recruits – that is, the activist groups' constituents – can access and share this material multiple times.

Bennett and Segerberg (2012) further examine the use of social media in relation to large-scale activist movements. In their analyses of global protests such as Occupy and Arab Spring, they distinguish between two ends: the idea of collective action (considered to be by them as more important to traditional social movements and based on a desire for what they call 'collective identifications') and what they term 'connective action'. The latter they see as based on large-scale 'personalized collective action' essentially organised through social media and not requiring the same levels of collective identifications (Bennett & Segerberg, 2012, p. 760). Of this latter form of action, they identify two key elements: (a) the 'personal action frames', which cover the various reasons as to why individuals might contest and work towards changing a state of affairs; and (b) the use of 'personal technologies' (e.g., YouTube, Twitter, Facebook or email), which enable the large-scale sharing of reasons for change (Bennett & Segerberg, 2012, pp. 744–745). As they note, it is the 'network mode' of social media that enables individuals to share 'grievances' broadly in what are 'very personalized accounts' (p. 742). The key point is that connective action networks can be mobilised without requiring the collective identity framing which social movements traditionally worked hard to develop; they only need to engage the network of 'weak ties' which make up an individual's social media network (p. 744). These weak ties should be considered significant for two reasons. First, it is the very weakness of connective action ties and networks that allows content to move quickly and broadly via trending topics and to go viral, keeping campaigns and messages at the top of news feeds (Poell & van Dijck, 2015). Second, they allow activists and social movements to not only facilitate the growth of their social networks and the sharing of ideas through social media but retain their organisation's brand identity in the background (Bennett & Segerberg, 2012, p. 757). As a consequence, while the campaign is trending and going viral, the activist group is raising their brand identity; however, once the limelight dims, the weak ties fall away.

A growing number of empirical studies show that activists are using social media towards numerous ends. For instance, in the case of Occupy Gainsville, social media platforms were used by activists to 'notify people of "real-time events" such as actions and arrests' as well as to inform participants about the instances of 'police brutality' (Sbicca & Perdue, 2014, p. 322). Researchers to date have studied activists' use of platforms such as Facebook, YouTube and Twitter, as well as email, with recent studies showing that certain platforms are most useful for specific kinds of actions and activism. Many studies, for example, point to social media platforms such as Facebook, YouTube and Twitter as playing major roles in sharing and spreading information, organising protests and mobilising individuals to participate in protests (cf. Enjolras, Steen-Johnsen & Wollebaek, 2012; Lindgren & Lundström, 2011; Sbicca & Perdue, 2014; Uldam & Askanius, 2013; Warren, Sulaiman & Jaafar, 2014). Some of the specific utilities for activists of these main platforms – Facebook, Twitter and YouTube, as well as email – are examined here, first with a focus on the affordances of specific platforms and then with regard to the general shared capacities of the platforms.

Platforms

Although the majority of our focus here is to do with social media platforms, it is worth briefly mentioning the affordances of standard websites for activist campaigning. Not only a database and an archive for multimedia content, websites also act as hubs for activist and broader community members. They can thus not only act as a repository for cause and campaign information but link visitors to other sites and organisations, as well as the organisation's own associated social media sites and sites for digital action. In addition, having a website can allow smaller and fringe organisations to compete with larger players as website development carries relatively low costs and web-based models of communication are cheap and efficient in reaching a large audience. In a similar vein, the general lack of editorial control on the World Wide Web also means that grassroots activist organisations have the potential to reach a much greater audience via their website than through traditional broadcast media forms (Oostveen, 2010).

Facebook, according to Poell (2014), has a crucial role in the planning and coordination stages of an activist campaign. It has also been argued – insofar as Facebook activity is typically constructed from an individualised and personal perspective, and users are encouraged to reconstruct their 'offline' lives and relationships on the platform via profile and status updates – that Facebook attracts 'fans' and provides an effective mechanism for the distribution of motivational and mobilising content (Ryan, Jeffreys, Ellowitz & Ryczek, 2013). In their study of Norway's Rose Marches – solidarity rallies, the largest since the Second World War, in remembrance of the seventy-six victims of bomb and gun attacks by a right-wing fanatic in 2011 – Enjolras et al. (2012) found that Facebook was a leading source of information about where demonstrations were being held. Their study of the Rose Marches revealed that Facebook has 'an independent effect on mobilization', which supplements already-established civil society campaign (2012, p. 902). As well as effective content distribution, Facebook arguably displays an individual's commitment to a cause. Raising awareness about a campaign through *liking* on Facebook – or even through changes to one's profile image – may appear to be a trivial act, but studies have shown that this can itself be considered a political action (Theocharis, 2015; Vie, 2014). For instance, Sumner, Ruge-Jones and Alcorn's (2017, p. 8) small study of Facebook's Like button revealed that when communicating 'content-related messages' Like tended to mean 'endorsement, agreement, amusement, or interest'. Here the idea is that pressing Like for a campaign – in front of one's broader Facebook network – can show that the individual identifies with that group and is sending a solid message of support for the campaign.

Platforms such as the microblogging platform Twitter have conversely been found to be 'highly significant' in circulating, facilitating and disseminating news (Enjolras et al., 2012, p. 899; also see Lindgren & Lundström, 2011). Twitter features – including retweeting which promotes broad dissemination of campaign messages, trending topics which raise the profile of the campaign, the breaking of *real-time* news more rapidly than mainstream news and public participation in reporting (Poell, 2014) – have meant that Twitter is often used for cause and campaign advertising (Ryan et al., 2013), 'triggering, organising, facilitating and accelerating' actions, 'broadcasting' and, in some cases, motivating (Kharroub & Bas, 2016, p. 1976). Lindgren and Lundström (2011) found, for instance, in their study of the Twitter campaign #wikileaks that tweets were typically used to circulate information (including published news items), share knowledge and call for donations. Twitter users, what is more, employed tweets to 'defend free speech and free press' by tweeting political and philosophical sayings (Lindgren & Lundström, 2011, p. 1006). Other tweets might be disseminated to facilitate the formulation of collective identities and communities by constructing 'the identity of the political enemy' (p. 15). Relatedly – in their study of three movements (Occupy Wall Street, Indignados and Aganaktismenoi) across three countries (Spain, Greece and the United States) – Theocharis, Lowe, van Deth and García-Albacete (2015) found that Twitter was mainly used for 'the distribution of information' and for 'conversational messages' (pp. 212–214).

YouTube as a user-generated video site can also provide several useful elements for activists. These include embedded links; a repository for (activist) videos and protest evidence – especially of police response and violence; the enhancement of the visual spectacle of activist events; the capacity to raise revenue through targeted advertising; and the ability to 'draw large numbers of users to the video it hosts' (Poell, 2014, p. 724). Some studies also conclude that YouTube can be valuable for producing and disseminating information before an event (Uldam & Askanius, 2013) – for instance, YouTube videos can be circulated globally to alert potential participants about an issue – but as it is not a content producer as such it is not considered a useful tool for organising a protest (Poell, 2014). Other studies, particularly of human rights activism, also found that video is a form of 'strategic witnessing' and is also useful for mobilising, generating visibility and building collective identities (Ristovska, 2016, p. 1036; also see Uldam & Askanius, 2013). As Cammaerts (2015, p. 6) points out, social media tools such as YouTube can be used as a tactic of counter-surveillance or 'sousveillance' (cf. Mann, Nolan & Wellman, 2003) – that is, hand-held cameras and mobile video devices can be used for the counter-surveillance of police, authoritarian regimes and industry (these issues are considered further in chapter 4).

Finally, literature on online activism also points out that email is an excellent vehicle for fast, efficient and inexpensive one-to-many communication (Osler & Hollis, 2001; Ward, Gibson & Lusoli, 2003). In Meikle's words: 'If there is a killer app for Internet politics, then it's email' (2002, p. 14). Email is part of the activist's cyber-toolkit, as Wall (2007) calls it, able to educate and mobilise movement participants by easily and quickly providing information updates, as well as easing logistical communication tasks. These capacities of email and mailing lists for activism have been borne out in Oostveen's (2010) study of an anti-e-voting campaign – 'Wij vertrouwen stemcomputers niet' ('We do not trust voting computers') – carried out in the Netherlands in 2006. As she found, email was used in five different ways by this activist group throughout the campaign: (a) as a way to distribute newsletters to citizens, journalists, government minsters and the vendors of the Dutch voting computers; (b) a distribution mechanism for press releases sent to specific journalists and the mainstream media; (c) as informing both a discussion mailing list used to 'stimulate debate' between subscribed members (neither subscription nor messages were moderated) and (d) an internal crew mailing list used to 'debate strategy and tactics' as well as facilitate decision-making, divide up the campaign work and maintain the group's commitment; and, finally, (e) as the basis for a general information mailing list through which the general public could contact the group with any questions or comments (pp. 800–808). As Oostveen found, although there was no formal organisation regarding how these emails were answered – they were answered by whoever in the group felt most capable of providing a good response, meaning that sometimes queries received multiple independent responses – this last tactic proved particularly productive. Although it took up a substantial amount of time, activists found the direct communication with members of the public useful for several reasons. By having to answer a lot of enquiries and explain the objectives of the campaign repeatedly, the activists were able to refine their own arguments and viewpoint. These emails also proved to include some original tactical advice and provide a feedback mechanism on strategic decisions made by the activists. In addition, in responding to almost all of this incoming email, the group established an approachable open image, which arguably also contributed to the success of the campaign. Finally, the provision and maintenance of this general information mailing list worked to connect potential and only loosely affiliated members more strongly with the campaign. As Oostveen (p. 815) noted regarding this matter, the 'positive experience of sending emails to a grassroots campaign and getting serious feedback can increase the sense of internal efficacy for supporters'.

Issues of Visibility

Social movements and activist groups prior to the Internet and the rise of digital participatory media relied mainly on the mass and mainstream media to spread their campaign, to attract supporters and to make their campaign visible (Poell & van Dijck, 2015; Rucht, 2004). However, because the mass media has a tendency to focus more on spectacle and acts of violence – and because it is a domain often highly moderated by institutional interests – the campaigns and actions of activists could be distorted, sensationalised and trivialised (Bennett & Segerberg, 2011; Uldam & Askanius, 2013). In either of these cases, the reach and significance of campaign messages was limited. The brief examinations earlier have made clear that for activists digital platforms fulfil several uses. The attraction of digital media platforms and tools for activists lies in (a) their communicative capacities – including their capacities to make issues, campaigns and proposed actions highly visible to a broad audience; (b) their capacities to attract people into committing to these issues, campaigns and actions; and finally (c) their capacities to facilitate the organisation of campaigns and actions. What these technologies expedite in particular is the mass circulation and recirculation of symbols, the development, in other words, of memes and the possibility of viral uptake. Of course, as we have noted previously, although Internet memes are highly effective in quickly raising awareness of an issue, they and other *trending* topics can be problematic for activist campaigning insofar as their operation means that users are constantly steered towards new topics. As Poell and van Dijck (2015, p. 531) have commented, 'Twitter algorithmically privileges breaking news and viral content dissemination'. This tendency is exacerbated when campaign supporters have only a weak connection or commitment to that campaign or group, often the case with social media–based supporters with whom a momentary commitment can easily give way to the next trend (Cammaerts, 2015; Poell & van Dijck, 2015).

One possible counter to this tendency rests in the multimedia capacities of these platforms, specifically their capacity to disseminate visual information, in the form of both images and video. This is important because it is well recognised that 'emotionally arousing images' are highly effective in drawing a response from viewers and facilitating participation in some form of collective action (as cited in Kharroub & Bas, 2016, p. 1977). Indeed, as will be demonstrated throughout this book, most social movements and activist groups use visuals as a 'tactical strategy' (Carty & Onyett, 2006, p. 237). Visuals, after all, can provide a compelling record of events to not just inform viewers but encourage their support (Ryan et al., 2013). Further, they interpellate viewers in a variety of ways, facilitating not just public debate but solidarity and mobilisation, which is the main aim for any activist campaigns. Indeed, while visual culture and non-governmental politics might be presumed to refer to two distinct realms – with the former somehow encoding and representing the latter – the two, in activism, need to be understood as mutually imbricated (McLagan & McKee, 2012, p. 9). Visuals make things public; they are an integral part of 'the relational processes through which particular relations of social power are reinscribed as issues of political concern and concrete transformation' (McLagan & McKee, pp. 9–10). Importantly, however, what matters for activism is not simply the image but its dissemination and proliferation, what McLagan and McKee have called the 'image complex' (p. 12). By this they mean the following: it is not only the image but the 'channels of circulation along which cultural forms travel; it is also the nature of the campaigns that frame them; it is the discursive platforms that display and encode them in specific truth modes'; and finally it is 'the imbrication of aesthetic form, medial practice, and political intent into one assemblage' (p. 12). Given this outline of the mutual entanglements of aesthetics, mediation and political movements, the various affordances of social media are particularly significant.

TENSIONS

There are, of course, tensions problematising these ideas that activism has moved effectively into the online domain. These concern not just Rhimes's (2014) point – mentioned at the beginning of this chapter – that a hashtag does not by itself change anything, but broader issues to do with the modern neoliberal era of consumerism and commercialism. These issues will be considered later and throughout subsequent chapters. To begin with is the long-standing debate concerning the efficacy of digital activism itself which operates between two major positions. First is the view that the digital technologies we have been talking about so far do offer productive vehicles for activism, more specifically, that the networked nature of Web 2.0 applications, in particular social media, as well as the explosion of users worldwide, provides activists with unprecedented tools to communicate their ideas, mobilise supporters and take action outside established hierarchical power structures. As de Ville (2013) notes:

> With their built-in feature allowing many-to-many communication, social media have revolutionised the way information is produced and shared: everyone is encouraged to participate, share opinions, pictures and videos on issues that they care about or witness and instantly upload them from their smartphone on the Internet. Institutions and individuals that represent public authority are now under constant citizen scrutiny. They know that any abuse, any mistake can spark online retaliation and take proportions that are hard to control. Many cyberactivists and academics see in digital networks a new source of power that will eventually force the ruling elite around the world to become more transparent, accountable and favour human rights and democracy.

Under this perspective, not only can digital technologies dramatically increase communication, but they can facilitate the building – as Roberts (2014, p. 177) puts it with reference to the Occupy movement – of 'people's assemblies' so as to 'empower member and not leaders'. This is an important point; under this perspective there is no need to see digital activism as a 'new species of social movement' (Castells, 2012, p. 5), although some have argued this point (see Jenkins et al., 2013; Shirky, 2011). Rather the view can simply be that digital technologies have enabled more efficient ways of carrying out such activist tasks as sharing and disseminating information, mobilising supporters, campaigning on a range of platforms and publicising this campaigning, fostering the building of collective identities, reaping resources and achieving efficiencies, connecting activists, mapping trending issues and linking to transnational movements (Hara & Huang, 2011; Rodan & Mummery, 2016).

Second are the opposing positions evident in several views. For starters there is the perspective, introduced earlier, that the (weak) networks that inform much digital activism are just not strong enough to facilitate social change. Weak ties based on an individual's response to trending issues, as noted earlier, tend to fall away as quickly as they were formed. This is Gladwell's point too in his famous 2010 article in *The New Yorker*, 'Small change: Why the revolution will not be tweeted', where he argued that the strong ties of offline relationships are significantly more effective than the weak tie relationships of near strangers who collaborate online. Furthermore, many of the actions facilitated through digital activism are, as Rhimes (2014) has insisted, 'short on useful action' (Gladwell, as cited in Shirky, 2011, p. 38). Here the view is that activities limited to the Internet such as clicking Like or Share, or signing electronic petitions – activities often summed up disparagingly as *clicktivism* or *slacktivism* – are simply 'less impressive to large publics and political decision makers than offline protests' (Rucht, 2013, p. 260). Under this view, because offline protests require people's time, resources and energy, they are considered to demonstrate more personal investment and belief (Gladwell, 2010; Rucht, 2004, 2013). A related view is to recognise the significance of digital technologies for some activist purposes – specifically communications and campaign visibility – while still arguing that activist groups still need to maintain face-to-face contact for the building of trust and collective identities and for the sustaining of long-term campaigning (Couldry, 2015). This is to say that while the 'Internet may facilitate the traditional forms of protest such as rallies, demonstrations, and collections of signatures . . . it will hardly replace these forms' (van de Donk, Loader, Nixon & Rucht, 2004, p. 18). Such a view may also take the form of seeing the online and offline realms as interdependent in activism, with online strategies targeting or supporting offline activities and vice versa (Bimber, 2000; Kneip & Niesyto, 2007; Van Laer & Van Aelst, 2009). As Van Laer and Van Aelst put it, activist groups now, after all, 'almost never use just one single tactic, but instead draw on a myriad of tactics both offline and online' (2009, p. 6). Our case studies in the subsequent chapter will bear witness to their claim.

A different critical perspective is expressed by Roberts (2014) and Sauter (2014), who both argue that the extensive surveillance, privatisation and securitisation typical of digital technologies must be recognised as problematic for activist struggles. Evgeny Morozov (2011), in turn, has proposed an authoritarian trinity of digital technology: censorship, surveillance and propaganda. As Sauter notes, 'There is nowhere online for an activist to stand with her friends and her sign' (2014, p. 4) – or at least while there may be places to stand, there are few chances of being read (except by the already like-minded), and many chances of running afoul of corporate and state interests. Sauter (p. 4) continues: 'Because of the densely intertwined nature of property and speech in the online space, unwelcome acts of collective protest become also acts of trespass'. Part of this issue is the basic point that while digital technologies clearly do dramatically enhance the communicative capacities of activist groups, they also similarly enhance the effectiveness of state surveillance, allowing governments and other bodies to monitor communications, disable access for certain users and even track dissidents (Akin et al., 2012; Couldry, 2015). These are issues we address in some detail in chapter 4.

A further critique is that the commercial disposition of social media platforms makes them 'technologically and commercially antithetical to community formation' (Poell & van Dijck, 2015, p. 534). Youmans and York (2012, p. 317) elaborate that there is a 'mismatch between the commercial logic of platforms' and the desire of activists to use platforms to broadcast information to the public. Facebook and YouTube, for instance, raise revenue through personalised advertising (Poell, 2014, p. 725; cf. Morrison, 2014), whereas Twitter raises revenue by selling the 'real-time character of the platform' (p. 723). YouTube is 'entirely funded by advertising' (Allen, as cited in Gillespie, 2010, p. 353), and the platform consistently looks to make a profit from commercial media and user-generated videos. Hence, as Couldry (2015, p. 621) points out, although social networking sites are 'the place where "we" come together', platforms are in fact motivated to 'sell the data-based value' which derives from these sites. This is to say that these platforms so often used by activists are actually only 'public' spaces as far as their corporate owners allow. As Internet commentator Ethan Zuckerman (2010) has thus noted, 'Hosting your political movements on YouTube is a little like trying to hold a rally in a shopping mall. It looks like public space, but it's not – it's a private space, and your use of it is governed by an agreement that works harder to protect YouTube's fiscal viability than to protect your rights of free speech'. This is also the reminder that because social media platforms were designed to appeal broadly to a range of users and advertisers – they were not designed for activist aims – changes to the platform rules and infrastructure have the potential to impact negatively on activist campaigning (Youmans & York, 2012, p. 317).

These are tensions problematising some of the more optimistic assumptions and ideals regarding the capacities of digital activism, but there are also tensions undercutting some of the broader ideals of activism itself, which need to be noted. Here the primary issue concerns whether activism – indeed any form of solidarity – can be taken seriously in today's neoliberally inflected world. Although it has been used to refer to all, some or some combination of ideology, theory, policy prescriptions, processes and practices, neoliberalism can broadly be understood as referring to 'a theory of political economic practices that proposes that human well-being' – in both individual and collective senses – can be best supported and 'advanced by liberating individual entrepreneurial freedoms and skills within an institutional framework characterized by strong private property rights, free markets and free trade' (Harvey, 2007, p. 2). With these various objectives gaining in global traction from the late twentieth century, their effects have been diverse and pervasive, but what is indubitable is that through endorsing a market logic across not only economic but political and social contexts – or, better, seeing these contexts as indistinguishable under a market logic – neoliberalism has come to hold the idea that both individual and societal well-being can only ensue from the 'unimpeded private pursuit of individual preferences and interests' (McCluskey, 2003, p. 786).

Under neoliberalism, therefore, given this prevailing assumption that individual freedoms are actually best guaranteed by freedom of market, freedom has come to mean individual strategising, consumer choice and the advocacy of free enterprise. It has been turned 'largely into the desire to consume and invest exclusively in relationships that serve only one's individual interests' (Giroux, 2014; cf. Roberts, 2014). Ideals regarding equality, in turn, have been stripped of their public good focus of reducing inequality in everyday life along with increasing realisable opportunities for all; the ideal of equality has come to point to the (alleged) equal capacity of all – no matter their lived experience – to strive for success. The neoliberal hegemonic norm has indeed become one of denying 'the legitimacy of state responsibility for the quality of life of its citizens' (McLagan & McKee, 2012, p. 11). These points together mean that individuals are personally responsible for empowering themselves to be successful in their work, in their communities and in their social life (Roberts, 2014), to the point that requiring 'assistance and support suggests a lack of enterprise and application' (Laster & Erez, 2000, p. 247; cf. Harvey, 2007). The broader result of this is that individual solutions will tend to be promoted 'over collective solutions' to injustice and inequality (Maddison & Martin, 2010, p. 104). So conceived, then,

> the model neoliberal citizen is one who strategizes for her- or himself among various social, political, and economic options, not one who strives with others to alter or organize these options. A fully realized neoliberal citizenry would be the opposite of public-minded; indeed, it would barely exist as a public. (Brown, 2005, p. 43)

There are two associated problems therefore that social movement and social change activists cannot but have with neoliberal ideology. First, social movements – whether these are protest movements, online activist movements or a combination of both – are by definition 'collective forms of protest or activism that aim to affect some kind of transformation in existing structures of power that have created inequality, injustice, disadvantage, and so on' (Martin, 2015, p. 1). That is, because they rely on individuals identifying – even weakly – with the collective interest and participating in communal activities toward social change, the assumptions and work of social movements and activists are clearly not in alignment with neoliberal assumptions concerning change. Second, relatedly, neoliberalism casts a facade of distrust over the work of social movements and activists. This work is considered unnecessary because the neoliberal attitude is that individuals would actually possess no rights either to challenge market distributions or to claim any distribution of resources other than that produced by the marketplace and their own marketplace activities. It is individual work that is also considered unreasonable in many ways. Because marketplace operation is considered under neoliberalism a matter of neutral, value-free laws (Handler, 2000), this means that the social effects of the marketplace are themselves to be understood as an inevitable rather than constructed order. This means, in turn, that challenging the operation of the marketplace can be seen as intrinsically wrong or nonsensical, and activists can easily become framed as dissidents (a framing becoming increasing typical within Australia).

These issues result in some interesting issues with which activist campaigns must engage. To begin with, the entrenchment of neoliberally inflected thinking means that there can be a disconnect between the activist desire for justice, say, and the neoliberal individual's desire for choice and pleasure (Glickman, 2009; Kozinets & Handelman, 2004). Activists may indeed portray non-activists – aka consumers insofar as neoliberalism has arguably achieved the conversion of 'the practice of citizenship into the art of shopping' (Lapham, 2012) – as 'unaware, hypnotized, selfish, and lazy' and themselves as 'aware, free, altruistic, and mobilized' (Kozinets & Handelman, 2004, p. 702). Under this view, activists recognise that individuals may profess a commitment to a cause but may well be enticed in a different direction by other preferences. Such perceptions further feed into the ideas that social media–inspired connections with activist movements may be inspired more by an awareness of what's trending rather than by any deep commitment to the activist cause. This would thus be an activism positioned by market forces, perhaps to the point that it is no longer activism in any strong sense. Certainly this is the view that has informed the derogation of digital activism as clicktivism or slacktivism.

Also pertinent here is the long-standing activist reliance on mobilising strategies based on emotion and affect. To the extent that neoliberalism has been successful in instilling norms that frame activism as a challenge to a 'fair' economic order – fair because marketplace operation is considered to be neutral – it has also transformed ideals and practices of deliberation concerning the public good. If deliberation is supposed to be reasoned and reasonable (cf. Habermas, 1998), and neoliberalism argues that it is most reasonable to give precedence to the operation of the marketplace, then many activist causes and campaigns become in effect unreasonable. This may be because the causes themselves challenge the precedence of the operation of the marketplace – this, for instance, is often how causes challenging the overriding of non-human animal and environmental interests by economic rationalisation are dismissed – or because campaigns deliberately rely on mobilising strategies based on emotion and affect. This is not a new practice, as noted previously activists have long recognised the importance of emotion for facilitating mobilisation and new forms of cause identification, but arguably the prioritising of emotion-led campaigning has been further exacerbated within the online domain of trends and clicktivism.

These are all issues that will turn up and be addressed repeatedly throughout the following chapters, where the focus will remain on how and to what extent the engagement of digital technologies might advance activist aims and social movements. This includes how participatory activism works within progressive organisations; we extend on this idea in chapter 5. This is, in turn, informed by the broader question as to how digital culture and the use of multi-platform tools might facilitate citizens' engagement, participation and deliberation in social issues, as well as promote subsequent collective action and advance social change. We draw on insights from media studies, cultural studies, social movement studies, social theory and a range of ethical and political perspectives regarding deliberation and ethics, to examine different facets of digital culture in each chapter. Alongside these insights we explore the engagement of both deliberative and affective models of communication by activist campaigning. In totality, then, this book examines how digital culture might be seen to offer productive mechanisms and spaces within the Australian context for shaping interested and involved citizens, public attitudes and society itself to support and facilitate the progression of social change. Our first detailed consideration of these issues takes the form of an examination of politically focused blogging with regard to prevailing assumptions concerning the role of deliberation in promoting active conceptions of citizenship and social change. The context for this discussion in this next chapter will be the work of Indigenous bloggers around issues of reconciliation and indigeneity.

REFERENCES

Akin, A. I., Encina, C., Restivo, M., Schwartz, M. & Tyagi, J. (2012). Old wine in a new cask? Protest cycles in the age of the new social media. *The Whitehead Journal of Diplomacy and International Relations*, *13*(1), 89–103.

AVAAZ. (2016). About us. Retrieved from https://secure.avaaz.org/page/en/about/.

Avritzer, L. (2002). *Democracy and the public space in Latin America*. Princeton, NJ: Princeton University Press.

Bennett, W. L., & Segerberg, A. (2011). Digital media and the personalization of collective action. *Information, Communication & Society*, *14*(6), 770–799.

Bennett, W. L., & Segerberg, A. (2012). The logic of connective action: Digital media and the personalization of contentious politics. *Information, Communication & Society*, *15*(5), 739–768.

Bimber, B. (2000). The study of information technology and civic engagement. *Political Communication*, *17*(4), 239–333.

Bimber, B., Flanagin, A. J. & Stohl, C. (2005). Reconceptualizing collective action in the contemporary media environment. *Communication Theory*, *15*(4), 365–388.

Breines, W. (1982). *Community and organization in the new left: 1962–1968: The great refusal*. New York, NY: Praeger.

Brown, W. (2005). *Edgework: Critical essays on knowledge and politics*. Princeton, NJ: Princeton University Press.

Bruns, A. (2005). *Gatewatching: Collaborative online news production*. New York, NY: Peter Lang.

Bruns, A. (2006). Towards produsage: Futures for user-led content production. In F. Sudweeks, H. Hrachovec & C. Ess (Eds.), *Proceedings Cultural Attitudes towards Communication and Technology* (pp. 275–284). Tartu, Estonia. Retrieved from http://eprints.qut.edu.au.

Buechler, S. M. (2011). *Understanding social movements: Theories from the classical era to the present*. Boulder, CO: Paradigm Publishers.

Burgess, J., & Green, J. (2009). *YouTube online video and participatory culture*. Cambridge, England: Polity Press.

Cadwalladr, C. (2013, November 17). Inside Avaaz – can online activism really change the world? *The Guardian*. Retrieved from https://www.theguardian.com/technology/2013/nov/17/avaaz-online-activism-can-it-change-the-world.

Cammaerts, B. (2015). Social media and activism. *LSE Research Online*. Retrieved from http://eprints.lse.ac.uk/62090/.

Carty, V., & Onyett, J. (2006). Protest, cyberactivism and new social movements: The re-emergence of the peace movement post 9/11. *Social Movement Studies*, *5*(3), 229–249.

Castells, M. (2007). Communication, power and counter-power in the network society. *International Journal of Communication*, *1*, 238–266.

Castells, M. (2012). *Networks of outrage and hope: Social movements in the internet age*. Cambridge and New York, NY: Polity Press.

Clarke, R. (2004). *Origins and nature of the Internet in Australia*. Retrieved from http://www.rogerclarke.com/II/OzI04.html.

Cohen, J., & Sabel, C. (1997). Directly-deliberative polyarchy. *European Law Journal*, *3*(4), 313–342.

Couldry, N. (2015). The myth of 'us': Digital networks, political change and the production of collectivity. *Information, Communication & Society*, *18*(6), 608–626.

De Ville, G. (2013). From optimism to delusion: Cyber-technologies, democracy and surveillance. Re.framing Activism. [Blog post]. Retrieved from http://reframe.sussex.ac.uk/activistmedia/2013/11/from-optimism-to-delusion-cyber-technologies-democracyand-surveillance/.

Diani, M. (1992). The concept of social movement. *Sociological Review*, *40*(1), 1–25.

Einwohner, Rachel L. (2002). Bringing the outsiders in: Opponents' claims and the construction of animal rights activists' identity. *Mobilization: An International Journal*, *7*(3), 253–268.

Enjolras, B., Steen-Johnsen, K. & Wollebaek, D. (2012). Social media and mobilization to offline demonstrations: Transcending participatory divides? *New Media & Society*, *15*(6), 890–908.

Faris, D. (2011). We are all revolutionaries now. In *Social media revolutions: All hype or new reality?* (pp. 4–14). Princeton, NJ: Liechtenstein Institute on Self-Determination, Princeton University. Retrieved http://blogs.roosevelt.edu/dfaris/files/2010/09/social media_2011-11.pdf.

Faris, D., & Meier, P. (2013). Digital activism in authoritarian states. In A. Deliche & J. J. Henderson (Eds.), *The participatory cultures handbook* (pp. 197–205). New York, NY: Routledge.

Fotopoulou, A. (2016). Digital and networked by default? Women's organisations and the social imaginary of networked feminism. *New Media & Society 18*(6), 989–1005.

Fuchs, C. (2006). The self-organization of social movements. *Systemic Practice and Action Research*, *19*(1), 101–137.

Gaventa, J. (2004). Towards participatory governance: Assessing the transformative possibilities. In S. Hickey & G. Mohan (Eds.). *From tyranny to transformation* (pp. 25–41). London, England: Zed Books.

Gillespie, T. (2010). The politics of 'platforms'. *New Media & Society*, *12*(3), 347–364.

Giroux, H. A. (2014, April 26). Neoliberalism's war on democracy. *Truthout*. Retrieved from http://www.truth-out.org/opinion/item/23306-neoliberalisms-war-on-democracy.

Gladwell, M. (2010). Small change: Why the revolution will not be tweeted. *The New Yorker*. Retrieved from http://www.newyorker.com/.

Glickman, L. B. (2009). *Buying power: A history of consumer activism in America*. Chicago, IL: University of Chicago Press.

Goodwin, J., & Jasper, J. M. (Eds.). (2003). *The social movements reader: Cases and concepts*. Hoboken, NJ: Wiley-Blackwell.

Gregg, M. (2011). *Work's intimacy*. London, England: Polity Press.

Gusfield, J. R. (1970). Introduction: A definition of the subject. In J. R. Gusfield (Ed.), *Protest, reform and revolt: A reader in social movements* (pp. 1–8). New York, NY: John Wiley and Sons.

Habermas, J. (1998). *Between facts and norms: Contributions to a discourse theory of law and democracy*. (W. Rehg, Trans.). Cambridge, MA: MIT Press.

Handler, J. F. (2000). The 'third way' or the old way? *University of Kansas Law Review*, *48*, 765–800.

Hara, N., & Huang, B. (2011). Online social movements. *Annual Review of Information Science and Technology*, *45*(1), 489–522.

Harvey, D. (2007). *A brief history of neoliberalism*. Oxford, England: Oxford University Press.

Hinton, S., & Hjorth, L. (2013). *Understanding social media*. London, England: Sage.

Hunt, S. A., & Benford, R. D. (2004). Collective identity, solidarity, and commitment. In D. A. Snow, S. A. Soule & H. Kriesi (Eds.), *The Blackwell companion to social movements* (pp. 433–457). London, England: Blackwell.

Jasper, J. M., & Poulsen, J. (1995). Recruiting strangers and friends: Moral shocks and social networks in animal rights and anti-nuclear protests. *Social Problems*, *42*(4), 493–512.

Jenkins, H., Ford, S. & Green, J. (2013). *Spreadable media*. New York, NY: New York University Press.

John, N. A. (2012). Sharing and Web2.0: The emergence of a keyword. *New Media & Society*, *15*(2), 167–182.

Kharroub, T., & Bas, O. (2016). Social media and protests: An examination of Twitter images of the 2011 Egyptian revolution. *New Media & Society*, *18*(9), 1973–1992.

Kneip, V., & Niesyto, J. (2007, October 5–6). *Interconnectivity in the 'public of publics' – the example of anti-corporate campaigns*. Paper presented at Changing Politics through Digital Networks: The Role of ICTS in the Formation of New Social and Political Actors and Actions, University of Florence, Florence, Italy.

Kozinets, R. V., & Handelman, J. M. (2004). Adversaries of consumption: Consumer movements, activism, and ideology. *Journal of Consumer Research*, *31*(3), 691–704.

Krinsky, J., & Crossley, N. (2014). Social movements and social networks: Introduction. *Social Movement Studies*, *13*(1), 1–21.

Laclau, E., & Mouffe, C. (2001). *Hegemony and socialist strategy: Towards a radical democratic politics* (2nd ed.). London, England: Verso.

Lapham, L. H. (2012, September 20). Feast of fools: How American democracy became the property of a commercial oligarchy. *Truthout*. Retrieved from http://truth-out.org/.

Laster, K., & Erez, E. (2000). The Oprah dilemma: The use and abuse of victims. In D. Chappell & P. Wilson (Eds.), *Crime and criminal justice in Australia: 2000 and beyond* (pp. 240–258). Sydney, Australia: Butterworths.

Levine, P., & Nierras, R. M. (2007). Activists' views of deliberation. *Journal of Public Deliberation*, *3*(1), 1–14.

Lievrouw, L. (2011). *Alternative and activist new media*. Cambridge, England: Polity Press.

Lindgren, S., & Lundström, R. (2011). Pirate culture and hacktivist mobilization: The cultural and social protocols of #Wikileaks on Twitter. *New Media & Society*, *13*(6), 999–1018.

Lummis, C. D. (1996). *Radical democracy*. Ithaca, NY: Cornell University Press.
Maddison, S., & Martin, G. (2010). Introduction to 'surviving neoliberalism: The persistence of Australian social movements'. *Social Movement Studies*, *9*(2), 101–120.
Mann, S., Nolan, J., & Wellman, B. (2003). Sousveillance: Inventing and using wearable computing devices for data collection in surveillance environments. *Surveillance & Society*, *1*(3), 331–355. Retrieved from https://ojs.library.queensu.ca/index.php/surveillance-and-society/article/view/3344.
Mansbridge, J. J. (1999). Everyday talk in the deliberative system. In S. Macedo (Ed.), *Deliberative politics: Essays on democracy and disagreement* (pp. 211–239). Oxford, England: Oxford University Press.
Martin, G. (2015). *Understanding social movements*. Oxon, England: Routledge.
Martin, J. (2009). Post-structuralism, civil society and radical democracy. In A. Little & M. Lloyd (Eds.), *The politics of radical democracy* (pp. 92–111). Edinburgh, Scotland: Edinburgh University Press.
McAdam, D. (1994). Culture and social movements. In E. Laraña, H. Johnston & J. R. Gusfield (Eds.), *New social movements: From ideology to identity* (pp. 36–57). Philadelphia, PA: Temple University Press.
McCluskey, M. T. (2003). Efficiency and social citizenship: Challenging the neoliberal attack on the welfare state. *Indiana Law Journal*, *78*(2), 783–876.
McLagan, M., & McKee, Y. (2012). Introduction. In M. McLagan & Y. McKee (Eds.), *Sensible politics: The visual culture of nongovernmental politics* (pp. 9–26). New York, NY: Zone Books.
Meikle, G. (2002). *Future active: Media activism and the internet*. New York, NY: Routledge/Pluto Press.
Meikle, G. (2016). *Social media: Communication, sharing and visibility*. New York, NY: Routledge.
Melucci, A. (1980). The new social movements: A theoretical approach. *Social Science Information*, *19*, 199–226.
Melucci, A. (1994). A strange kind of newness: What's 'new' in new social movements. In E. Laraña, H. Johnston & J. R. Gusfield (Eds.), *New social movements: From ideology to identity* (pp. 101–132). Philadelphia, PA: Temple University Press.
Melucci, A. (2013). The process of collective identity. In H. Johnston & B. Klandermans (Eds.), *Social movements and culture* (pp. 73–109). Hoboken, NJ: Taylor & Francis.
Mercea, D. (2012). Digital prefigurative participation: The entwinement of online communication and offline participation in protest events. *New Media & Society*, *14*(1), 153–169.
Morozov, E. (2011). *The net delusion: The dark side of internet freedom*. New York, NY: Public Affairs.
Morrison, A. (2014). Facebook and coaxed affordances. In A. Poletti & J. Rak (Eds.), *Identity technologies: Constructing the self online* (pp. 112–131). Madison, WI: University of Wisconsin Press.
Mummery, J. (2017). *Radicalizing democracy for the twenty-first century*. London and New York, NY: Routledge.
Munster, A., & Murphie, A. (2009). Web 2.0 is a doing word. *The Fibreculture Journal*, *14*. Retrieved from http://fourteen.fibreculturejournal.org/.
Oberschall, A. (1973). *Social conflict and social movements*. Englewood Cliffs, NJ: Prentice-Hall.

Oostveen, A. (2010). Citizens and activists. *Information, Communication & Society, 13*(6), 793–819.

O'Reilly, T. (2005). *What is Web2.0: Design patterns and business models for the next generation of software*. Retrieved from http://www.oreilly.com/lpt/a/1.

Osler, F., & Hollis, P. (2001). *The activist's guide to the Internet*. London, England: Prentice Hall.

Papacharissi, Z. A. (2010). *A private sphere: Democracy in a digital age*. Cambridge, England: Polity Press.

Permanent Culture Now. (2013). Introduction to activism. [Bog post]. Retrieved from http://www.permanentculturenow.com/what-is-activism/.

Piven, F. F. (2006). *Challenging authority: How ordinary people change America*. Lanham, MD: Rowman & Littlefield.

Poell, T. (2014). Social media and the transformation of activist communication: Exploring the social media ecology of the 2010 Toronto G20 protests. *Information, Communication & Society, 17*(6), 716–731.

Poell, T., & van Dijck, J. (2015). Social media and activist communication. In C. Atton (Ed.), *The Routledge companion to alternative and community media* (pp. 527–537). London, England: Routledge.

Poletta, F., & Jasper, J. M. (2001). Collective identity and social movements. *Annual Review of Sociology, 27*, 283–305.

Poore, M. (2014). *Studying and researching with social media*. London, England: Sage.

Postmes, T., & Brunsting, S. (2002). Collective action in the age of the Internet: Mass communication and online mobilization. *Social Science Computer Review, 20*(3), 290–301.

Reisch, M. (2005). Radical community organizing. In M. Weil (Ed.), *The handbook of community practice* (pp. 287–304). Thousand Oaks, CA: Sage.

Rhimes, S. (2014). Shonda Rhimes '91, Commencement address.[Speech]. Retrieved from http://www.dartmouth.edu/~commence/news/speeches/2014/rhimes-address.html.

Ristovska, S. (2016). Strategic witnessing in an age of video activism. *Media, Culture & Society, 38*(7), 1034–1047.

Roberts, J. M. (2014). *New media and public activism: Neoliberalism, the state and radical protest in the public sphere*. Bristol, England: Polity Press.

Rodan, D., & Mummery, J. (2016) Doing animal welfare activism everyday: Questions of identity. *Continuum: Journal of Media & Cultural Studies, 30*(4), 381–396.

Rucht, D. (2004). The quadruple 'A': Media strategies of protest movements since the 1960s. In W. van de Donk, B. D. Loader, P. G. Nixon & D. Rucht (Eds.), *Cyberprotest: New media, citizens and social movements* (pp. 29–56). London, England: Routledge.

Rucht, D. (2013). Protest movements and their media usages. In B. Cammaerts, A. Mattoni & P. McCurdy (Eds.), *Mediation and protest movements* (pp. 249–268). Bristol, England: Intellect.

Ryan, C., Jeffreys, K., Ellowitz, T. & Ryczek, J. (2013). Walk, talk, fax or tweet: Reconstructing media-movement interactions through group history telling. In B. Cammaerts, A. Mattoni & P. McCurdy (Eds.), *Mediation and protest movements* (pp. 133–157). Bristol, England: Intellect.

Ryan, J. (2010). *A history of the internet and the digital future*. London, England: Reaktion.

Sauter, M. (2014). *The coming swarm: DdoS actions, hacktivism, and civil disobedience on the internet*. New York, NY: Bloomsbury.

Sbicca, J., & Perdue, R. T. (2014). Protest through presence: Spatial citizenship and identity formation in contestations of neoliberal crisis. *Social Movement Studies, 13*(3), 309–327.

Shirky, C. (2011). The political power of social media: Technology, the public sphere, and political change. *Foreign Affairs*, *90*(1), 28–41. Retrieved from https://www2.warwick.ac.uk/fac/arts/theatre_s/applying/postgraduate/ma-theatre-performance-research/option_modules/th988/schedule/shirky.pdf.

Snow, D. A., & McAdam, D. (2000). Identity work processes in the context of social movements: Clarifying the identity/movement nexus. In S. Stryker, T. J. Owens & R. W. White (Eds.), *Self, identity, and social movements* (pp. 41–67). Minneapolis, MM: University of Minnesota Press.

Sumner, E., Ruge-Jones, L. & Alcorn, D. (2017). A functional approach to the Facebook Like button: An exploration of meaning, interpersonal functionality, and potential alternative response buttons. *New Media & Society*, 1–19. doi:10.1177/1461444817697917.

Tatarchevskiy, T. (2011). The 'popular' culture of internet activism. *New Media & Society*, *13*(2), 297–313.

Theocharis, Y. (2015). The conceptualization of digitally networked participation. *Social Media + Society*, *1*(2), 1–14. doi:10.1177/2056305115610140.

Theocharis, Y., Lowe, W., van Deth, J. W. & García-Albacete, G. (2015). Using Twitter to mobilize protest action: Online mobilization patterns and action repertoires in the Occupy Wall Street, Indignados, and Aganaktismenoi movements. *Information, Communication & Society*, *18*(2), 202–220.

Tilly, C. (1978). *From mobilization to revolution*. Reading, MA: Addison-Wesley Publishing Company.

Touraine, A. (2002). The importance of social movements. *Social Movement Studies*, *1*(1), 89–95.

Uldam, J., & Askanius, T. (2013). Calling for confrontational action in online social media: Video activism as auto-communication. In B. Cammaerts, A. Mattoni & P. McCurdy (Eds.), *Mediation and protest movements* (pp. 159–178). Bristol, England: Intellect.

Van de Donk, W., Loader, B. D., Nixon, P. G. & Rucht, D. (2004). Introduction: Social movements and ICTs. In W. van de Donk, B. D. Loader, P. G. Nixon & D. Rucht (Eds.), *Cyberprotest: New media, citizens and social movements* (pp. 1–22). New York, NY: Routledge.

Van Deth, J. (2014). A conceptual map of political participation. *Acta Politica*, *49*(3), 349–367.

Van Laer, J., & Van Aelst, P. (2009). Cyber protest and civil society: The internet and action repertoires of social movements. In Y. Jewkes & M. Yar (Eds.), *Handbook on internet crime* (pp. 230–254). New York, NY: Willan Publishing.

Vie, S. (2014). In defense of 'slacktivism': The human rights campaign Facebook logo as digital activism. *First Monday, 19*(4–7). Retrieved from http://firstmonday.org/article/view/4961/3868.

Wall, M. (2007). Social movements and email: Expressions of online identity in the globalization protests. *New Media & Society*, *9*(2), 258–277.

Ward, S., Gibson, R. & Lusoli, W. (2003). Online participation and mobilisation in Britain: Hype, hope and reality. *Parliamentary Affairs*, *56*, 652–668.

Warner, M. (2002). *Publics and counterpublics*. Brooklyn, NY: Zone Books.

Warren, A. M., Sulaiman, A. & Jaafar, N. I. (2014). Facebook: The enabler of online civic engagement for activists. *Computers in Human Behavior*, *32*, 284–289.

Wieviorka, M. (2005). After new social movements. *Social Movement Studies*, *4*(1), 1–19.

Wrenn, C. L. (2012). Applying social movement theory to nonhuman rights mobilization and the importance of faction hierarchies. *Peace Studies Journal*, *5*(3), 27–44.

Wu Song, F. (2010). Theorizing Web 2.0. *Information, Communication & Society*, *13*(2), 249–275.

Youmans, W., & York, J. (2012). Social media and the activist toolkit: User agreements, corporate interests, and the information infrastructure of modern social movements. *Journal of Communication*, *62*, 315–329.

Zuckerman, E. (2010, October 1). Public spaces, private infrastructure – open video conference. [Blog post]. Retrieved from http://www.ethanzuckerman.com/blog/2010/10/01/public-spaces-private-infrastructure-open-video-conference/.

Chapter 2

Political Blogging: Can Public Deliberation Realise Activist Aims?

Public deliberation practices involving interested and engaged citizens that aim for equity-driven social change correlate with ideas that are standard practice for democratic societies. It is the ideals of both democratic and much activist politics that these standard arguments stress, namely (a) the facilitating of active citizen participation, (b) the forging (and re-forging) of political consensus and the framework for a desired society via this involvement and (c) the fostering and implementing of public policies that ground not only a productive economy but a healthy society in which all citizens can flourish and realise their potential (Fung & Wright, 2003). These ideals and procedures not only are essential for the robust practice of democracy, but they require a broad promotion and take-up of public deliberation. The point here is that insofar as deliberation stresses the pursuit of reciprocal understanding across those who may hold to different frameworks or ideologies, in due course it helps members of a community determine what issues are of communal concern and what the relevant factors are for a constructive public discussion regarding these issues. Facilitating popular participation, it also helps community members to express the public good they support (Turner, Tomlinson & Pearce, 2006) as well as work towards intermediate goals, such as public action, and, most important, work towards the strengthening of democracy as a whole.

More broadly, since deliberation as a process requires not only the proposition of ideas but listening to and reflecting on the opinions of others – being a form of exchange that accepts the need for the ongoing revision of judgements and preferences – it has also been framed as requiring citizens to be responsive to each other's interests and needs. Citizens also need to be constitutively open to negotiating and renegotiating ideas of the public good. Pellizzoni in fact sums up the benefits of deliberation as its ability to produce better citizens: that is, ones who 'are more informed, active, responsible, open to the arguments of others, cooperative, fair, able to deal with problems, ready to alter their opinions' (2001, p. 66), as well as always striving to make decisions that are attuned to the larger public good. These are all important attributes for the achievement of progressive social change.

It is in this sense that deliberative practice has also been presented as important for activist practice. Not only are the processes of public deliberation often presented in contemporary democracies such as Australia as the only legitimate mode of action for activists (and anyone) to utilise in their attempts to advance a substantive political or social goal or outcome – this aim informing Levine and Nierras's (2007) definition of an activist – but activists too clearly recognise the importance of public debate and deliberation. Hence, as noted in the previous chapter, activists work towards raising public awareness of issues and thereby towards oft-stated goals of achieving a democratic order in which deliberation and the pursuit of common agreement would be able to fairly shape political participation (see Stears, 2013). The trouble is that there are also counterarguments about the possible utility of public deliberation for activists, an influential one being that activists may despair of the processes of deliberation as actually being able to drive substantial social change. This is to say that activists, by definition, are promoting specific social changes – ones they consider to be right or fair – and that while deliberative processes might deliver socially legitimate decisions, there 'are no reasons to expect the right decision to emerge automatically from a deliberative procedure' (Arias-Maldonado, 2007, p. 247). This indeed is the question as to whether a *right* decision can arise from a deliberative process aside from whether it has been legitimately reached (although, of course, it is arguable that a lack of public deliberation will always make a decision impacting on the public good illegitimate).

Activists may thus contend that deliberation can too easily tend towards conservatism: (a) foregrounding what can often be narrow and exclusionary conceptions of its requirements and processes; (b) functioning primarily as a critical or justificatory activity divorced from any real exercise of power; (c) functioning as little more than the handmaiden of existing institutions; or (d) being seen as an exercise best left to authorised elites (bureaucrats, experts, members of dominant social groups or institutions). In addition, (e) practices of deliberation may be critiqued for their (unintended) skewing of discussions towards the interests of dominant or higher-status groups. Such criticisms see deliberative frameworks as overly prioritising narrow conceptions of rationality and models for communication and negotiation, along with the achievement of consensus. The framework further suggests that when participants are strongly oriented in deliberative practice towards the need for a common result, they may tend only to use those arguments that they expect to be acceptable to others, entailing the seeming inadmissibility of other positions and arguments (Pattie, 2008). According to such arguments, activists may believe they need to reject the conventional constraints of deliberative procedures or principles, given that such principles would seemingly require them to drop or substantially alter some of their demands in order to gain broad public support for an issue. What is more, seeing themselves as facing the intransigence built from the vested interests of powerful adversaries, activists may resort – out of perceived necessity – to intentionally cultivated practices of direct and adversarial confrontation, perceiving them as the most effective form of activity (D'Arcy, 2007; Young, 2003).

It is these arguments and the relations – tensions – between deliberation and activism that inform this chapter, relations that will be shown to be further problematised once reference is also made to contemporary arguments concerning the various roles and affordances of the Internet and digital participatory media for the work of both deliberation and activism. Largely, then, this chapter uses a detailed analysis of politically focused blogging to examine the theories and practice of public deliberation and its roles in promoting active conceptions of citizenship that would support progressive social change. Although blogs may not necessarily be activist in aim and authorship, political blogging – as already, by definition, oriented to discussion of issues of public concern – appears well able to promote, support and facilitate deliberative and indeed civic practices and exchanges. In particular, in holding the potential to inform and engage people's participation in the public and political spheres with regard to issues of public concern, politically focused blogging would thus seem a productive mechanism for the furthering of activist aims and social movement calls for social change. However, as we demonstrate in our analysis, there are important questions concerning the relations between deliberative exchange and its presumption of reason-based communicative practices and the facilitation of social change. Drawing on insights from the previous chapter as well as engaging with diverse perspectives and critiques of Jürgen Habermas's and others' work on deliberation and public spheres, this chapter explores these various issues through a comparative examination of some facets of the Australian blogosphere. Our focus, in this instance, is on Indigenous authored politically focused blogs with specific regard to issues of indigeneity, reconciliation and social change.

DEBATING DELIBERATION AND THE PUBLIC SPHERE

Definitions of public deliberation do vary. One version, which has been particularly influential in what has come to be called deliberative democracy (Chambers, 2003; Fishkin, 1991), presents it as an 'ideal speech situation' in which all participants – contrary to actual practice – possess equal influence and argue from positions of full information, and in which the best argument prevails (see, e.g., Habermas, 1984, 2008). As will be shown, objections to this conception are mostly practical: even if this sounds ideal and desirable, it may seem impossible or unlikely to achieve in practice. Conversely, public deliberation can also be considered to refer to everyday conversations, debates and communications about issues, as conducted in a diffused way throughout society – especially evident in private associations, parties, legislatures and courts, as well as through the media. Such practices, in their turn, certainly exist, but they can be criticised as poorly informed, inequitable, unbalanced and so on (Levine & Nierras, 2007). What is not in debate, whatever the definition, is the idea that decision-making with regard to issues of public concern should engage the public generally; this is the basic democratic assumption that issues which affect the public should allow for their involvement in any decision-making. This connects with what Habermas has termed the public sphere, which, he contends, comes into being when people communicate about issues of public interest. Conceived as a 'multiple, anonymous, heterogeneous network of many publics and many conversations' (Benhabib, 1994, p. 87; Habermas's original framing of this space was seen by critics as being too narrow and homogenised and has as such been broadened and pluralised), the public sphere stands for the 'constellation of communicative spaces in society that permit the circulation of information, ideas, debates – ideally in an unfettered manner – and also the formation of political will (i.e., public opinion)' (Dahlgren, 2005, p. 148).

What Habermas and his critics agree upon is that the aim of debate in the public sphere(s) is for citizens to reach collective agreement on issues of public concern – to deliberate, in other words – with the corollary of this being a stress on the use of communication strategies that contribute to greater understanding and the chance for genuine collective agreement to be attained. The view here is that communication strategies that attempt to manipulate or coerce individuals for strategic aims can never be considered to support genuine attempts at public deliberation (Dahlberg, 2005; Habermas, 1984). The only appropriate communication strategies would rather be those that promote reasonableness and dialogue, and allow for agreement to be developed 'only as the result of more or less exhaustive controversy in which proposals, information and reasons can be more or less rationally dealt with' (Habermas, 1998, p. 362). Participants would thus ideally take part in public debate in fair and reasonable ways. In this fashion participants would not only be up front about their interests and prejudices but committed to reflexivity, discursive equality and inclusion and what Dahlberg (2001) has called ideal role-taking, by which he means a commitment to trying to see arguments from others' perspectives. These are the norms in Habermas's eyes of any kind of reasonable public dialogue – they are especially fundamental for public deliberation.

Habermas contends that in public deliberation, agreement on issues should be reached only after proposals are subjected to what he calls 'discursive verification', a process whereby a proposed 'truth claim is first rendered problematic and then redeemed' (1987, pp. 361–364). More specifically, this process requires truth claims to be 'justified' not simply by participants on a personal level (e.g., where one would draw on one's personal experience) but also through a broader community-level process of dialogue and 'argumentative reasoning' (Habermas, 1987, p. 364). Under this process, all participants would need to feel 'free to raise and challenge claims without fear of coercion, intimidation, deceit, or the like and . . . have equal chances to speak, to make assertions, self-presentations, and normative claims and to challenge others' (Warnke, 1995, p. 126). Furthermore participants would be expected to (a) recognise, raise problems about and justify all proposed claims to truth; and (b) accept that their individual preferences may be 'mistaken: inaccurate, incoherent, or incomplete' (Dzur, 2002, p. 325). Put into practice this would mean first of all that deliberation involves no more and no less the capacity of the better argument to emerge through reasoned communal dialogue. And, second, that deliberation should be understood as that 'debate and discussion aimed at producing reasonable, well-informed opinions in which participants are willing to revise preferences in light of discussion, new information, and claims made by fellow participants' (Chambers, 2003, p. 309).

Habermas also makes the point that any instance of deliberative consensus can only be partial and contingent, open to further debate and revision. No consensus reached can exemplify universality in any absolute sense (Knops, 2007), which in turn makes clear that deliberative quality rests on the meeting of procedural conditions. Practical implementation presumes 'that reasonable or fair results are obtained' to the degree that information flow is not interrupted or stymied and the process, properly handled, has 'not been obstructed' (Habermas, 1998, p. 296). The trouble, as a range of critics have pointed out, is that even with the recognition that deliberative outcomes can never be final – outcomes always being open to revision as new information is brought to light – such a view of deliberation does appear to place an excessive emphasis on both the requirements of reasoned argumentation and the achievement of consensus. In other words, such an understanding of public deliberation appears to leave little space for (a) forms of expression that are not conditioned primarily by rationality and impartiality and (b) contestatory, conflictual exchanges. This is the earlier point that perhaps such a model requires deliberation to take place under what are actually unattainable conditions.

A further problem is that this Habermasian proceduralist conception of deliberation appears, despite itself, to entail a certain curtailing of pluralism and diversity, in this instance through its prioritising and legitimising of certain forms of expression and discussion over others. This may, as critics have noted, impact unevenly, potentially marginalising or dismissing those voices and factions already little heard in the public domain (see Tully, 2002; Young, 2000). As Iris Marion Young has noted, for example, the problem is that any instance of deliberation can only ever take place within a context that itself most probably possesses 'a given history' of inequality and systemic discrimination (2003, p. 113). The legacy of such inequality, Young continues, is not redressed simply by promoting open deliberation. This is because in practice the different groups and individuals to be engaged in deliberation come to it with differing levels of experience and expertise in the process. In Young's (2003, p. 116) words:

> Parties to deliberation may agree on premises, they may accept a theory of their situation and give reasons for proposals that the others accept, but yet the premises and terms of the account mask the reproduction of power and injustice.

As Young sees it, even purportedly open deliberation may end up reproducing existing structural inequalities. This problem is made clear in Levine and Nierras's (2007) interviews with activists. One interviewee, Joel Rocamora, a Philippino activist for democracy, for instance, expressed his concerns that while formally educated people from the middle classes may well be clear and forceful communicators within the processes of deliberation, the 'discourse of peasants is often not explicit – often hard to understand' (as cited in Levine & Nierras, 2007, p. 4). Furthermore, setting people into a deliberative space who are not well prepared to participate may merely serve to demoralise or alienate them. As Bettina von Lieres, an activist from South Africa, observed, 'In a situation where people have no experience of effective representative democracy . . . to take groups of people like that into deliberative processes . . . it can be completely threatening' (as cited in Levine & Nierras, 2007, p. 4). Far from resulting in the kind of open and productive exchange among diverse perspectives promoted as exemplary of deliberation, such practices may not only see a failure in the deliberative exercise but effectively mean the alienation of these cohorts from participation in future activities. Fatma Yusuf, also from South Africa, similarly said, 'I get the feeling that deliberation is an elitist discourse . . . That it has to be a certain level of maturity and there has to be a certain level of power in order to deliberate' (as cited in Levine & Nierras, 2007, p. 4).

Such concerns have led to the development of decolonising reconceptions of deliberation, with Seyla Benhabib, for example, outlining what she sees as the three essential features for comprehensively inclusive deliberation:

> (a) Participation in such deliberation is governed by the norms of equality and symmetry; all have the same chance to initiate speech acts, to question,

> interrogate, and to open debate; (b) all have the right to question the assigned topics of conversation; (c) all have the right to initiate reflexive arguments about the very rules of the discourse procedure and the way in which they are applied or carried out. There is no *prima facie* rule limiting the agenda or the conversation, nor the identity of the participants, as long as each excluded person or group can justifiably show that they are relevantly affected by the proposed norm under question. (1994, p. 31, emphasis in original)

Achieving this may take, as Benhabib also notes, some special affordances – often presented as positive discriminations – towards the members of disadvantaged groups, at least initially. It has also been argued that deliberation – to be inclusive – must be framed as able to recognise and engage diverse forms of reasoning and justification along with broadly affective and values-based judgements. It should thus be able to engage with non-conventionally rational forms of communication, such as rhetoric, testimony or storytelling, as well as explicitly contestatory forms of discussion (Bächtiger, 2011). Framing deliberation in contestatory terms might also mean being able to see it as a confrontational and adversarial process in which participants passionately engage with each other, getting to the heart of the matter by persistently questioning and challenging each other's proposals and arguments. Such a frame has indeed been presented as more effective than that of a consensus orientation insofar as the latter may be reductive of the content and range of claims and arguments considered in a deliberative process (Bächtiger, 2011; Pattie, 2008).

There is another thread now often woven through these arguments, which refers to the perceived affordances of new digital communications technologies for enabling and enhancing public deliberation. In these instances, the idea is that such technologies not only dramatically increase the networks and communicative spaces comprising the public sphere, along with their overall scope and reach, but further alleviate some of the entrenched inequities with regard to access and participation that have so concerned critics. Under this view, due to their 'enacting a global, horizontal network of communication' that provides 'an organizing tool and a means' for both synchronous and asynchronous dialogue, debate and collective decision-making (Castells, 2008, p. 86; cf. Drezner & Farrell, 2008; Papacharissi, 2010), digital communications technologies are presented as particularly able to facilitate open deliberative practices and exchanges (Hands, 2011; Mummery & Rodan, 2013). Such forms of communication are thus considered capable of building 'people's assemblies' so as to 'empower members and not [just] leaders' (Roberts, 2014, p. 177). According to this view, then, as Tsagarousianou has argued, new communications technologies have the potential to 'enable both deliberation (citizen to citizen communication) and "hearing" (citizen to authority communication)' (1999, pp. 195–196; also see Dahlgren, 2005). The assumed point here is that such technologies can sustain both communicative enclaves and shared nodes, both of which can facilitate the inclusion of previously marginalised or excluded voices, as well as allowing multiple publics to engage in deliberation within and across public boundaries (Simone, 2010).

These, however, as with all models for deliberative exchange, are contested views, with counterarguments being made that such technologies may facilitate factionalism instead of deliberation (Bellamy & Raab, 1999; Davis & Owen, 1998; Sunstein, 2007). They may also simply reproduce existing hegemonic power relations and inequities (Roberts, 2014). As we noted in the previous chapter, Sauter's (2014) point with regard to the increased public sphere supposedly afforded activists by digital communications technologies is also telling. Even if there are more places for an activist to stand (in effect) in protest, there are few chances of being read (except by the already like-minded), and many chances of running afoul of corporate and state interests. This is her point that unwelcome acts of collective protest within the digital sphere can all too easily become acts of trespass.

And yet we would argue in line with others that while these points do have traction, these technologies do have the capacity to support deliberative exchange. Such arguments propose that while the affordances of these technologies can indeed entail factionalism – with people 'talking without listening, confirming rather than problematizing dogmas, convicting rather than convincing adversaries' (Barber, 1999, p. 40; cf. Wilhelm, 2000) – given it is possible to design public spaces and processes that facilitate deliberative exchanges, it must equally be possible to design virtual forums that support this same work. This rests on the recognition too that no single forum could ever achieve full engagement and participation, that online exchanges – like face-to-face exchanges – constitutively take place in 'several culturally fragmented cyberspheres that occupy a common virtual space' (Papacharissi, 2002, p. 22; cf. Downey & Fenton, 2003). Forum designs, then, that may provide possibilities for engagement and deliberative exchange might feature (a) asynchronous communication (allowing thoughtful reflection), (b) some version of moderation (maintaining a minimum level of respect and civility so as to facilitate ongoing deliberative exchanges), (c) threaded messages (allowing participants to identify and follow discussions of interest) and (d) a capacity for anonymity (supporting the presentation and discussion of non-majority aligned views) (Coleman & Gøtze, 2001; Sack, 2005; Wright & Street, 2007). Under such a framework, we propose that Internet communication can enable deliberative practices and exchanges, insofar as it should enable participants to (a) engage in debate over issues of public concern, (b) introduce additional issues into the debate, (c) argue for preferred views and (d) engage with differing viewpoints. Similarly, social media platforms arguably also enable ordinary people to express themselves about specific issues of concern to them, thereby nurturing both public engagement and spaces for activist dissent and exchange that can also provide effective mechanisms for offline mobilisation (Eltantawy & Wiest, 2011; Lim, 2012).

BLOGGING DELIBERATION IN THE PUBLIC SPHERE

With regard to the achievement of deliberative practices via the use of new communications technologies, then, blogs (web logs) seem a strong proposal. The term 'blog', however, has been applied to a vast array of sites since its introduction and its definitions are multiple (Thompson, 2003). Initial definitions have described them as 'a type of online publishing best characterized as an interactive diary' (Maynor, 2007, p. 5; also see Gil de Zúñiga, Puig-I-Abril & Rojas, 2009), but most basically they typically comprise a web page with the following features: 'minimal to no external editing, providing an online commentary, periodically updated and presented in reverse chronological order, with hyperlinks to other online sources' (Drezner & Farrell, 2008, p. 2). Overall, a typical blog entry consists of a hyperlinked 'summary of a story posted somewhere else on the Web' and 'the blogger's opinion, commentary, or analysis' (Leccese, 2009, p. 581). Blogs as such can function as personal or group diaries, but their additional feature of being able to not only transmit information but receive comments means that they can also enable discussion. This could be technical or interest-oriented discussion, celebrity gossip or the discussion of issues of public interest, whether sports or politics.

Within these frames, comments can take the form of such practices as supplying information, requesting clarification of issues, debating a point, asking a question or disputing a claim made by others. In addition, more elaborate forms of participation are supported through such linking and tracking services as syndication software and commands (RSS) and permalinks. The latter, in particular, play a significant role regarding a blog's facilitation of discussion insofar as permalinks are a unique and stable URL for every blog posting that can be linked to individually (even when that posting is no longer current and has been archived) (Lankshear & Knobel, 2006). Overall, then, in not necessarily being edited by third parties, and due to their ease of creation and use, blogs can clearly encourage participation, giving people the 'opportunity to participate and express their opinions without intellectual or political restrictions' (Gil de Zúñiga et al., 2009, p. 556).

Political blogging or blogging oriented to discussion of issues of public concern, as a specific genre, was initially considered in terms of its relation to political campaigns, with the idea being that blogs can be used in political campaigns to both communicate with and 'organize and motivate' citizens (Drezner & Farrell, 2008, p. 2). Given this focus, there has been consideration – mainly in the United States (e.g., Drezner & Farrell, 2008) – of the impact of political blogging on politics, but a second line of inquiry has focused on the more general question as to whether participation in blogs can enhance levels of public engagement and deliberation with issues of public concern (Gil de Zúñiga et al., 2009; Lawrence, Sides & Farrell, 2009; Meraz, 2007). Framed with regard to its deliberative potential, political blogging has been considered in terms of its capacity to allow participants to seek and comment on information, and engage in deliberation regarding topics of public interest (Johnson, Kaye, Bichard & Wong, 2007). All this has in turn led to the view that, even though individual bloggers may not themselves be overly concerned with objectivity or fairness, blogged discussion has at least the potential to be 'self-correcting through the process of contestation and deliberation' (Maynor, 2007, p. 18). For instance, given its capacity to enable 'conversations and debates about public policies in the hope of positively shaping their resolution', there are arguments that blogging may enable the public presentation and consideration of 'reasons and arguments acceptable in deliberative forums' (Maynor, 2007, pp. 12–18; also see Mummery & Rodan, 2011, 2013).

Political blogging as such has several elements that suggest that it can enable deliberative exchanges about the public good and politics. First, McKenna and Pole (2008, p. 102), for instance, found that most political blogs (about 80 percent) concern themselves with topics such as 'media and politics, economics and politics, and campaigns and elections'. Second, political bloggers tend to provide 'specialised information to their readers' – information that many political bloggers argue is not being supplied by the mainstream media (p. 102). Under these circumstances, political bloggers are understood as offering alternative perspectives to the mainstream media (Ekdale, Namkoong, Fung & Perlmutter, 2010), thereby giving voice to different perspectives and dialogues, and, through their common utilisation of hyperlinks, connecting others to additional resources and information (Woodly, 2008). In this sense, political bloggers can themselves clearly be described as interested and involved citizens (Lawrence et al., 2009; Woodly, 2008), and, as Ken Parish (a blogger in the Australian group blog Club Troppo) argues, 'a critical dimension' of such blogging is the 'conversation and community, developed through comment threads' (as cited in Garden, 2010, p. 20).

In the Australian context, as Highfield and Bruns (2012) have noted, political blogs are rarely purely focused on political issues. Rather they 'often also cover other, non-political subjects in their posts, and may at times bridge one or several topical areas in their activities'. Similarly, political topics can be considered in 'sites dedicated to economics, parenting, health, craft, sport and personal journals, and these thematic groups remain active sections of the Australian blogosphere' (Highfield & Bruns, p. 90). Also considered typical of Australian political blogging is that bloggers pay 'attention' to the writing of others. That is, they often link to and discuss 'sites with opposing views to highlight alternative, or possibly "wrong", interpretations of issues' (p. 92). Furthermore, while researchers in the United States and New Zealand (Hopkins & Matheson, 2012) found that political blogs may often have partisan interests – such as supporting specific political candidates or political parties – this is not always the case in the Australian political blogosphere. Certainly Australian political blogs often array themselves on the left or right of the political spectrum, but this does not necessarily translate into the support of any particular politicians.

There are, however, three main limitations with seeing political blogs as sites for public deliberation:

(i) The demographic of those who use and write politically interested blogs is limited. Political bloggers 'tend to be well-educated, white middle-class' males with an average age of '43.3 years' (Dailey, Demo & Spilman, 2008; Johnson et al., 2007; Lawrence et al., 2009, p. 10; McKenna & Pole, 2008; Perlmutter, 2008). Another demographic issue concerns access to necessary infrastructure. In Australia, with the National Broadband Network not yet fully rolled out, the cost and reliability of broadband and wireless services, and the pressure of commercial interests, can affect an individual's ability to access fast Internet services and thereby his or her chance of participation in political blogging and its deliberation. These issues may entail, in Australia, a differentiation between the deliberative engagements – within the political blogosphere at least – of people living in rural, regional and remote areas as opposed to those living in the major cities.

(ii) Lawrence et al. (2009, p. 11) have found that about '94% of political blog readers consume only blogs from one side of the ideological spectrum'. Because political blog networks tend to seek and reinforce existing political opinions, they tend to be 'homophilous', falling 'well short of the deliberative ideal' (Lawrence et al., pp. 6–7). A number of researchers further point to the 'balkanization' of the blogosphere, meaning (a) 'the isolation of individuals within groups that share their values and beliefs' (Maynor, 2007, p. 13; also see Xenos, 2008), entailing (b) their limited 'opportunity for revising their opinions' (Lawrence et al., 2009, p. 17).

(iii) Bloggers may be limited in their ability to enable public debate because they serve what Habermas has called a ' "parasitical" function of criticizing and correcting the mainstream press' (as cited in Lawrence et al.,

> 2009, p. 4). Kenix (2009, p. 814; also see Xenos, 2008) states that that 'rather than "answering" to public concerns about content', the political blogs she sampled 'were driven by individual interests created within the culture of mainstream media'.

These limitations, although certainly real, are perhaps however not as problematic as they initially look. First, while it is true that in Australia, as for instance in the United States, the main political bloggers and their readers look primarily to be educated, white and male (Young, 2011), the overall Australian politically oriented blogosphere has been argued to be comprised of a 'far greater diversity of voices, professional backgrounds and personal interests' (Highfield & Bruns, 2012, p. 91). Second, what needs to be remembered is that when considered with regard to their deliberative potential, individual blogs themselves may not need to be non-partisan. That is, bias itself has been identified as an important attribute of political blogs insofar as it means that bloggers can deliver 'more detailed and in depth examination of issues' than mainstream media can, given the latter's required maintenance of standards of fairness and balance (Johnson et al., 2007, p. 114). In this sense, political blogs may be considered to be 'more credible over-all' than 'traditional media or other online sources' (p. 114). Even partisan blogs, then, can support deliberative practices and exchanges insofar as they clearly do enable participants to (a) engage in debate over issues of public concern, (b) introduce additional issues into the debate, (c) argue for preferred views and (d) engage with differing viewpoints. That is, even partisan blogged discussion holds the potential to inform and engage people's participation in the public and political spheres.

Similarly, even if political blogs do tend to be driven by concerns present in the mainstream media (McKenna & Pole, 2008, p. 102) – and Highfield and Bruns (2012) do contend that Australian political bloggers primarily act as commentators and watchdogs – they can still facilitate deliberation of these concerns insofar as they do not necessarily follow the agendas set by the mainstream media (see Highfield & Bruns, 2012). Finally, regardless of these points, we would suggest first that to expect complete non-partisanship and freedom from all commercial interests within public spheres which facilitate public deliberation is to forget that the Habermasian-desired deliberative framework is first of all a normative ideal; second that public spheres are multiple; and third, and more significantly, that deliberation is unending. What this entails is that any deliberative engagement exceeds its frame. In other words, deliberative exchanges may start between citizens in one space for public sphere discussion and then be picked up in new ways in another.

BLOGGING FOR SOCIAL CHANGE: RECONCILING WITH INDIGENOUS AUSTRALIA

The beginning of an Information Sheet put out by the Australian Human Rights Commission (n.d.) entitled 'Social Justice and Human Rights for Aboriginal and Torres Strait Islander Peoples' reads as follows:

> A LIFE of opportunity and dignity, free from discrimination and disadvantage, should not be an ideal. It is, in fact, a basic human right – one that we all share in common.

As has been and still is manifest in every cross-comparison of non-Indigenous and Indigenous Australians lives, however, this is not a right that is equally delivered. Indigenous Australians – by which is meant, following the Australian Human Rights Commission, members of Aboriginal and Torres Strait Islander peoples – consistently rank lower than non-Indigenous Australians when it comes to health and well-being, relative wealth and economic status, educational involvement and outcomes. They show, however, higher rates of involvement in the legal system and of imprisonment. As Torres (2015) has written:

> Loss of land, culture and self-determination has already resulted in a state of emergency in Aboriginal Australia, already experiencing chronic rates of poverty, homelessness, forced child removals, alcoholism, incarceration, trauma, suicide and ongoing deaths in custody. On top of this, the number of Aboriginal and Torres Strait Islander people in our prisons has risen more than 80% in ten years.

Indigenous Australians also rank higher in their experience of negative forms of discrimination, with a 2014 report from TNS Social Research (commissioned by *beyondblue*), indicating that 'discrimination against Indigenous Australians is considered one of the most prevalent forms of discrimination in Australia' (p. 2). This same report indicates that discrimination against Indigenous Australians – including, for instance, verbal abuse and racist jokes, employment discrimination, racial profiling, the acceptance of negative stereotypes – is greater than that suffered by people with mental health conditions or who are gay, lesbian or bisexual. The only persons who are ranked higher by TNS Social Research (2014) with regard to their being discriminated against are those who do not speak English.

It is this unequal delivery to all of lives 'of opportunity and dignity, free from discrimination and disadvantage', which drives home the need in Australia for social justice and for social change, and the development of Indigenous Australian activism (Maddison, 2009; Maynard, 2008). The Australian Human Rights Commission (n.d.) presents the goals of social justice as not just the meeting of the 'practical, day-to-day realities of life', these being about such everyday things as

> waking up in a house with running water and proper sanitation; offering one's children an education that helps them develop their potential and respect their culture. It is the prospect of satisfying employment and good health,

but also entailing broader recognition and acceptance by the non-Indigenous Australian community of the 'distinctive rights that Indigenous Australians hold as the original peoples of this land'. This is to stress the importance of general respect for and acceptance of

- the right to a distinct status and culture, which helps maintain and strengthen the identity and spiritual and cultural practices of Indigenous communities;
- the right to self-determination, which is a process where Indigenous communities take control of their future and decide how they will address the issues facing them;
- the right to land, which provides the spiritual and cultural basis of Indigenous communities.

Such issues are arguably being worked on throughout the broad Australian community through a variety of mechanisms. There is, for example, the work facilitated by institutionalised markers – themselves the result of extensive political and public deliberation. These include the Australian High Court's 1992 decision in Mabo (which rejected the idea that Australia was *terra nullius* – land belonging to no one – at the time of European settlement recognition); the institution of the Native Title Act 1993 (which recognises a property right reflective of the relationship to land foundational for Indigenous religion, culture and well-being); the reports from various Royal Commissions and National Inquiries into the situation of Indigenous Australians (e.g., the 1991 report from the Royal Commission into Aboriginal Deaths in Custody, the 1997 report from the National Inquiry into the Separation of Aboriginal and Torres Strait Islander Children from Their Families); the actual creation in 1992 by the federal parliament of the position of the Aboriginal and Torres Strait Islander Social Justice Commissioner; and the growing feeling in the last few years that the Australian Constitution needs to be brought up to date – that is, so that it explicitly recognises and includes Aboriginal and Torres Strait Islander peoples – so as to reflect the reality of Australia in the twenty-first century. There are two other key institutionalised markers: the then Australian Prime Minister Kevin Rudd's apology in 2008 to Indigenous Australians on behalf of the country and the instituting of National Sorry Day, NAIDOC (National Aboriginal and Islander Day Observance Committee)

Week and Reconciliation Week. At the same time, however, as the TNS Social Research (2014) report shows, there is continuing need for an ongoing raising of awareness regarding Indigenous issues and respect for Indigenous Australians, with many of those surveyed for this report demonstrating (a) a lack of understanding as to what discriminatory behaviour actually consists of, (b) an evident lack of motivation to modify discriminatory behaviours shown towards Indigenous Australians (up to one-third of the non-Indigenous Australians surveyed indicated that discriminatory behaviours are undertaken automatically, even unconsciously, and over a quarter did not see addressing discrimination as important) and (c) high levels of acceptance of racist beliefs and negative stereotypes within the Australian community.

These are tendencies, then, in clear need of change, the desired aim being for all non-Indigenous Australians to reject beliefs, attitudes and actions (physical and verbal) that discriminate against Indigenous Australians. These are also issues that have recently been explicitly framed with reference to the work of ideal public deliberation, with the former Australian Human Rights Commissioner, Tim Wilson, arguing in 2014 for the repeal of section 18C of the Racial Discrimination Act – this is the section which makes it unlawful to insult people based on their race or ethnicity – on the basis that allowing free speech will actually help cure bigotry. As he put it: 'Bigotry comes from ignorance that does not go away if silenced, it just hides in dark corners and festers. No law can abolish bigotry, nor is the law the solution to all of society's ills' (Wilson, 2014). Presumably Wilson saw open public deliberation on the norms of appropriate speech – or, as he put it, 'speaking up when we hear something objectionable' – as the best mechanism for 'promoting pluralism, opposing reprehensible racism and highlighting the importance of [individual] responsibility', all of which he agrees are important. Of course, as many critics of his views have pointed out, such a vision once again seemingly assumes that all those engaged in such deliberation are constitutively equal in their capacity to participate and be listened to, and that no participants are responding from a context of historic and/or structural inequality. Wilson clearly assumes – incorrectly unfortunately – that there is a level-playing field between Indigenous and non-Indigenous people within Australian society.

All of these issues – including Tim Wilson's proposal – are themselves under public debate, with diverse perspectives and arguments being presented and debated in manifold ways throughout the public sphere. The mode in specific focus here, for two reasons, is the blogosphere: first, because of its aforementioned affordances of public engagement and deliberation (via detailed posts and analyses, hyperlinking, interlinking comments and archive and search capacities); and second, and more important, because of the development and early mapping, by Indigenous activist and entrepreneur

Leesa Watego, of a specifically Indigenous (and activist) blogosphere, Deadly Bloggers. Starting from Watego's initial collation in 2009 of a list of Aboriginal and Torres Strait Islander peoples who blogged – which was presented as a link list on her personal blog – by 2012 Deadly Bloggers had evolved to include a Facebook page, blogspot directory and a Twitter account, and by 2013 it had moved from Watego's site to its own WordPress site. As described in the site, Deadly Bloggers is the 'first and only directory of Aboriginal and Torres Strait Islander bloggers' who, using a range of platforms including WordPress, Blogger and Tumblr, post 'on everything from design to business, literature to pop culture' (Deadly Bloggers, 2014). As is stressed within the site, one of the core goals of Deadly Bloggers has been 'to encourage Aboriginal and Torres Strait Islander people to use digital platforms to express their ideas, histories, voices, opinions, and stories', with an added focus of increasing audience and reader numbers for affiliated bloggers (Deadly Bloggers, 2017). And indeed, while Watego blogs in 2013 that she has 'deliberately not positioned Deadly Bloggers in the "how to blog" market', she not only provides advice on 'how to help your audience share your posts' (2013) but has developed The Deadly Bloggers Blog Carnival (#DBBC) which runs from July 1 to 31 and is aimed at increasing both Indigenous blogging and broader public engagement with Indigenous bloggers and issues. As Jackie Huggins has put it in a set of essays devoted to Indigenous digital excellence, Indigenous participation in the digital public sphere has the capacity to 'enhance the recognition and the status of Indigenous people and help close the gap' (2014, p. viii). Indigenous participation is thus, arguably, constitutively activist.

INDIGENOUS BLOGGING TOWARDS RECONCILIATION AND SOCIAL CHANGE

> Blogging, & other forms of online publication, allow writers to define themselves (and their Aboriginality). It can provide a space where First Nations Peoples can play, explore, create, debate, rant and vent, satirise, and philosophise the world in which we live. (Watego, 2014)

As Watego (2014) has noted in a presentation entitled '"I found my voice": Indigenous narratives enduring through digital participation', given that Indigenous Australians are often the subject of research and media stories, blogging is one mechanism through which to speak back and 'to speak in my own voice', and share culture and personal and collective struggles. Indeed, the tools of participatory digital media are being recognised as significant for facilitating the proliferation of Indigenous voices in the public sphere (Dreher, McCallum & Waller, 2016), with social media channels being recognised in particular as important for keeping diverse opinions alive and visible. Four voices for consideration here are the blogs The Koori Woman and 1 Deadly Nation, and the microblogging or Twitter movements of @ IndigenousX and #sosblakaustralia. All of these are delivered by Indigenous activists concerned to speak to and share their experiences of life in Indigenous Australia.

The Koori Woman: Gomeroi. This Is My Truth

> This is where I say what I want. About Aboriginal Affairs, politics, life, Black feminism & occasionally, Star Trek. I do NOT want to hear you tell me what YOU would prefer I say. (TheKooriWoman, n.d.)

Written by Kelly Briggs, named one of the top twenty women shaking things up on Twitter in 2013, by the online publication *The Shake*, and an active participant in the online IndigenousX movement discussed later, The Koori Woman was itself named the 2014 Commentary Blog of the Year by The Australian Writers Centres. Primarily focused on Aboriginal issues, blog categories include Aboriginal Australia, Aboriginal employment, Aboriginal health, Aboriginal politics, Aboriginal women, Aboriginal anti-racism, Colonialism, Empowered communities, Indigenous, NAIDOC, Politics, Racism, Stereotypes and The Intervention. Most posts are categorised under several of these tags. Describing her blogging with reference to the importance of practising self-determination, she has made the point:

> I started blogging because I wanted to express myself. I say if you're black and have an Internet connection, get a blog, start talking and people talk back. (Briggs, as cited in Krusche, 2014)

Comments are enabled although mostly sparse, with most posts receiving fewer than ten comments and only one (in a search examining posts between mid-2016 and mid-2013) garnering over twenty comments. Of the comments that have been posted, most are single posts responding to the original blog post, and very rarely does Briggs reply to any comments. Given these attributes, it would seem that this site does little to facilitate deliberative exchanges. This, however, would be to forget the multiple points of engagement blogging can have with the deliberative process. What existing comments primarily all remark on is Briggs's capacity to provide readers with an honest appraisal of Indigenous life, and her capacity to provide a rich but critical corrective to mainstream assumptions about life in Australia.

For instance, respondents make such comments as 'I think you articulate the issues really well and I always learn so much when I read your blogs' (Rochelle Jones, 2014, April 8); 'The way you write your experiences is raw, touching, humorous at times and always thought provoking' (Jenny Sparks, 2014, October 15); 'I started reading your blogs over a year ago and am impressed with your raw honesty and commitment' (Tara, 2014, November 8); 'Your writing is giving me an insight into what you & your children are enduring & I am in awe of your practical strength' (Elizabeth Marr, 2014, January 10).

Here respondents are commenting on blog posts telling in several ways of what it is like to be Indigenous and out of work and struggling financially, of the first-hand experiencing of discriminatory treatment and of having to talk with Aboriginal sons about how to behave with the police. Alongside are posts concerning Indigenous rates of incarceration, anti-racism campaigns, government policies and the chronic discrepancies in health and mortality rates within Australia between Indigenous and non-Indigenous people. Briggs's blog posts also themselves respond to, source material from and link directly to a range of materials such as independent online media such as *Crikey*, political reports and items in the mainstream media; and her posts may also be cross-published in other online spaces, including *Crikey*, *Croakey*, @Aboriginaloz, @IndigenousX, the *Guardian*, *New Matilda* and the *Hoopla*. Respondents also mention sharing Briggs's posts on Facebook.

1 Deadly Nation: Unity in Diversity

> 1 Deadly Nation – With Music, art, sport, news, interviews, opinion and activism we uplift our society, feed our souls, grow our bond and live in 1 Deadly Nation! (1 Deadly Nation, n.d.)

With 1 Deadly Nation, blogger, writer and activist Martin Hodgson talks of his dream for a deadly nation – 'Dead·ly (ddl) adj. dead·li·er, dead·li·est – Australian aboriginal lingo for really excellent' – in which 'we can improve and inform ourselves, our community and this nation we share' (n.d.). He explicitly presents his site as having a role in this work, with focuses on activism and news as well as on art, music and sport. The site also links to Hodgson's Twitter feed (the Deadly Feed), which lists over 10,000 followers. In particular, however, this blog is tied to information sharing, disseminating news about and critically evaluating the policies and events affecting Indigenous Australians. Blogs are categorised into the following sets and ordered here with regard to number of posts (high to low): For your information, Uncategorised, Get involved!, News, Politics, Music, Hero/Villain,

Must watch movies, Sport and Television. As with The Koori Woman, comments are enabled although sparse, with most posts receiving fewer than ten comments and many posts not receiving any comments. Only two posts (in a search examining posts between mid-2016 and mid-2013) garnered over twenty comments. Again, as with The Koori Woman, the majority of comments are single posts responding to the original blog post, and only very rarely does Hodgson reply to comments.

Respondents, however, not only are commenting about the importance of posts – 'Thank you so much for sharing this – I have shared this article' (Renee Davis, 2013, August 14), 'Thanks for your astute summary of the issue' (Dave Bryant, 2013, July 18), 'I needed to thank you for this great read!! I definitely loved every bit of it. I have you saved as a favorite to check out new things you post' (esthetician salary, 2013, August 18) – but they are also engaging in some discussion of various posts' contents. In such instances they are addressing not only the author but, in a few cases, each other. This is visible in the two posts receiving more than twenty comments: 'Abbott, the Truth and Cost of His Indigenous Volunteering' (posted 13 August 2013, receiving twenty-six comments) (1 Deadly Nation, 2013) and 'Ferguson Australia, Murder under the Red, White and by Blue' (posted 25 November 2014, receiving twenty-eight comments) (1 Deadly Nation, 2014). For instance, in the Abbott post, the twenty-six comments are made by twenty-five authors (one author posts twice), including Hodgson who addresses one respondent's challenge on content. Aside from Hodgson's response to an author, there are only two instances of respondents addressing each other in their posts. The majority of comments provide commentary on the original post (mostly positive, only the one direct challenge), sometimes drawing further connections and conclusions; only five comments take the form of being simply praise or a statement of the post being shared.

A different balance of response is visible in the Ferguson post. Here there are fifteen authors of comments, including Hodgson, with three of these – Turtle, Stop Race Baiting, BlackCard – each making three or more posts. Also prevalent in this comment set is that authors are responding to each other, with eighteen of the comments making a direct response to others; Turtle in particular responds to eight different authors, including Hodgson, and three respondents – again including Hodgson – address Turtle directly. These exchanges are broadly deliberative insofar as they do tend to take the form of clarifications and corrections of each other's points, although they tend also to be critical in nature, sometimes to the point of being derogatory: 'You have a very unbalanced view'; 'Actually your facts are totally incorrect. Why don't you educate yourself'; 'You really should educate yourself'; 'It is a shame you have both joined this conversation and left facts behind as you entered'.

@IndigenousX

> The beauty of Twitter that you don't get from Facebook is that anyone can comment and chime in. Rather than constantly speaking to the converted, you're creating a platform where you can have conflicting ideas and values but also ultimately reach common ground. (Benson Saulo, as cited in Morris, 2015)

Sometimes described as standing for Indigenous Excellence, @IndigenousX is, in turn, an example of user-driven innovation and of how Indigenous voices and perspectives are emerging strongly in the digital landscape. Founded by activist Luke Pearson in 2012, @IndigenousX was initially a rotating Twitter account that featured a different Indigenous commentator examining a new topic each week (Kelly Briggs from The Koori Woman was, for example, one such commentator in November 2013). These commentators provide perspectives from remote, rural, urban and metropolitan areas across Australia, giving readers access to a wide range of personal and professional insights and experiences from Indigenous people working in, or impacted by, Indigenous programs. The more than 180 commentators have encompassed lawyers, performers, community workers, bloggers, academics, politicians and advisors all of whom share their personal stories as well as the issues they're passionate about. Commentators have included in particular the first host and director of the National Indigenous Youth Leadership Academy, a textile artist who released a range of swimwear as part of the inaugural Indigenous Fashion Week, and the former National President of the Australian Labour Party and Chair of the current government's Indigenous Advisory Council. As Pearson has stressed in an interview in AWAYE! On Radio National in 2015, the site has an open-door policy with every Indigenous person who has asked to host the account receiving that opportunity (Morris, 2015). Commentators and the account more generally also link readers to organisations such as the Indigenous Literacy Foundation, the National Centre for Indigenous Excellence and The Thin Black Line which delivers 'news and current affairs from an Indigenous perspective' (Thin Black Line, n.d.).

The account's overall aim was and still is to raise awareness of the various issues, programs, stories and perspectives significant for Indigenous life (Thin Black Line, n.d.). As Pearson (2014, p. 46) has stressed:

> Digital technologies, and in particular social media, can be a significant tool for connection, empowerment, education, employment, the ongoing struggle for social justice, and Reconciliation. In fact, whatever issue is being addressed (or is not, as the case may be), I believe the digital world can assist.

This capacity is particularly important, Pearson (p. 47) also stresses in this essay, because of Indigenous Australia's 'history of being excluded from, and ridiculed within, the national dialogue', and of having voices and stories neither 'heard, respected [n]or appreciated'. Digital participation – in particular the bringing of stories online, of putting 'your own truth out there in a way of your own choosing, on your own terms, and in your own time' – will see, he says, the 'opening of a Pandora's Box'.

Although Twitter still remains @IndigenousX's most recognised platform, with nearly 29,000 followers online and over 27,000 likes, @IndigenousX has also expanded to develop partnerships with the online news site *Guardian Australia*, the crowdfunding platform StartSomeGood (raising so far over $250,000 for Indigenous projects) and the Australian Institute of Aboriginal & Torres Strait Islander Studies. It has, in addition, sparked the developments of a sister account in Canada (@IndigenousXca) and complementary social media accounts on Facebook, Instagram and YouTube, as well as a business account (@IndigenousXLtd) (@IndigenousX, n.d.). Pearson has talked also of a radio show and of web-tv (as cited in Latimore, 2013). Sweet, Pearson and Dudgeon (2013, p. 108) have argued that the account's effectiveness in terms of online and offline deliberation ranges from its provision of the means to 'both scale and tear down barriers to participation'; foster emotional, social and cultural well-being; and mark a journalistic innovation as well as a community development innovation. Such views are also reflected in the account's nominations in 2013 for a Shorty Award (a US initiative which recognises achievement in social media), which consistently applauded its capacities to share Indigenous stories and knowledge, encourage Indigenous voices and opinions, challenge prevailing stereotypes and reflect the diversity of Indigenous peoples (Sweet et al., 2013).

With regard to @IndigenousX and deliberation, while there is little direct deliberative exchange of views – tweets by hosts are primarily retweeted or liked rather than replied to – the account is recognised for its capacity to disseminate Indigenous views broadly. Specifically it: presents diverse perspectives on issues of public interest, facilitates the development of communities of interest, enables grassroots advocacy and increases the participation and visibility of Indigenous voices in the public sphere. As another past commentator has written:

> It had such a positive effect on me to know that there is such a deadly and wonderfully rich community that shares the same thought patterns around a certain topic. It also boosted my confidence to be able to share things publicly online and have conversations in that forum. (Kylie Farmer, as cited in Morris, 2015)

sosblakaustralia

The #sosblakaustralia campaign reflects concerns at the denial of services to remote Indigenous communities as symptomatic of a widespread move

> by state and federal governments away from Indigenous self-determination and land rights and towards policies designed to force Indigenous people into the mainstream economy. (Dreher, McCallum & Waller, 2016, p. 32)

An example of community-led social media activism, with a website presence, as well as Twitter, Facebook and Instagram presences, the sosblakaustralia campaign launched in March 2015 to protest against a plan to forcibly close up to 150 remote Aboriginal communities in Western Australia. With three official hashtags (#SOSBLAKAUSTRALIA, #Noconsent and #Lifestylechoice), this campaign began with a single Facebook post from Wangkatjungka, a remote Aboriginal community in the Kimberley region of Western Australia. This post by Nelson Bieundurry was written in response to remarks by then Australian Prime Minister Tony Abbott, who had told *ABC News* that the Commonwealth could no longer afford to fund essential services like electricity and power in remote Aboriginal communities. Abbott had said then that Indigenous people living in these areas were making a *lifestyle choice* as opposed to fulfilling a cultural obligation (Medhora, 2015). Bieundurry's post led to a call for protest, which circulated around Australia and then internationally, trending in Twitter and giving rise to ninety-seven rallies in Australia and overseas, including 10,000 people marching in sixty locations within Australia (Clark, 2015). As Sam Cook, one of the blaktivist founders of sosblakaustralia and a guest tweeter for @IndigenousX between 1 and 14 April 2015, explained:

> This action was initiated on 13 March by a small group of Kimberley women and in six days we mounted a national call to action activating every state and territory in Australia. We mobilised upwards of 20,000 people on the streets and led a virtual campaign that has reached everyone from Angela Davis to Hugh Jackman to the Australian union movement, AFL footballers and bilateral support politically. The online virtual protest is still raging and in 18 days we have just under 50,000 on our Facebook page alone, with a reach of over 1 million. Artists have written songs, painted works and are documenting this through their writings. Protests are being held internationally in Canada, UK, New Zealand and Europe to support this. We made history and have mobilised the country while shining light on Australia globally. (2015b)

A second global call to action (1 May 2015) was held with 98 global actions and over 60,000 marching; by the fifth global call to action, the campaign had attained an audience of 20 million. Sosblakaustralia has been called the biggest Aboriginal-led action of the twenty-first century. Overall, however, the sosblakaustralia social media campaign is much more than a protest movement; it is also a call for Aboriginal communities to register their needs and for individuals to offer skills that could aid the community. As Cook (2015a) explains in a different post:

> At the back end, the plan goes far beyond calls to action. What has been at the heart of SOSBLAKAUSTRALIA is a humanitarian effort we are aiming to drive alongside the communities. It is our plan to make all of our communities sustainable through alternative power, water, and waste solutions, as well as to repair years of neglected infrastructure. This is in line with our sovereignty, and we have individuals in the community already looking into the potential to file a class action on behalf of our Aboriginal Nations against the state and federal governments. Our communities have issued a vote of no confidence in both state and federal governments, and we are all aware that this is an epoch of upheaval.

What is also important about the campaign is its reach. The campaign's Facebook site, for instance, shows over 70,000 likes, with each post garnering multiple likes, shares and comments, some posts showing hundreds of such responses. Some posted video content has garnered over half a million views. The Twitter campaign in its turn has over 5,500 followers.

Campaigns are still current in their drawing of public attention and deliberation to the still-extant possibility of remote community closures, with sosblakaustralia challenging the new Western Australian Labor state government (which took power in March 2017) to clarify its remote Aboriginal community *reform* position (sosblakaustralia, 2017). Although this statement has not as yet been made (as of late August 2017), the Indigenous Treasurer in the newly elected government, Ben Wyatt, had made his views on the former government clear, labelling it 'belligerent and disrespectful', and has stated that he is hopeful that the previous government's planned community closures will not happen (as cited in Cromb, 2017). Given its aims, sosblakaustralia is in the process of becoming a more formal organisation so as to more effectively conduct the humanitarian work which underpins the campaign. As Cook has also pointed out: 'The future republic of Australia will be forced into a new relationship with Indigenous sovereign nations and we [sosblakaustralia] should collectively and proactively be looking to broker this dialogue' (as cited in Tan, 2015).

INDIGENOUS ACTIVISM, PARTICIPATORY MEDIA AND DELIBERATION FOR SOCIAL CHANGE

> Social media provides opportunities for Indigenous young people to feel a sense of power and control over their own identities and communities. (Rice, Haynes, Royce & Thompson, 2016, p. 10)

Certainly it is true, as has been noted in the previous chapter, that the platforms of participatory digital media are constrained in a variety of ways. They are not neutral tools as Lim (2012) and Sauter (2013) point out, being rather constrained by the companies and corporations that develop and own them, by the governments that regulate their use and by their own technological capacities. Tensions are, thus, always going to be inevitable between these Indigenous aims of self-expression and recognition and those of corporate success. Such constraints, however, despite suggesting for some a problem for deliberation, must be considered alongside the sheer ubiquity of social media technology, its embeddedness in broad swathes of social life and its 'ability to communicate with a broad, accessible, and engaged audience' (Petray, 2013). Furthermore, once these issues are factored in, given that blogging is such a broadly relational platform, it clearly shows capacity to enhance deliberative exchange.

Our examination of the Indigenous blogging sphere is thus a small but rich sample of the ways in which blogging can be used to facilitate deliberative processes, albeit while also showing the limitations – both systemic and self-imposed – of the practice. Of course, there are many more than these voices comprising the Indigenous blogosphere, and many more Indigenous activists similarly utilising participatory digital media as tools. Overall, what is clear is that these tools are being used for 'empowerment, education, creation, identity affirmation, cultural preservation, protection and reclamation, and for creating a sense of solidarity' (Pearson, 2014, pp. 52–53; cf. Booth, 2014; Rice et al., 2016). More specifically, as Petray (2013) has noted, not only do these tools allow everyone (with access) to effectively 'write themselves into being' – facilitating the negotiation of both individual and collective forms of identity for both bloggers and readers – but they enable Indigenous activists to challenge essentialist 'mainstream imagery' of Indigenous life by self-writing and widely disseminating 'alternative understandings about what it means to be Indigenous'.

It is this capacity, in particular of making alternatives visible, fundamental for the success of activist aims, that, we suggest, also must be understood as significant in deliberative practice. Furthermore, if we return to our earlier discussion about the need to widen the process of deliberation beyond the reaching of consensus, to leave space for posters to express their opinions in ways that would not necessarily be considered instantiations of rational and impartial discussion and to allow contestatory and conflictual exchanges, then our analysis also sheds light on the value of blogging. Finally, not only do these bloggers and posters facilitate understanding about contemporary Indigenous life and living, supplementing and often challenging representations gleaned from mainstream media, the explicit subjectivity informing and indeed enabling such deliberative exchanges underscores the importance of affective resonance in this process. Although these are issues to be picked up in the following chapter where we examine the role of affect in deliberation explicitly (this time with reference to calls for social change regarding animal welfare), what is important to note here is that the capacity to be able to really hear the voice and perspective of another – and respond to it – rests on that of connecting with that other, and, as we have noted in the previous chapter, even weak connections require some form of identification. Affective resonance and emotional appeals, as we discuss next, are highly effective in enabling identification and the making of such connections.

REFERENCES

Arias-Maldonado, M. (2007). An imaginary solution? The green defence of deliberative democracy. *Environmental Values, 16*(2), 233–252.

@IndigenousX. (n.d.). About. Retrieved from http://indigenousx.com.au/about/#.WLTt2zuGM2w.

Australian Human Rights Commission. (n.d.). Social justice and human rights for Aboriginal and Torres Strait Islander peoples. [Information sheet]. Retrieved from https://www.humanrights.gov.au/our-work/aboriginal-and-torres-strait-islander-social-justice/guides/information-sheet-social.

Bächtiger, A. (2011, October 22). *Contestatory deliberation*. Paper presented at the Epistemic Democracy Conference, Yale University, New Haven, Connecticut. Retrieved from https://www.uio.no/english/research/interfaculty-research-areas/democracy/news-and-events/events/seminars/2011/papers-yale-2011/Yale-Bachtiger.pdf.

Barber, B. (1999). The discourse of civility. In S. Elkin & S. Karol (Eds.), *Citizen competence and democratic institutions* (pp. 39–48). University Park, PA: Pennsylvania State University Press.

Bellamy, C., & Raab, C. D. (1999). Wiring up the deck-chairs? In S. Coleman, J. Taylor & W. Van de Donk (Eds.), *Parliament in the age of the internet* (pp. 156–172). Oxford, England: Oxford University Press.

Benhabib, S. (1994). Deliberative rationality and models of democratic legitimacy. *Constellations: An International Journal of Critical and Democratic Theory, 1*(1), 26–52.

Booth, G. (2014). Foreword. In *Making the connection: Essays in Indigenous digital excellence* (pp. v–vii). Fremantle, Australia: Vivid Publishing.

Bryant, D. (2013, July 18). Re: 1 Deadly Nation [Web log comment]. Retrieved from https://1deadlynation.wordpress.com/2013/07/18/trayvon-the-license-to-kill/.

Castells, M. (2008). The new public sphere: Global civil society, communication networks, and global governance. *The Annals of the American Academy of Political and Social Science, 616*, 78–93.

Chambers, S. (2003). Deliberative democracy theory. *Annual Reviews of Political Science, 6*, 307–326.

Clark, A. (2015). How a single Facebook post inspired thousands to stand up for Indigenous rights. *BuzzFeed*. Retrieved from http://www.buzzfeed.com/allanclarke/how-a-single-facebook-post-inspired-thousands-to-stand-up-fo#.lykjeayPj.

Coleman, S., & Gøtze, J. (2001). *Bowling together: Online public engagement in policy deliberation*. London, England: Hansard Society.

Cook, S. (2015a). #SOSBLAKAUSTRALIA: Stop the forced closure of Aboriginal communities. *Cultural Survival Quarterly Magazine*, *39*(2). Retrieved from https://www.culturalsurvival.org/publications/cultural-survival-quarterly/sosblakaustralia-stop-forced-closure-aboriginal.

Cook, S. (2015b, April 1). #SOSBLAKAUSTRALIA: Stop the forced closure of Aboriginal communities – IndigenousX. *The Guardian Australia*. Retrieved from http://www.theguardian.com.

Cromb, N. (2017, April 17). Newly elected WA state government asked to clarify their position on remote communities. SBS *NITV*. Retrieved from http://www.sbs.com.au/nitv/article/2017/04/17/newly-elected-wa-state-government-asked-clarify-their-position-remote-communities.

D'Arcy, S. (2007). Deliberative democracy, direct action, and animal advocacy. *Journal for Critical Animal Studies*, *5*(2). 1–16.

Dahlberg L. (2001). Computer-mediated communication and the public sphere: A critical analysis. *Journal of Computer-Mediated Communication*, *7*(1). doi:10.1111/j.1083-6101.2001.tb00137.x.

Dahlberg, L. (2005). The Habermasian public sphere: Taking difference seriously? *Theory and Society*, *34*(2), 111–136.

Dahlgren, P. (2005). The internet, public spheres, and political communication: Dispersion and deliberation. *Political Communication*, *22*(2), 147–162.

Dailey, L., Demo, L. & Spillman, M. (2008). Newspaper political blogs generate little interaction. *Newspaper Research Journal*, *29*(4), 53–65. Retrieved from http://elibrary,bigchalk.com.ezproxy.ecu.edu.au.

Davis, R. (2013, August 14). Re: 1 Deadly Nation [Blog comment]. Retrieved from https://1deadlynation.wordpress.com/2013/08/13/abbott-the-truth-and-cost-of-his-indigenous-volunteering/.

Davis, R., & Owen, D. (1998). *New media and American politics*. Oxford, England: Oxford University Press.

Deadly Bloggers. (2014). Home. Retrieved from http://deadlybloggers.com/.

Deadly Bloggers. (2017). Deadly Bloggers Blog Carnival. [Blog post]. Retrieved from http://deadlybloggers.com/events/deadly-bloggers-blog-carnival/.

Downey, J., & Fenton, N. (2003). New media, counter publicity and the public sphere. *New Media & Society*, *5*(2), 185–202.

Dreher, T., McCallum, M. & Waller, L. (2016). Indigenous voices and mediatized policy-making in the digital age. *Information, Communication & Society*, *19*(1), 23–39.

Drezner, D. W., & Farrell, H. (2008). Introduction: Blogs, politics and power. *Public Choice*, *134*, 1–13.

Dzur, A. W. (2002). Public journalism and deliberative democracy. *Polity*, *34*(3), 313–336.

Ekdale, B., Namkoong, K., Fung, T. & Perlmutter, D. (2010). Why blog? (then and now): Exploring the motivations for blogging by popular American political bloggers. *New Media & Society*, *12*(2), 217–234.

Eltantawy, N., & Wiest, J. B. (2011). Social media in the Egyptian revolution: Reconsidering resource mobilization theory. *International Journal of Communication*, *5*, 1207–1224.

esthetician salary. (2013, August 8). Re: 1 Deadly Nation [Web log comment]. Retrieved from https://1deadlynation.wordpress.com/2013/08/13/abbott-the-truth-and-cost-of-his-indigenous-volunteering/.

Fishkin, J. (1991). *Democracy and deliberation: New directions for democratic reform*. New Haven, CT: Yale University Press.

Fung, A., & Wright, E. O. (2003). Thinking about empowered participatory governance. In A. Fung & E. O. Wright (Eds.), *Deepening democracy: Institutional innovations in empowered participatory governance* (pp. 3–42). London, England: Verso.

Garden, M. (2010). Newspaper blogs: The genuine article or poor counterfeits? *Media International Australia Incorporating Culture and Policy*, *135*, 19–31.

Gil de Zúñiga, H., Puig-I-Abril, E. & Rojas, H. (2009). Weblogs, traditional sources online and political participation: An assessment of how the Internet is changing the political environment. *New Media & Society*, *11*, 553–574.

Habermas, J. (1984). *The theory of communicative action. Vol. 1: Reason and the rationalization of society* (T. McCarthy, Trans.). Boston, MA: Beacon Press.

Habermas, J. (1987). *Knowledge and human interests* (J. J. Shapiro, Trans.). Cambridge, England: Polity Press.

Habermas, J. (1998). *Between facts and norms: Contributions to discourse theory of law and democracy* (W. Rehg, Trans.). Cambridge, MA: MIT Press.

Habermas, J. (2008). *Between naturalism and religion: Philosophical essays*. Cambridge, England: Polity Press.

Hands, J. (2011). *@ is for activism: Dissent, resistance and rebellion in a digital culture*. London, England: Pluto Press.

Highfield, T., & Bruns, A. (2012). Confrontation and cooptation: A brief history of Australian political blogs. *Media International Australia Incorporating Culture and Policy*, *143*, 89–98.

Hodgson, M. (n.d.). About1Deadly Nation. Retrieved from https://1deadlynation.wordpress.com/about/.

Hopkins, K., & Matheson, D. (2012). Talking in a crowded room: Political blogging during the 2008 New Zealand general election. *Media International Australia Incorporating Culture and Policy*, *144*, 108–117.

Huggins, J. (2014). Foreword. In *Making the connection: Essays in Indigenous digital excellence* (pp. viii–x). Fremantle, Australia: Vivid Publishing.

Johnson, T., Kaye, B., Bichard, S. & Wong, W. (2007). Every blog has its day: Politically-interested Internet users' perceptions of blog credibility. *Journal of Computer-Mediated Communication*, *13*(1), 100–122.

Jones, R. (2014, April 8). Re: The Koori Woman [Web log comment]. Retrieved from https://thekooriwoman.wordpress.com/about/.

Kenix, J. (2009). Blogs as alternative. *Journal of Computer-Mediated Communication, 14*, 790–822.

Knops, A. (2007). Debate: Agonism as deliberation – on Mouffe's theory of democracy. *Journal of Political Philosophy, 15*, 115–126.

Krusche, D. (2014). Finding voice amid the internet chatter. *The Citizen*. Retrieved from http://www.thecitizen.org.au/media/finding-voice-amid-internet-chatter.

Lankshear, C., & Knobel, M. (2006). Sampling 'the new' in new literacies. In M. Knobel & C. Lankshear (Eds.), A new literacies sampler (pp.1–24). Retrieved from http://everydayliteracies.net/files/NewLiteraciesSampler_2007.pdf.

Latimore, J. (2013, August 30). Social media giving voice to Indigenous communities. *The Citizen*. Retrieved from http://www.thecitizen.org.au/media/social-media-giving-voice-indigenous-communities.

Lawrence, E., Sides, J. & Farrell, H. (2009). Self-segregation or deliberation? Blog readership, participation, and polarization in American politics. *Perspectives on Politics, 8*(1), 141–157.

Leccese, M. (2009). Online information sources of political blogs. *Journalism and Mass Communication Quarterly, 86*(3), 578–593.

Levine, P., & Nierras, R. M. (2007). Activists' views of deliberation. *Journal of Public Deliberation, 3*(1), 1–14.

Lim, M. (2012). Clicks, cafes, and coffee houses: Social media and oppositional movements in Egypt, 2004–2011. *Journal of Communication, 62*, 231–248.

Maddison, S. (2009). Voice and diversity in Indigenous politics. *Indigenous Law Bulletin*, 14, *7*(11). Retrieved from http://www.austlii.edu.au/au/journals/IndigLawB/2009/14.html.

Marr, E. (2014, January 10). Re: The Koori Woman [Web log comment]. Retrieved from https://thekooriwoman.wordpress.com/about/.

Maynard, J. (2008). *Fight for liberty and freedom. The origins of Australian Aboriginal activism*. Canberra, Australia: Aboriginal Studies Press.

Maynor, J. W. (2007, April 12). *Blogging for democracy: Deliberation, autonomy, and reasonableness in the blogosphere*. Paper presented at the Annual Meeting of the Midwest Political Science Association, Palmer House Hotel, Chicago, Illinois.

McKenna, L., & Pole, A. (2008). What do bloggers do: An average day on an average political blog. *Public Choice, 134*, 97–108.

Medhora, S. (2015, March 10). Remote communities are 'lifestyle choices', says Tony Abbott. *The Guardian*. Retrieved from https://www.theguardian.com/australia-news/2015/mar/10/remote-communities-are-lifestyle-choices-says-tony-abbott.

Meraz, S. (2007). Analyzing political conversation on the Howard Dean candidate blog. In M. Tremayne (Ed.), *Blogging, citizenship and the future of media* (pp. 59–82). London, England: Routledge.

Morris, E. (Presenter). (2015, August 10). AWAYE, Radio National [Radio broadcast]. Australian Broadcasting Commission. Retrieved from http://www.abc.net.au/radionational/programs/awaye/the-voices-behind-indigenousx/6680348.

Mummery, J., & Rodan, D. (2011). Chewing the communal cud: Community deliberation in broadsheet letters and political blogs. In J. Yearwood & A. Stranieri (Eds.), *Technologies for supporting reasoning communities and collaborative decision making: Cooperative approaches* (pp. 296–318). Hershey, PA: Information Science Reference, IGI Global.

Mummery, J., & Rodan, D. (2013). The role of blogging in public deliberation and democracy. *Discourse, Context & Media*, *2*(1), 22–39.

1 Deadly Nation. (2013, August 13). Abbott, the truth and cost of his indigenous volunteering [Web log post]. Retrieved from https://1deadlynation.wordpress.com/2013/08/13/abbott-the-truth-and-cost-of-his-indigenous-volunteering/.

1 Deadly Nation. (2014, November 25). Ferguson Australia, Murder under the red, white and blue [Web log post]. Retrieved from https://1deadlynation.wordpress.com/2014/11/25/ferguson-australia-murder-under-the-red-white-and-by-blue/.

1 Deadly Nation. (n.d.). About. Retrieved from https://1deadlynation.wordpress.com/about/.

Papacharissi, Z. A. (2002). The virtual sphere: The internet as a public sphere. *New Media & Society*, *4*(1), 9–27.

Papacharissi, Z. A. (2010). *A private sphere: Democracy in a digital age*. Cambridge, England: Polity Press.

Pattie, J. W. (2008). Arguments-based collective choice. *Journal of Theoretical Politics*, *20*(4), 379–414.

Pearson, L. (2014). Reflections on engaging with the Indigenous digital world. In *Making the connection: Essays in Indigenous digital excellence* (pp. 45–53). Fremantle, Australia: Vivid Publishing.

Pellizzoni, L. (2001). The myth of the best argument: Power, deliberation and reason. *British Journal of Sociology*, *52*(1), 59–86.

Perlmutter, D. (2008). Political blogging and campaign 2008: A roundtable. *The International Journal of Press/Politics*, *13*(2), 160–170.

Petray, T. (2013). Self-writing a movement and contesting Indigeneity: Being an Aboriginal activist on social media. *Global Media Journal: Australian Edition*, 7(1). Retrieved from http://www.hca.westernsydney.edu.au/gmjau/wp-content/uploads/2013/08/GMJAU_V7-1_Self-Writing.pdf.

Rice, E., Haynes, E., Royce, P. & Thompson, S. C. (2016). Social media and digital technology use among Indigenous young people in Australia: A literature review. *International Journal for Equity in Health*. doi:10.1186/s12939-016-0366-0.

Roberts, J. M. (2014). *New media and public activism: Neoliberalism, the state and radical protest in the public sphere*. Bristol, England: Policy Press.

Sack, W. (2005). Discourse architecture and very large-scale conversations. In R. Latham & S. Sassen (Eds.), *Digital formations: IT and new architectures in the global realm* (pp. 242–282). Princeton, NJ: Princeton University Press.

Sauter, T. (2013). *Governing self on Facebook: Social networking sites as tools for self-formation*. Unpublished doctoral dissertation. Queensland University of Technology, Brisbane.

Sauter, M. (2014). *The coming swarm: DdoS actions, hacktivism, and civil disobedience on the internet*. New York, NY: Bloomsbury.

Simone, M. A. (2010). Deliberative democracy online: Bridging networks with digital technologies. *The Communication Review*, *13*(2), 120–139.

sosblakaustralia. (2017, April 12). Media release [Facebook post]. Retrieved from https://www.facebook.com/sosblakaustralia/?hc_ref=PAGES_TIMELINE&fref=nf.

Sparks, J. (2014, October 15). Re: The Koori Woman [Web log comment]. Retrieved from https://thekooriwoman.wordpress.com/about/.

Stears, M. (2013). *Demanding democracy: American radicals in search of a new politics*. Princeton, NJ: Princeton University Press.

Sunstein, C. (2007). *Republic.com 2.0*. Princeton, NJ: Princeton University Press.

Sweet, M., Pearson, L. & Dudgeon, P. (2013). @ IndigenousX: A case study of community-led innovation in digital media. *Media International Australia Incorporating Culture Policy*, *149*, 104–111.

Tan, M. (2015, September 21). Emma Donovan calls on Australia to save its remote Indigenous communities. *The Guardian*. Retrieved from https://www.theguardian.com/music/2015/sep/21/emma-donovan-calls-on-australia-to-save-its-remote-indigenous-communities.

Tara. (2014, November 8). Re: The Koori Woman [Web log comment]. Retrieved from https://thekooriwoman.wordpress.com/about/.

TheKooriWoman. (n.d.). About. Retrieved from https://thekooriwoman.wordpress.com/about/.

Thin Black Line. (n.d.). Thin black line. [Twitter update]. Retrieved from https://twitter.com/ttbl_2ser.

Thompson, G. (2003). Weblogs, warblogs, the public sphere, and bubbles. *Transformations*, *7*, 1–12. Retrieved from http://transformations.cqu.edu.au/journal/issue_07/article_02.shtml.

TNS Social Research. (2014). *Discrimination against Indigenous Australians: A snapshot of the views of non-Indigenous people aged 25–44*. Retreived from https://www.beyondblue.org.au/docs/default-source/research-project-files/bl1337-report—tns-discrimination-against-indigenous-australians.pdf?sfvrsn=2.

Torres, M. (2015). #SOSBLAKAUSTRALIA actions to continue – our communities need certainty. [Facebook press release]. Retrieved from https://www.facebook.com/sosblakaustralia/posts/1105435579473251.

Tsagarousianou, R. (1999). Electronic democracy: Rhetoric and reality. *Communications*, *24*(2), 189–208.

Tully, J. (2002). The unfreedom of the moderns in comparison to their ideals of constitutional democracy. *Modern Law Review*, *65*(2), 204–228.

Turner, G., Tomlinson, E. & Pearce, S. (2006). Talkback radio: Some notes on format, politics and influence. *Media International Australia Incorporating Culture and Policy*, *118*, 107–119.

Warnke, G. (1995). Communicative rationality and cultural values. In S. K. White (Ed.), *The Cambridge companion to Habermas* (pp. 120–142). Cambridge, England: Cambridge University Press.

Watego, L. (2013, March 30). Help me subscribe and share your work [Web log post]. Retrieved from http://deadlybloggers.com/help-me-subscribe-and-share-your-work/.

Watego, L. (2014). 'I found my voice': Indigenous narratives enduring through digital participation [Slideshow]. Retrieved from https://www.slideshare.net/leesawatego/deadly-bloggers-wipce-presentation.

Wilhelm, A. G. (2000). *Democracy in the digital age: Challenges to political life in cyberspace*. London, England: Routledge.

Wilson, T. (2014, March 26). Free speech is best medicine for the bigotry disease. *The Australian*. Retrieved from http://www.theaustralian.com.au/.

Woodly, D. (2008). New competencies in democratic communication? Blogs, agenda setting and political participation. *Public Choice*, *134*, 109–123.

Wright, S., & Street, J. (2007). Democracy, deliberation and design: The case of online discussion forums. *New Media & Society*, *9*(5), 849–869.

Young, I. M. (2000). *Inclusion and democracy*. Oxford, England: Oxford University Press.

Young, I. M. (2003). Activist challenges to deliberative democracy. In J. Fishkin & P. Laslett (Eds.), *Debating deliberative democracy* (pp. 102–120). New York, NY: Blackwell.

Young, S. (2011). *How Australia decides: Election reporting and the media*. Cambridge, England: Cambridge University Press.

Xenos, M. (2008). New mediated deliberation: Blog and press coverage of the Alito nomination. *Journal of Computer-Mediated Communication*, *13*(2), 485–503.

Chapter 3

Animals Australia, Multi-Platform Campaigning and the Mobilisation of Affect

One of the questions underpinning this book has been how digital culture and digital participatory media tools can support activists in their drives for social change, specifically with regard to how they might use these tools and capacities to appeal to and influence citizens. With activism understood as generally meaning the taking of action 'to effect social change' (Permanent Culture Now, 2013), and activists defined in the previous chapter as those committed to advancing a substantive political or social goal or outcome (Levine & Nierras, 2007), activists are well known – and sometimes criticised – for making use of a variety of means to get their messages across. They may engage both direct and indirect forms of action – with some direct forms of action contravening state expectations regarding citizen action – as well as utilise both deliberative and affective modes of engagement. This is to say that activist activities focused towards the achievement of social change are not limited to the deliberative practices of reasonable public contestation but also explicitly draw on affective modes of expression, aiming at an emotional as well as a rational response from stakeholders. To use popular parlance, activist campaigns strive to appeal to the heart as well as the mind. This dual focus is integral given activist aims of forging and promoting not just new individual and collective practices but new individual and collective identities.

This chapter, then, examines the capacity of multi-platform digital activist campaigning to engage and mobilise individuals through both deliberative and affective practices and thereby support activist calls for social change. To do this it examines the contentious but highly effective campaigning work undertaken on animal welfare by the peak national animal protection organisation Animals Australia. In engaging multiple media throughout their various campaigns – the use of print and broadcast media with digital media technologies and tools – Animals Australia provides a clear demonstration of the capacity of multi-platform campaigning to foreground and keep an activist issue in the mainstream public sphere. Two aspects are of particular interest also in this case: first how various digital tools and technologies facilitate the deliberate production and mobilisation of affect by Animals Australia and second how their facilitation of subjective investment aims at reforming citizens into, in this case, ethical consumers who consider animal welfare in their consumption practices. Framed by a brief discussion of animal activism within Australia, this chapter examines the main tenets and multiple tactics comprising Animals Australia's multi-platform 'Make It Possible' campaign. More specifically, this chapter explores (a) the contested framing of affect by both deliberative and ethical theories, (b) the question of the significance of affect and affective economies in facilitating social change (engaging in particular with social movement theories) along with (c) broader theories and issues concerning ethical consumerism. These are all important issues for activists – particularly in the fields of animal welfare and environmentalism – given the oft-cited arguments that social change should be based on and informed by public deliberative reasoned exchange culminating in a reasoned consensus and that activist actions operating outside of this remit disrupt the public sphere in unproductive and unjustifiable ways. These various issues inform (d) our final discussions concerning how affect and deliberation should be understood as inseparable in the functioning and use of digital culture and digital media tools – an entanglement we argue is explicitly leveraged in digital activism.

ANIMAL ACTIVISM IN THE AUSTRALIAN CONTEXT

Animal welfare in Australia is a highly contested issue engaging standpoints and stakeholders representing multiple perspectives: animal protectionist and liberationist, economic, agricultural/industrial, cultural and legal. The specific balance given to these interests further varies between Australia's states and territories. Legal protection of animal welfare in Australia, as in many countries, is, however, particularly problematic for livestock – defined here as all animals farmed for use and profit, including poultry and aquatic animals – insofar as they are effectively excluded from the majority of existing animal protection statutes. Despite explicit recognition of the necessity for reform in Australian animal law – in 2008 the Australian Law Reform Commission journal, *Reform*, described animal welfare and animal rights as the 'next great social justice movement' (Weisbrot, 2007, p. 2) – current practices concerning livestock welfare give the most weight to the industry's Model Codes of Practice for the Welfare of Animals. These are commissioned by the Primary Industries Standing Committee and endorsed by the

Primary Industries Ministerial Council. Varying across the Australian states and territories, these codes are best described as sets of guidelines detailing minimum rather than best welfare standards, and which are furthermore neither compulsory nor practically enforceable. This model has come under increasing pressure from animal advocates and activists who have argued that there is an inherent conflict of interests between welfare and production, and that livestock animals, as sentient beings, should have their welfare requirements properly recognised and protected. There is also increasing recognition that, despite the existing network of statutes and codes, Australia's current laws 'fail to provide meaningful protections to farm animals' (Sharman, 2009, p. 36; also see Bagaric & Akers, 2012).

Similar to other countries, animal activism within Australia has gained a reputation for extremism, with some activist groups engaging in more or less serious acts of unlawfulness to promote their cause. The latter have included trespass, damage to public and private property, the infliction of mental or physical injury on participants in animal cruelty (or on their families) and economic sabotage (Bagaric & Akers, 2012). Such acts, however, even if considered to be morally justifiable by some, have caused a public opinion backlash. Currently, as in other parts of the world, animal activists who covertly access private property to record acts of animal cruelty are being framed in industry and some political contexts as economic saboteurs and even 'terrorists' (*ABC News*, 2013b), and there are attempts to institute what have come to be called 'Ag-gag' laws within Australia. An 'Ag-gag' law is the name given to legislation designed to curb the rise in animal activist (and environmental) monitoring and investigative activities within the livestock sector in particular. Proposals to introduce such legislation first arose in the United States in the late 1990s and, where these laws have been enacted, they typically contain one or more of the following provisions:

- A prohibition of taking photographs or video footage on or in an agricultural facility or property without the permission of the proprietor;
- A prohibition on seeking employment with an agricultural business under false pretences or without disclosing ties to animal rights organisations; and
- A requirement that any documentary evidence of animal mistreatment is reported to relevant authorities within a short time frame, often a 24 to 48 hour period. (RSPCA, 2016)

Such laws seek to duplicate existing trespass laws, but with a twist. Seriously increasing penalties, making it illegal to distribute or broadcast images that have not been surrendered to the police and making it a crime to seek employment with the aim of exposing animal suffering would mean that animal activists would be unable to let the broader community know about socially invisible animal suffering (O'Sullivan, 2015). Interest in enacting such legislation arguably corresponds with a sharp increase in the use of direct monitoring and investigative activities by animal activists. The increasing prevalence – and perhaps effectiveness – of these investigations has led to calls for the introduction of similar laws in Australia (the unsuccessful Criminal Code Amendment [Animal Protection] Bill 2015 in the Australian Senate being one such example).

ANIMALS AUSTRALIA AND 'MAKE IT POSSIBLE'

For several years now, Animals Australia – a not-for-profit representing some forty member groups and over 1.5 million individual supporters – has been recognised as Australia's foremost national animal protection organisation. Along with its global arm, Animals International, the organisation has a well-recognised international and national track record in investigating and exposing animal cruelty and for conducting strategic public awareness campaigns (Animals Australia [Web], n.d.) In 2015, for example, the organisation was recognised as a 'standout charity' by the US-based Animal Charity Evaluators, this being the first time an Australian-based organisation has been so selected. With this designation being the second-highest ranking the organisation awards, the evaluation recognised that although Animals Australia is based in Australia, its mission, investigations, reach and, ultimately, positive impact for animals all extend globally (Animals Australia, 2016). As stated by the Animal Charity Evaluators of this award, 'Animals Australia has shown the ability to steer public conversation in Australia in a more animal friendly direction and make concrete achievements on behalf of animals like getting McDonald's to phase out eggs from hens in battery cages' (Smerdon, 2015).

Within the Australian context, footage from Animals Australia's national and international investigations into animal cruelty (in such contexts as factory farming, live export, slaughterhouses, greyhound racing, duck shooting and puppy farming) has been featured on every current affairs program within Australia – both commercial and public channels – including *Four Corners*, *60 Minutes*, *Today Tonight*, *A Current Affair*, *7.30*, *The Project*, *Lateline* and *Landline*. The organisation also uses these materials to develop a range of broader multimedia public campaigns around these issues. What is clear is that the organisation sees its remit as to undertake two interwoven roles: to be both a peak body representing a large number of grassroots groups and a campaign-focused organisation working to raise community awareness of animal cruelty and promote reform. The organisation's mission, as detailed in its main website, is thus to (a) investigate, expose and raise community awareness of animal cruelty; (b) provide animals with the strongest representation possible to government and other decision-makers; (c) educate, inspire, empower and enlist the support of the community to prevent and prohibit animal cruelty; and (d) generally strengthen the animal protection movement (Animals Australia [Web], n.d.). In delivery of its mission, the organisation thus engages not only the platforms of public rallies and protests, government and industry submissions, corporate outreach and various forms of print and broadcast media (television, radio, newspapers and billboards) as well as the web to present its campaigns, but multiple forms of digital participatory media, including Facebook, YouTube and Twitter. These latter are further tailored around key campaigns and audience demographics (Animals Australia Unleashed! being, for instance, the youth-targeted sites), with the organisation supporting multiple forms of web presence. These are detailed in table 3.1 along with an indication, where possible, of each platform's reach via numbers of subscribers, followers, likes and views.

Table 3.1. Animals Australia's platforms, sites and reach as of 11 January 2017.

Platform	*Site*	*Reach (As of 11 January 2017)*
Web	Animals Australia [Web]. (n.d.)	No data of views available
	Animals Australia Unleashed! [Web]. (n.d.)	No data of views available
	Ban Live Export [Web]. (n.d.)	No data of views available
	Make it Possible [Web]. (n.d.)	No data of views available
		Total unavailable
Facebook	Animals Australia [Facebook]. (n.d.)	1,452,112 followers 1,498,350 likes
	Animals Australia Unleashed! [Facebook]. (n.d.)	91,858 followers 94,283 likes
	Ban Live Export [Facebook]. (n.d.)	22,569 followers 24,227 likes
	Make it Possible [Facebook]. (n.d.)	66,123 followers 67,551 likes
		Total followers: 1,632662 Total likes: 1,684,411
YouTube	Animals Australia [YouTube]. (n.d.)	9,347 subscribers 3,877,758 views
	Animals Australia Unleashed! [YouTube]. (n.d.)	383 subscribers 149,915 views
		Total subscribers: 9,730 Total views: 4,027,673
Twitter	Animals Australia [Twitter]. (n.d.)	39,891 followers 16,273 likes
	Animals Australia Unleashed! [Twitter]. (n.d.)	3,653 followers 1,408 likes
	Ban Live Export [Twitter]. (n.d.)	4,692 followers 529 likes
		Total followers: 48,236 Total likes: 18,210

Launched in October 2012, the Make It Possible campaign began with a video made by LOUD advertising agency, which was uploaded by Animals Australia on YouTube on 21 October 2012. The video also screened for periods as a cinema and television advertisement on commercial stations during peak time – reaching 3 million viewers across the country – and featured in major Australian magazines and newspapers. An extended eleven-minute video, including a sequence of celebrity endorsements (by a variety of high-profile Australians, including actors, singers, comedians, sportspeople and chefs), was also uploaded by Animals Australia on its own website and YouTube, as well as being translated into Spanish, Portuguese and Italian and shared through international social media platforms. The campaign message remains simple and the same: factory farming is a major cause of animal cruelty; all factory-farmed animals experience a life of intolerable and unnecessary suffering; each of us can and should work to end the factory farming of animals (see Lyn White, as cited in Clark, 2013). As Animals Australia Campaign Director Lyn White stated in 2012: 'We know that factory faming only exists because their secrets are secured behind high walls and closed doors – and that an informed community would not knowingly support such cruelty' (as cited in Neales, 2012). Such awareness raising is thus the remit of Animals Australia and the Make It Possible campaign. In White's words, 'Our vision, our work is towards ensuring that all animals . . . especially in human care, have protection from cruel treatment and are treated with compassion and respect. That is what we work towards on a daily basis' (as cited in Clark, 2013).

Combining *Babe* (1995) style animation effects with real footage from Australian factory farms – visual effects which won the makers a Mobius Award in 2012 – the Make It Possible YouTube video presents animals as being fundamentally *like* the viewers, possessing a similar interest in living a life of well-being. Engaging viewers' tacit knowledge of how it feels to be restricted, along with their empathy, animals in factory farms are presented in the campaign video (see the transcript, Animals Australia, 2012) as yearning for a better life, for 'a new way of living'. They are described as 'living lives of abject misery' denied 'the simple joys in life that we take for granted, freedom, sunshine, fresh air and exercise', as 'waking up each day, just to suffer', descriptions which are reinforced with images of overcrowding, confinement, lightlessness and industrial sterility. The campaign reminds viewers that the animals kept in these barren and constrictive conditions are 'no different to our pets at home'; that they are 'highly intelligent creatures who feel pain, and who will respond to kindness and affection – if given the chance'; and that they are 'someone, not something'. Further driving this message home, animals are anthropomorphised, given human voice, expression and desires; they are also individuated, with recurring close-ups of real animal faces and eyes, directly challenging any tendency to see these animals as nothing more than a resource to be used, as livestock. With its final scene of a winged pig escaping confinement, the video draws on a powerful social narrative of exile, alienation and hope. As Anthony Ritchie, one of the campaigners with Animals Australia, stressed with regard to the development of the video, this deliberate focus on likeness and facilitation of empathy was integral:

> Pigs and chickens aren't animals that people instantly connect with or have empathy for so our first task was simply getting people to like them – to think about them in a different way and to understand that these animals share the same capacity to suffer and to feel love as our dogs and cats at home. The success of movies like *Charlotte's Web* and *Babe* gave us a great formula to work with and that's what we had in mind when we created our 'hero pig'. The rest of the TVC uses real footage from factory farms in Australia – it was critical that what we were showing reflected the current situation for most animals raised for food in Australia today. Finding the song 'Somewhere' and obtaining the rights to use it brought the vision together. We always knew that if animals could plead their own case for a kinder world then factory farming would have ended long ago and the words to 'Somewhere' so beautifully encapsulate our core message – that at the very least animals raised for food should be provided with a life worth living. (as cited in van Gurp, 2012)

Make It Possible, then, is a campaign that works explicitly to activate affect along with viewers' ethical agency, their recognition and acceptance of individual responsibility. It interpellates viewers to recognise themselves as being essentially compassionate and caring but ignorant of the real situation of animals in factory farming. As explained in the video, viewers are positioned as not knowing of the 'terrible price' paid by animals in the consumer demand for cheap animal products, as not knowing that this demand has culminated in an 'animal welfare disaster of a magnitude this planet has never known'. This interpellation further encompasses a call to act. Viewers are reminded that consumer choice can 'create a kinder world for these animals'. They are reminded that although 'there are many things in this world that we are powerless to change . . . this is not one of them', that by 'refusing to buy factory farmed products, and making kinder choices', they can end this cruelty. Such framing of the campaign message presents two dichotomies, between (a) knowledge and ignorance and (b) compassion and cruelty. These contend that once viewers realise the cruelty inherent in factory farming they cannot but call for it to end – to do otherwise is to sanctify cruelty for purely selfish reasons. Such framing calls every viewer into the same position, as holding to the same goal, recognising the same duty.

In direct response to this message, as of the end of November 2013, over 173,000 Australians publicly pledged through the campaign site to boycott factory-farmed animal produce, reduce consumption of animal products and, in some cases, to become meat-free. By the beginning of 2017 this number increased to close to 288,000. Also within the period from release to late 2013, the extended YouTube video was viewed nearly 118,000 times, shared nearly 2,000 times and received 780 comments, 88 percent supportive (by the beginning of 2017 YouTube received over 569,000 views and was shared over 4,700 times). Public response has also extended to donations enough for television and print advertising (including a full-page poster in multiple national newspapers which was made possible by 100,000 supporters), and grassroots outreach initiatives, and to generally increase Animals Australia's lobbying power towards ending legal exemptions that permit cruelty to animals in factory farms.

COLES AND THE SHORT-LIVED FLIGHT OF THE WINGED PIG SHOPPING BAG

Along with its public outreach and desired effects on consumer identification and action (to be discussed later), the Make It Possible campaign, along with additional lobbying work carried out by Animals Australia, has been credited as being instrumental in the recent shifts within Australia by major supermarket and fast-food chains away from factory-farmed eggs and pork, the main targets of the campaign. One of Australia's supermarket giants, Coles – which with Woolworths control approximately '80% of the grocery market' (Maher, 2013; cf. Deloitte Access Economics Pty Ltd., 2012; Mortimer, 2013) – explicitly referred to its ongoing dialogues with Animals Australia and other animal welfare organisations regarding issues of animal welfare and sustainability (Sampson, 2013) as the basis for its decision in early 2013 to discontinue the use of sow stalls and battery hen cages for Coles brand products (Nason, 2013) – a year earlier than initially scheduled. (As of early 2017, Aldi, Hungry Jacks, McDonald's, Subway and Woolworths have also all taken steps to phase out cage eggs from their supply chains in Australia, along with multiple Foodworks and IGAs (Independent Grocers of Australia), as has the food manufacturer Simplot, the parent company of Bird's Eye, Lean Cuisine, Edgell and Leggo's; *Marketing Magazine*, 2015.) Coles, however, took a further step in May 2013 in agreeing to publicly partner with Animals Australia and sell *winged pig* campaign shopping bags in-store, with some of the proceeds going directly to support the Make It Possible campaign (Frazer, 2013).

Coles's decision to partner with Animals Australia in this way garnered extensive media coverage across a wide variety of mainstream Australian print, digital and online sites. It also gained widespread coverage through social media. It proved to be a controversial decision. When news of the Coles-Animals Australia bag sale broke, 'beef and lamb producers threatened to stop supplying Coles with products, while other farmers threatened to stop buying fertiliser and insurance from Coles' parent company, Wesfarmers' (Malone, 2013). In the view of the National Farmers Federation (NFF), Coles's support of the Make It Possible campaign would cause 'serious harm to many parts of animal agriculture in this country' (*The Land*, 2013). As was expressed by farmers in a variety of ways across multiple media outlets, Coles selling these shopping bags in-store to help raise funds for Animals Australia could only be seen as a kick in the face or the guts for Australian primary producers (as cited in Bettles, 2013). In the words of the Sheepmeat Council of Australia CEO Ron Cullen,

> Coles have made statements about being concerned for their suppliers – but teaming up with an activist group that wants to close down Australian livestock production seems to be inconsistent with that previously stated support. . . . Our members are incredibly concerned that Coles is moving closer to an activist group with an agenda to end livestock production. (as cited in Bettles, 2013)

Along with such expressions of anger and disappointment with Coles's decision, the NFF and other farming organisations also turned to social media campaigning, using Facebook and Twitter to mobilise antipathy towards the Make It Possible campaign, Animals Australia and other animal advocacy organisations. These exchanges in turn received wide-ranging news coverage and generated extensive public commentary in the form of social media posts and responses to online news articles. Commentary and responses crystallised around three contrasting affectively charged positions: (a) that farmers have successfully shown that they cannot be bullied by, what the NFF CEO Matt Linnegar called, an 'extremist animal activist group' (as cited in Nason, 2013); (b) that farmers have shown themselves to be uncaring about animal welfare; and (c) that caring about animal welfare is not in itself an extremist position (Rodan & Mummery, 2014b). The controversy resulted in Animals Australia releasing Coles from its obligation regarding the shopping bags. As Animals Australia then framed these events, 'the take-home message for shoppers' can only be that 'farmers are opposed to an initiative that aims to improve the lives of animals produced for food' (*ABC News*, 2013a). Such reporting gained Animals Australia enough donated funds to reintroduce the Make It Possible television advertisements on prime-time commercial television.

Associated with perceived bullying tactics and/or animal welfare concerns (the latter affirmed or denigrated), what became clear through analysis of this coverage (Rodan & Mummery, 2014b) was that the winged pig shopping bag itself had become 'saturated with affect' (Ahmed, 2004b, p. 11). That is, it mobilised individuals into seemingly opposed cohorts, calling them towards some form of activism regarding Animals Australia's attempts to raise consciousness and entrench new norms of animal welfare. Hence, while Animals Australia presented itself as speaking on behalf of animals and all *caring* Australians, calling on consumers to change their behaviour and hold the livestock industry accountable for the inhumanity of its practices, the NFF presented itself as speaking on behalf of the industry and sector, mobilising Australian farmers to reject Animals Australia's campaigns as extremist attacks on the industry. This interpellation of individuals into affectively charged cohorts, although not demonstrating majority alignment of individuals with the campaign, was nonetheless extremely effective in generating and harnessing affect able to be mobilised by Animals Australia.

This interpellation was played out deliberatively in many ways, insofar as coverage of the debate from each perspective called directly for community participation. More specifically, each position called, in effect, on community members to participate in the renegotiation of ideas of the public good sparked by the campaign and the kinds of change considered desirable and/or necessary with regard to these issues. Each position called, therefore, on community members to become better informed and to challenge each other over their understandings of the public good, to become, in other words, involved deliberatively in the debate. The social media forums in use, in turn, supported that other major requirement of deliberation, that all participants would 'have equal chances to speak, to make assertions, self-presentations, and normative claims and to challenge others' (Warnke, 1995, p. 126). The fact that a community consensus on these issues has not been forthcoming is not of itself a problem to deliberative procedure, insofar as no consensus reached can exemplify universality in any absolute sense (Knops, 2007). What is instead important is that deliberative quality rests on the meeting of procedural conditions, specifically 'the presumption that reasonable or fair results are obtained insofar as the flow of relevant information and its proper handling have not been obstructed' (Habermas, 1998, p. 296). In this instance, and despite claims from each perspective that other positions are biased, overly emotional, invested and/or ignorant, what is evident is that public debate over these issues remains not just unobstructed but explicitly promoted by key stakeholders. If deliberation is taken, as we have suggested in the previous chapter, as needing to meet the minimal standards of enabling participants to (a) engage in debate over issues of public concern, (b) introduce additional issues into the debate, (c) argue for preferred views and (d) engage with differing viewpoints, then public discussion concerning this campaign has clearly met these standards, even if it was mobilised through emotion.

THE PROBLEM OF AFFECT

It is, however, the generation of affect and affective alignment that is often presented as problematic in activist campaigning. This problem was clearly pointed to by then Australian Parliamentary Secretary for Agriculture, Sid Sidebottom, who said, in reference to the aforementioned controversy, that there needs to be greater understanding of farming and food production among the Australian public rather than the existing furore driven by high emotion over animal welfare issues. As he stated, 'Sometimes I despair that we can't have a sensible debate on these types of issues' (as cited in Bettles, 2013). This is an important point in that this wariness concerning emotion comprises one of the reasons activism is often framed as radical extremism. Here the view is that a focus on emotions can divert attention 'from objective information', as was written explicitly in critique of Animals Australia's affectively driven campaigning tactics (Keogh, 2015).

Following this same line, many deliberative and ethical theories do tend to denigrate emotion and affect as getting in the way of sensible debate, as effectively impeding *proper* decision-making over public issues (Ben-Ze'ev, 1997). As was discussed in the previous chapter, insofar as deliberation stresses the pursuit of reciprocal understanding between those who may hold to different frameworks or ideologies and comprises a form of exchange that accepts the need for the ongoing revision of judgements and preferences, it is typically framed as needing to prioritise forms of rational exchange over emotional ones. Deliberation hence is typically understood as that public 'debate and discussion aimed at producing reasonable, well-informed opinions in which participants are willing to revise preferences in light of discussion, new information, and claims made by fellow participants' (Chambers, 2003, p. 309). Consequently, as Jürgen Habermas – one of the heavyweights of deliberative theorising (see, e.g., Habermas, 1998) – has proclaimed, the only appropriate communication strategies for deliberation would be those that promote reasonableness and dialogue. Fitting strategies, as discussed in the previous chapter, would thus develop agreement 'only as the result of more or less exhaustive' discussions through which 'proposals, information and reasons can be more or less rationally dealt with' (Habermas, p. 362). Although this orientation towards rationality is under debate within deliberative theorising, with a variety of proponents disputing the levels and kinds of rationality that should be considered appropriate for deliberative decision-making within the public sphere (see Young, 2000), the basic requirement of reasoned and reasonable decision-making stands.

Similarly, concerned with the question of how one should act, morally speaking, normative ethics is recognised as functioning through the use of rules or handrails – better known as moral principles or reasons – which allow subjects to determine and justify whether a proposed action is right or wrong. Such moral principles are typically desired to be universalisable and rationally defensible, and they – and the moral reasoning they drive – are typically required to be compartmentalised away from our emotive, affect-driven responses. Indeed, what is clearly visible in the outline of theories of normative ethics – such as deontological or duty-based ethics, utilitarian ethics, social contract ethics and human rights – is that each of these theories remains suspicious of any attempts to give preference or moral value on anything other than rational, universalisable and impartial grounds. Any other grounds are likely to mean, as the argument goes, the loss of consistency in the application of moral principles, and such a loss is typically understood as meaning the loss of not just the principles as principles – and thereby as reasons able to guide behaviour – but ethical behaviour itself. After all, not only is consistency in the way we treat people at the heart of our notions of impartiality and fairness, but the loss of consistency makes it appear that our moral decisions are arbitrary. As Rachels (1986, p. 149) has thus stated of ethical decision-making:

> The idea cannot be to avoid reliance on unsupported 'sentiments' (to use Hume's word) altogether – that is impossible. The idea is [rather] always to be suspicious of them, and to rely on as few as possible, only after examining them critically, and only after pushing the arguments and explanations as far as they will go without them.

Emotion and affect – the latter here defined initially as the sticky residue or impression left by the movement of emotion (Ahmed, 2004b, p. 6) – are thus considered problematic for deliberative decision-making that aims for decisions attuned to the larger public good. Here the idea is that emotions and affect too easily work to polarise people, making them less able to hear and understand others' perspectives, let alone revise their own perspectives on the basis of others' views. The flip side of this position is that while this all may be the case, emotion and affect are always more than private matters belonging to individuals. Distributed across both social and psychic fields, emotions and affect, Ahmed (2004a) continues, ripple stickily, moving sideways and backwards, sliding from one object to a completely different one. Such circulation of emotion between people, as well as between people and images or objects, is what Ahmed refers to as the 'affective economy' (2004a, p. 120). Emotions and affect hence *do* things; they align and bind individuals into communities, forming collectivities and solidarity (Ahmed, 2004a, 2004b; Kuntsman, 2012; Watkins, 2010). They are both as such – by definition – markers of value and investment.

ROLES FOR AFFECT IN SOCIAL CHANGE

Emotions and affect in other words provide 'a motivating force for consciousness' (Watkins, 2010, p. 269) as well as for solidarity; their work in aligning and binding individuals means they can inform the mobilising of subjects to struggle for (and against) social change. In effect – to draw on a metaphor of static electricity – they can *charge* subjects to the point that they will and do *spark*, mobilise and seek change. This is to stress the point that achieving action and social change requires what in social movement theory has been called motivational framing, the actual mobilising of people so that they become inclined to and carry out ethical and political action (Jasper & Nelkin, 1992; Jasper & Poulsen, 1995). This mobilising has, in turn, been theorised, as discussed in chapter 1, as needing some forms of identification and personal investment of belief, and these, we would argue, are driven by affect as much as if not more than reason. Mobilisation, after all, is also an activation of solidarity, and solidarity arguably 'arises from affective stakes – caring for someone, outrage about an injustice, or aspiration for a changed world' (Shotwell, 2011, p. 100).

These are points social movement theories consistently stress. Snow and Benford (1988), for instance, identify three main tasks for social movements: diagnostic, prognostic and motivational framing. Under this model, diagnostic framing identifies some event or condition as problematic. According to the Make It Possible campaign, for example, the diagnosis is that intensive livestock farming is wrong because it is fundamentally inhumane. Linked to the diagnostic task, the prognostic task is to outline a potential solution; for Animals Australia this means, as noted earlier, mobilising consumers to change their everyday behaviour so as to influence both the livestock and retail industries. The third task, motivational framing, involves Animals Australia actually mobilising this support and having consumers behave differently. Thus, the important shift for activists and social movements is that from prognostic to motivational work. Jasper and Poulsen (1995, p. 498; cf. Jasper & Nelkin, 1992), examining the animal rights movement, argue that one common strategy in use in this context is the use of 'moral shock', meaning 'when an event or situation raises such a sense of outrage in people that they become inclined toward political action'. Moral shocks are most effective when they are 'embodied in, or translatable into, powerful condensing symbols' able to 'neatly capture – both cognitively and emotionally – a range of meanings, and convey a frame, a master frame, or theme' (Jasper & Poulsen, 1995, p. 498). As animal rights and welfare movements have long realised, representations of animals are effective condensing symbols able to convey a master frame of cruelty and suffering to produce the moral shock – what we would also call the affective charge – required to engage and motivate people both individually and collectively (Lowe, 2006; Nabi, 2009; Wrenn, 2013). Consequently, animal activists have a history of using disturbing images of animal suffering, with the common argument being that such 'shock tactics' are necessary because the suffering of animals is 'a hidden taboo that society is very reluctant to notice, let alone address' (Aaltola, 2014, p. 28). Indeed, as has been argued with reference to the controversy surrounding the live export industry within Australia since Animals Australia's investigations and the airing of its footage of animal cruelty on national television, 'the public's ire' is raised 'not by persuasive intellectual arguments, but rather by the moral shock of seeing animal suffering on television' (Munro, 2015, p. 10). Importantly, however, it is also recognised in this space that such shock tactics will be most effective when viewers are also pointed to an action that they can take to help the situation (Aaltola, 2014). Given the capacity, then, for the affective work of moral shocks – when strategically used and linked to achievable actions – to align individual respondents into collectivities and to mobilise them, activist campaigns must all strive to be 'affectively charged' so as to gain recognition and build momentum and action around issues (Kuntsman, 2012, p. 7).

THE AFFECTIVE CHARGE OF THE MAKE IT POSSIBLE CAMPAIGN

The Make It Possible campaign can clearly be read in this light as striving to affectively charge individuals, mobilising them towards a change in behaviour both individually and collectively. This is demonstrated through consideration of both the comments addressed by viewers to the YouTube campaign and the broader narratives of individual change requested and shared in one of the campaign sites. For instance, affective charging is clearly visible throughout the first 780 comments that responded to the extended YouTube video (comments were collected from the period extending from the YouTube release in October 2012 to the end of November 2013). Content analysis (Rodan & Mummery, 2014b) on these comments has shown that the vast majority (88 percent) of comments were supportive of the campaign message. Longer comments generally also explicitly foregrounded one or more of the following affective themes: (a) the highly emotive nature of the campaign (34 percent), (b) the high levels of suffering manifest in the livestock industry (19 percent) and (c) preferences regarding veganism and vegetarianism (20 percent). There was also a small number of explicit objections to the campaign (8 percent). Importantly, all comments supportive of the campaign accepted the campaign's affectively charged message that these animals are sentient and deserving of a much better life than that they currently experience in the factory farming system (such a view was also held by some of the campaign critics although they contended that change was impossible given the necessity of meeting human needs).

The major discursive focus of the comments suggests that, for the majority of respondents, the Make It Possible campaign successfully facilitated their development of an affectively charged understanding of animal welfare; they clearly identified their affective alignment with the movement's aims. What is therefore of interest is whether this understanding also translated, for respondents, into a desire to change their own behaviour and perhaps advocate for social change more broadly. Analysed against these aims, 35 percent of total comments articulated explicit advocacy aims. These aims were both personal and advocacy oriented to (a) *go vegan* or at least stop eating factory farm–produced animal products, (b) shop responsibly (read labels, lobby for free-range products, boycott inhumane products and companies), (c) share the campaign and (d) donate to Animals Australia. As expressed by one respondent, it 'makes me ashamed to be part of the human race when I see videos like this. Fortunately, I am human and I have the power of choice. I will never eat meat again'. There was a common stress on choice: 'It's the choices we make everyday that can make the biggest difference' and 'Consumer choice can make the change. We are all part of the system and it is high time we say no to factory farming'.

Such affective charging is also very clear in the option added by Animals Australia in October 2013 for viewers of the campaign to share their responses online (see Rodan & Mummery, 2014b). In the 'My Make It Possible Story' site, viewers were asked two questions, both targeting affective responses: 'How did you feel when you discovered that most eggs, poultry and pork products come from animals in factory farms?' and 'How has becoming informed changed your life?' In responding, viewers could choose whether to make their responses public, with public responses then used by Animals Australia to make a nationally broadcast radio advertisement (Rodan & Mummery, 2014b). Stories thus exemplify testimonials of personal feelings and action as well as constituting a further form of consumer surveillance of animal welfare practices.

Between October 2013 and January 2014, over 2,200 stories were posted onto the site. The highest number of stories posted on any one day in this period was 1,065, all posted on 21 October 2013. With every story supportive of the campaign message that animals are sentient and deserving of a much better life, content analysis of these stories (Rodan & Mummery, 2014b, 2016) unsurprisingly showed that the top-seven feeling words used by respondents were 'sickness', 'horror', 'disgust', 'anger', 'sadness', 'shock' and 'being brought to tears'. Respondents also articulated feeling misled by politicians, the government and farming industries generally and their consequent feelings of guilt in being misled. Our analyses of the stories uploaded on 21 October 2013 (Rodan & Mummery, 2014b, 2016) showed three themes emerging: commitments to vegan/vegetarianism (13 percent), consumer action (35 percent) and broad-scale animal advocacy (52 percent). Of these three, the first theme groups self-declared pre-existing vegans and/or vegetarians. In this group, respondents promote this diet as minimising cruelty to animals but do not explicitly articulate commitments to broader animal advocacy. The second theme of consumer action sees respondents pledging to change their shopping habits and those of family and friends. Many declared they still eat meat but stated their commitment to more ethical consumption. The third theme comprised a broader commitment to animal advocacy, with respondents declaring for either personal or public activist roles. Of these, personal activist commitments typically saw respondents vowing to consume more ethically and educate others, while public activist roles saw respondents also committing to broader political actions: contacting politicians, writing letters, protesting, donating and so on. What is important regarding these commitments is that respondents were self-selecting into particular communities of both feeling and action. The site thus encouraged respondents to articulate and share not just their affective charging and their response to the moral shock provided by the campaign but their subsequent mobilisation and activism.

THE PRACTICES OF ETHICAL CONSUMERISM

As is clearly articulated earlier, this is an affectively driven mobilisation fundamentally focused on what can be called the practices of ethical purchasing or consumerism. This is the idea that purchasing should be understood as a form of consumer activism where consumers are conceived as having power to promote and enable change. Ethical consumerism thus stands for a situation where consumers seek to 'engage and influence the suppliers of products and services through their actions in the marketplace' (Shaw, Newholm & Dickinson, 2006, p. 1050). Such an aim would thus see consumers – typically understood as responding to 'reports of questionable practices such as child labour, environmental pollution and/or animal welfare abuse' (p. 1050) – utilising the strategies of boycotting and positive buying (now known as buycotting) in order to change traditional production practices. Ethical consumerism is thus most commonly described as comprising both 'the intentional purchase of products considered to be made with minimal harm to humans, animals and the natural environment' (Burke, Eckert & Davis, 2014, p. 2237; also see Bray, Johns & Kilburn, 2011) and 'the avoidance of particular kinds of products because their consumption is thought to be morally wrong for particular reasons' (Neo, 2014, p. 2). In all cases, the idea is that purchasing and consumption are neither passive nor isolated private actions but rather an integral way in which people 'relate to themselves and the world . . . through a relationship of reflexivity and choice' (Slater, 2001, p. 124). The idea is thus that these choices in effect work as a form of collective action, and they have indeed been described as a form of both voting and vigilantism (Roddick, 2001).

Several current studies (Bray et al., 2011; Burke et al., 2014; Eckhardt, Belk & Devinney, 2010) have also, however, indicated that although consumers may well have several motivations to purchase ethically, there may well still be an attitude-intention-behaviour gap in practice. This is where everyday practices simply do not live up to stated commitments to ethical buying, with studies giving a variety of explanations, including a lack of information, a lack of appropriate substitutes, dissatisfaction with the quality – variously defined – and the cost of ethically produced items, convenience and, most damningly, apathy (Auger, Burke, Devinney & Louviere, 2003; Bedford, 2011; Yeow, Dean & Tucker, 2014). And yet the minimalist argument for ethical consumerism does stress that as long as consumer satisfaction and aesthetic pleasure are equal, and if given relevant information and choice, aware consumers will prefer companies and products that do not pollute, disregard human rights or subject people and animals to inhumane treatments (Scammell, 2003). This, indeed, is the basic ethical assumption the Make It Possible campaign depends on, that the gaining of knowledge must come to mean the taking of ethically informed action.

At the same time, however, there are questions as to whether ethical consumerism is simply too entangled in consumer capitalism to achieve long-lasting social change and new norms in, for instance, production with regard to animal welfare. One question has been whether ethical consumption is ultimately ineffective because it has become the province of an elite or professional middle class, and basically 'used by a minority as a panacea for middle-class guilt' (Littler, 2011, p. 27), or because it continues to stress individualistic aspirational action over collective solidarity. Such issues can suggest disconnect between the consumer activist's desire for justice and mainstream consumers' desire for choice and pleasure in consumption. Activists, for instance, may 'portray mainstream consumers as unaware, hypnotized, selfish, and lazy', conversely representing themselves as 'aware, free, altruistic, and mobilized' (Kozinets & Handelman, 2004, p. 702). Likewise, Glickman (2009, p. 25) reveals an ongoing tension between 'leaders of these movements' and 'their followers', with leaders often declaring 'their followers to be too few, too irresolute, too ignorant, or just too incompetent to sustain their cause'.

CONSUMER IDENTITY AND ACTIVISM

What Animals Australia and its Make It Possible campaign make clear, however, is that the affective interpellation of activist campaigns impacts not just individual and collective behaviour in the form of promoting the practices of ethical consumerism but identity. This is to say that the campaign makes tangible the connections between affective charging, ethical purchasing (and other advocacy and activism actions) and the identification, recognition and performance of oneself as a caring and ethical person. For example, it is clearly evident that the contributors to the Animals Australia My Make It Possible Story website, along with the majority of those responding to the YouTube video, desire to become more ethical in their consumption practices as well as to raise people's awareness about the need for action and change. Contributors also clearly identify with the animal welfare movement described through the campaign, an identification demonstrated through their accepting and sharing of the stated actions/objectives of the campaign: consuming ethically (whether this means committing to veganism or vegetarianism, or choosing cruelty-free produce) and spreading the word about factory farming. In this way – strengthened further through their sharing of their stories and commitments – they individually and collectively normalise practices of what is arguably an everyday activism, seeing them as integral components of their everyday identities and lives. Such normalisation is further reinforced by the organisation's provision of ongoing support for these changed practices in the form of vegetarian and vegan recipes (including a vegetarian starter kit, as well as holiday recipes), information packs on core issues, ideas and techniques for activist and advocacy actions and ongoing social media engagement with the Animals Australia community and mission.

Such individual commitments and practices can be understood as contributors accepting and adhering to a specific collective identity, that of an animal advocate/activist insofar as they function as a member of (at the very least) the animal advocacy/activist community that is supported by Animals Australia through their online and offline campaigning. Melucci (2013, p. 79) describes the development of a collective identity as a three-pronged process involving (a) a sharing of cognitive definitions concerning the ends, means and field of action; (b) the development of 'a network of active relationships between actors, who interact, communicate, influence each other, negotiate, and make decisions'; and (c) 'a certain degree of emotional investment, which enables individuals to feel like part of a common unity'. Importantly, as Melucci (2013) stresses, cognition comes with feeling and meaning comes with emotion. Along similar lines, Poletta and Jasper (2001, p. 285) define collective identity 'as an individual's cognitive, moral, and emotional connection with a broader community, category, practice, or institution'. The individual, in other words, perceives a 'shared status or relation, which may be imagined rather than experienced directly, and [which] is distinct from personal identities, although it may form part of a personal identity' (p. 285). All of these aspects of collective identity are clearly identifiable with respect to the Make It Possible campaign. Not only does the campaign itself, along with its links to the broader Animals Australia website and its plethora of additional information and campaigns, clearly set out the ends, means and field of action, but it provides the mechanisms that interrelate participants. Further, it is a feature of this campaign that respondents are brought to affectively invest in it, as well as to articulate and share their mobilisation and actions (see Mummery, Rodan, Ironside & Nolton, 2014; Rodan & Mummery, 2014a, 2014b). These processes work in turn to strengthen their identification and recognition of themselves as animal advocates.

These are important points because while several researchers have found that 'identity issues' in new social movements, such as animal welfare, can became mobilising factors (see McAdam, 1994; Melucci, 1994; Jasper & Poulsen, 1995), others (Johnston, Lanaña & Gusfield, 1994, p. 23) have also commented that this is dependent on how well the activist focus is linked into 'the everyday lives of the participants'. For participants taking part in the animal welfare movement represented by Animals Australia and the Make It Possible campaign, then, what is thus arguably integral is that their respective individual and collective identities merge as they make meaningful (to them) everyday life choices to take action: to choose cruelty-free products, commit to changing eating and living habits, inform others, raise awareness and spread the word. To put this another way, drawing here also on Horton's examination as to how common sense and hence practice for a particular cultural group can be acquired and sustained, what matters is the 'reiterative performance' (2003, p. 69) through which the doing of activism – as detailed earlier – comes to coalesce with identification with the animal welfare movement as activists/advocates. Arguably, then, it is by embedding animal-welfare-friendly everyday actions into everyday life that campaign participants can be identified as not only ethical consumers but activists.

SUPPORTING ACTIVISM AND SOCIAL CHANGE VIA DIGITAL CULTURE

Animals Australia (2015) makes the point in the *Animals Australia Supporter Update January 2015* that it has become the first Australian not-for-profit organisation to reach 1 million followers on Facebook (in early January 2017, as detailed earlier, it was close to 1.5 million). As the organisation also notes in that document, this makes animal welfare the single-biggest cause in Australian social media. It is also stated in that document that, in the course of every week, the organisation's social media posts reach between 10 and

20 million (and at times have been tracked as reaching over 100 million people). Indeed the Animal Charities Evaluator estimated in its report on the organisation that Animals Australia was reaching about half of all Australians in 2015 with its campaigns (ACE, 2017). One example of the impact of this reach, drawn from the broader remit of the Make It Possible campaign, is that of the organisation's 2014 Facebook campaign targeting McDonald's as the biggest user of eggs – specifically cage eggs – in the fast-food industry. As McDonald's, as with other corporations, tends to use social media as a platform for communicating with its public, Animals Australia targeted Facebook as its main platform for the campaign (Marks, 2016). The campaign started with a single Facebook post released on 18 June 2014 – itself a response to an earlier media release by McDonald's stating that it did not see a need to change its egg sourcing practices – combining an evocative image of a caged and listless hen with the following text:

> McDonald's doesn't think you care enough to let her out of here. Prove them wrong. For every egg she lays, she will have endured thirty hours of this. McDonald's Australia use 91 million eggs from battery hens like her every year. Why? Because they don't think you care enough for them to do anything about it. (as cited in Marks, 2016)

This post – receiving 8,400 likes, 1,400 comments and 8,427 shares – also advised viewers to 'Tell McDonald's what you really care about' and to 'Head to McDonald's' facebook [*sic*] page . . . and help cover their wall with messages of kindness for hens!' This advice saw cage eggs being the most talked-about issue on McDonald's own Facebook wall for the next eighty-seven days (Marks, 2016). Several weeks into the campaign, Animals Australia then released distressing footage received from a New South Wales battery cage farm owned by PACE (one of McDonald's suppliers) of an emaciated hen teetering on top of a vast manure pile under the battery cages (Marks, 2016). Receiving substantial news coverage (through, e.g., *ABC News*, the *Daily Mail*, *News.com*, the *Sydney Morning Herald*), this footage gave additional impetus to public discussion of McDonald's practices. Further impetus was delivered with Animals Australia's next step of using supporter-submitted video messages to put together a video directly addressing the corporation. Uploaded to social media on 23 August 2014, the *Please McDonald's* video features Australian children pleading with the corporation to stop using cage eggs and switch to kinder alternatives. Reported across national media, this video appeal quickly went viral. Animals Australia then began a public fundraising campaign to have the video appeal to be aired as an advertisement on commercial television. In the week prior to the advertisement going to air – the organisation having received enough donations for the advertisement to screen for a fortnight – Animals Australia secured a story about cage eggs on the current affairs program *The Project* for 12 September 2014. That same evening came the announcement that McDonald's Australia would phase out its use of cage eggs by the end of 2017. (Animals Australia targeted other corporations similarly, leading to others, as noted earlier, also taking steps to phase out cage eggs from their supply chains in Australia.)

The organisation's reach and effectiveness is also demonstrated in website figures, stating the number of activist actions undertaken by visitors to the Animals Australia sites. For instance, Ban Live Export lists 1,343,136 online actions taken as of 20 April 2017 (including sharing the campaign through social media, lobbying politicians, writing to the press, donating); Animals Australia Unleashed! includes a 'Lives Saved' counter registering pledges made through its sites to vegetarianism each year which as of 20 April 2017 stands at 129,751 (Animals Australia Unleashed! [Web], n.d.); and Make It Possible counts the numbers of visitors pledging to (a) refuse factory-farmed products, (b) eat fewer animal products, (c) go meat-free or (d) donate, and as of 20 April 2017, this counter listed 288,402 pledges. Although never definitive, such metrics do give some indication of the reach of a campaign message (McCafferty, 2011), with reach and impact also mappable through donation rates and the shifting affective positions articulated in online comments forums and in corporate reactions.

These are significant figures and drive home the point that social change movements and activists – including animal activists – are strongly colonising digital and social media platforms. This is no surprise given that these fundamentally participatory platforms offer highly productive vehicles for (at least some of) the communicative exchanges – and demands – important for effective activist action. Indeed, online participatory realms have been understood, as discussed in chapter 1, as facilitating the emergence of new kinds of highly fluid mobilising structures and networks that tend to low levels of vertical and hierarchical structuration, remaining, as such, open and participatory (Mercea, 2011). Hence, in 'enacting a global, horizontal network of communication' able to provide 'both an organizing tool and a means' for both synchronous and asynchronous dialogue, deliberation and collective decision-making (Castells, 2008, p. 86; cf. Drezner & Farrell, 2008; Papacharissi, 2010), as well as very effectively supporting the movement of an affective economy, digital media platforms and tools can very effectively facilitate activist practices and exchanges. Indeed, given their capacity to coordinate forms of protest, these platforms have been presented as not only able to dramatically increase the scope, scale and reach of the networks and communicative spaces comprising the public sphere but also able to facilitate the inclusion of previously marginalised or excluded voices, as well as allowing multiple publics to engage in deliberation within and across public boundaries (Simone, 2010).

Digital media platforms and practices have furthermore been recognised to influence both the nature of publics and the means through which they engage with issues (Bruns & Burgess, 2015), not only providing the stage on which public debates play out but also shaping their topics and dynamics (Burgess & Matamoros-Fernández, 2016). Indeed, there are arguments that it is a constitutive feature of the digital media environment that its multiplying publics are increasingly *issue-ified* (Marres, 2015), partially at least to do with how digital communications technologies and social media are well able – in a way the mainstream media is not – to keep topics continually foregrounded within their public spheres, a capacity clearly demonstrated with Animals Australia's challenge to McDonald's Australia to discontinue its use of cage eggs.

Arguably most important for the activist remit, however, is that these platforms are all about narrative exchange, connectivity and social interaction – all processes informed by emotion and affect – as well as effective information foregrounding and distribution, and deliberation. That is, these platforms facilitate the sharing of 'emotionally-charged' (Nabi & Green, 2015, p. 151) personal stories, responses and reactions across social networking sites. Indeed, it is these capacities that support not only the organising and implementing of collective activities but the promotion of community and collective and networked identities (Eltantawy & Wiest, 2011). Furthermore, it has particularly been argued that activist groups have been able to extend their capacities in mobilising collective action via their engagement of Web 2.0 tools insofar as they all blur the borderlines 'between private and public life' (Bimber, Flanagin & Stohl, 2005, p. 366). That is, what is significant regarding the capacity of digital media to facilitate community mobilisations and collective actions is their interconnection of 'personal spheres of representation with public or semi-public spheres of political interaction' (Miloni & Triga, 2012, p. 5). Such intertwining of private feelings and public issues and life gives further strength to the activist assumption that a personalised participatory politics can be – needs to be – invoked by emotion to be effective in mobilising broader political and social actions (Theocharis, 2015). After all, it is through recirculating, retweeting, sharing, liking activist campaigns and connecting them to private feelings and beliefs – private feelings and beliefs that are notably themselves also shared and recirculated publicly, often within the domain of activist sites – that individuals can come to identify and connect much more easily and instantaneously with activist causes (Burgess & Vivienne, 2013; Rodan & Mummery, 2016).

It is thus of no surprise that, recognising that digital environments can function as 'mediators and repositories of affect' able to be 'shaped and reshaped' (Kuntsman, 2012, pp. 6–7) and 'mined for value' (Clough, 2010, p. 220) – as well as facilitating a range of deliberative exchanges – Animals Australia and other activist and advocacy organisations explicitly work to mobilise consumer action. The work is done by circulating affective content through multiple forms of both traditional and social media. This content, in operating to mobilise a variety of actions – including increased public deliberation as well as practices of ethical consumerism and animal advocacy, and the reconception of identity – in turn clearly demonstrates the capacity of Animals Australia's multi-platform digital activist campaigning to engage citizens/consumers through both deliberative and affective practices in the attempt to effect social change. More broadly, however, it draws attention to a further point which is that, contrary to the dream of keeping affect and deliberation separated in debate of the public good, they should rather be understood as inseparable. Indeed, their constitutive entanglement is made abundantly clear in the functioning and use of digital culture and digital media tools, and it is an entanglement we see as being explicitly leveraged in the domain of digital activism. This will become clearer as we explore other campaigns and digital campaign tactics through the following chapters.

REFERENCES

Aaltola, E. (2014). Animal suffering: Representations and the act of looking. *Anthrozoos*, *27*(1), 19–31.

ABC News. (2013a, June 5). Coles ditches Animals Australia bags opposing factory farming conditions. Retrieved from http://www.abc.net.au/news/2013-06-05/coles-ditches-animals-australia-bags/4734358.

ABC News. (2013b, July 18). Animal rights activists 'akin to terrorists', says NSW minister Katrina Hodgkinson. Retrieved from http://www.abc.net.au/news/2013-07-18/animal-rights-activists-27terrorists272c-says-nsw-minister/4828556.

ACE. (2017). Animals Australia comprehensive review. Retrieved from https://animal charityevaluators.org/research/charity-review/animals-australia/#comprehensive review.

Ahmed, S. (2004a). Affective economies. *Social Text*, *79*(2), 117–139.

Ahmed, S. (2004b). *The cultural politics of emotion*. Edinburgh, Scotland: Edinburgh University Press.

Animals Australia. (2012). Make it possible [Video file and transcript]. Retrieved from http://www.youtube.com/watch?v=fM6V6lq_p0o.

Animals Australia. (2015). *Animals Australia supporter update 2015*. Retrieved from https://issuu.com/animalsaustralia/docs/animals-australia-supporter-update-.

Animals Australia. (2016, June 30). *Animals Australia chosen as a 'standout charity' on world stage*. Retrieved from http://www.animalsaustralia.org/features/standout charity-listing.php.

Animals Australia [Web]. (n.d). Who is Animals Australia? Retrieved from http://www.animalsaustralia.org/about/.

Animals Australia [Facebook]. (n.d.). Animals Australia community. [Facebook statistics]. Retrieved from https://www.facebook.com/pg/AnimalsAustralia/community/?ref=page_internal.

Animals Australia [Twitter]. (n.d.) Animals Australia [Twitter statistics]. Retrieved from https://twitter.com/AnimalsAus?ref_src=twsrc%5Egoogle%7Ctwcamp%5Eserp%7Ctwgr%5Eauthor.

Animals Australia [Web]. (n.d.). Animals Australia. Retrieved from http://www.animalsaustralia.org/.

Animals Australia [YouTube]. (n.d.). Animals Australia [YouTube statistics]. Retrieved from https://www.youtube.com/user/animalsaustralia.

Animals Australia Unleashed! [Web]. (n.d.). Animals Australia unleashed. Retrieved from http://www.unleashed.org.au/.

Animals Australia Unleashed! [Facebook]. (n.d.). Animals Australia unleashed! Community [Facebook statistics]. Retrieved from https://www.facebook.com/pg/AnimalsAustraliaUnleashed/community/?ref=page_internal.

Animals Australia Unleashed! [Twitter]. (n.d.). Animals Australia Unleashed! [Twitter statistics]. Retrieved from https://twitter.com/AAUnleashed.

Animals Australia Unleashed! [Web]. (n.d.). Animals Australia Unleashed! Retrieved from http://www.unleashed.org.au/.

Animals Australia Unleashed! [YouTube]. (n.d.). AnimalsUnleashed [YouTube statistics]. Retrieved from https://www.youtube.com/user/AnimalsUnleashed.

Auger, P., Burke, P., Devinney, T. & Louviere, J. (2003). What will consumers pay for social product features? *Journal of Business Ethics*. doi:10.1023/A:1022212816261.

Bagaric, M., & Akers, K. (2012). *Humanising animals: Civilising people*. Sydney, Australia: CCH Australia.

Ban Live Export [Facebook]. (n.d.). Ban live export community. [Facebook statistics] Retrieved from https://www.facebook.com/pg/BanLiveExports/community/?ref=page_internal.

Ban Live Export [Twitter]. (n.d.). Ban live export. [Twitter statistics]. Retrieved from https://twitter.com/Ban_Live_Export?ref_src=twsrc%5Egoogle%7Ctwcamp%5Eserp%7Ctwgr%5Eauthor.

Ban Live Export [Web]. (n.d.). Ban live export. Retrieved from http://www.banliveexport.com/.

Bedford, T. (2011). *Negotiating ethical consumerism in everyday life*. RESOLVE series 13–11. [Working paper]. Retrieved from http://resolve.sustainablelifestyles.ac.uk/publications?page=8.

Ben-Ze'ev, A. (1997). Emotions and morality. *The Journal of Value Inquiry*, *31*(2), 195–212.

Bettles, C. (2013, June 8). Coles cops more criticism. *The Land*. Retrieved from http://www.theland.com.au/story/3589497/coles-cops-more-criticism/.

Bimber, B., Flanagin, A. J. & Stohl. C. (2005). Reconceptualizing collective action in the contemporary media environment. *Communication Theory*, *15*(4), 365–388.

Bray, J., Johns, N. & Kilburn, D. (2011). An exploratory study into the factors impeding ethical consumption. *Journal of Business Ethics*, *98*(4), 597–608.

Bruns, A., & Burgess, J. (2015). Twitter hashtags from ad hoc to calculated publics. In N. Rambukkana (Ed.), *Hashtag publics* (pp. 13–28). New York, NY: Peter Lang.

Burgess, J., & Matamoros-Fernández, A. (2016). Mapping sociocultural controversies across digital media platforms: One week of #gamergate on Twitter, YouTube, and Tumblr. *Communication Research and Practice*, *2*(1), 79–96.

Burgess, J., & Vivienne, S. (2013). The remediation of the personal photograph and the politics of self-representation in digital storytelling. *Journal of Material Culture*, *18*(3), 279–298.

Burke, P., Eckert, C. & Davis. S. (2014). Segmenting consumers' reasons for and against ethical consumption. *European Journal of Marketing*, *48*(11/12), 2237–2261.

Castells, M. (2008). The new public sphere: Global civil society, communication networks, and global governance. *The Annals of the American Academy of Political and Social Science, 616*(1), 78–93.

Chambers, S. (2003). Deliberative democratic theory. *Annual Review of Political Science, 6*(1), 307–326.

Clark, C. (2013, June 16). Animals Australia under the microscope. *ABC Landline*. Retrieved from http://www.abc.net.au/landline/content/2013/s3782456.htm.

Clough, P. (2010). The affective turn: Political economy, biomedia, and bodies. In M. Gregg & G. J. Seigworth (Eds.), *The affect theory reader* (pp. 206–225). London, England: Duke University Press.

Deloitte Access Economics Pty Ltd. (2012). *Analysis of the grocery industry*. Canberra, Australia: Deloitte Access Economics.

Drezner, D. W., & Farrell, H. (2008). Introduction: Blogs, politics and power. *Public Choice, 134*, 1–13.

Eckhardt, G., Belk, R. & Devinney, T. (2010). Why don't consumers consume ethically? *Journal of Consumer Behaviour, 9*(6), 426–436.

Eltantawy, N., & Wiest, J. B. (2011). Social media in the Egyptian revolution: Reconsidering resource mobilization theory. *International Journal of Communication, 5*, 1207–1224.

Frazer, S. (2013, June 5). Animals Australia backdown on Coles campaign. *ABC News*. Retrieved from http://www.abc.net.au/news/2013-06-05/animals-australia-backdown-on-coles-campaign/4735834.

Glickman, L. B. (2009). *Buying power: A history of consumer activism in America*. Chicago, IL: University of Chicago Press.

Habermas, J. (1998). *Between facts and norms: Contributions to a discourse theory of law and democracy* (W. Rehg, Trans.). Cambridge, MA: MIT Press.

Horton, D. (2003). Green distinctions: The performance of identity among environmental activists. *The Sociological Review, 51*(Issue supplement s2), 63–77.

Jasper, J. M., & Nelkin, D. (1992). *The Animals rights crusade: The growth of a moral protest*. New York, NY: Free Press.

Jasper, J. M., & Poulsen, J. (1995). Recruiting strangers and friends: Moral shocks and social networks in animal rights and anti-nuclear protests. *Social Problems, 42*(4), 493–512.

Johnston, H., Lanaña, E. & Gusfield, J. R. (1994). Identities, grievances, and new social movements. In E. Lanaña, H. Johnston & J. R. Gusfield (Eds.), *New social movements: From ideology to identity* (pp. 3–35). Philadelphia, PA: Temple University Press.

Keogh, M. (2015, June 16). Realities of animal welfare getting lost in personalities and emotion. Australian Farm Institute. [Blog post]. Retrieved from http://www.farminstitute.org.au/ag-forum/realities-of-animal-welfare-getting-lost-in-personalities-and-emotion.

Knops, A. (2007). Debate: Agonism as deliberation – on Mouffe's theory of democracy. *The Journal of Political Philosophy, 15*(1), 115–126.

Kozinets, R. V., & Handelman, J. M. (2004). Adversaries of consumption: Consumer movements, activism, and ideology. *Journal of Consumer Research, 31*(3), 691–704.

Kuntsman, A. (2012). Introduction: Affective fabrics of digital culture. In A. Karatzogianni & A. Kuntsman (Eds.), *Digital cultures and the politics of emotion:*

Feeling, affect and technological change (pp. 1–17). Basingstoke, England: Palgrave Macmillan.

The Land. (2013, June 5). Coles withdraws AA bags. Retrieved from http://www.theland.com.au/.

Levine, P., & Nierras, R. M. (2007). Activists' views of deliberation. *Journal of Public Deliberation, 3*(1), 1–14.

Littler, J. (2011). What's wrong with ethical consumption? In T. Lewis & E. Potter (Eds.), *Ethical consumption: A critical introduction* (pp. 27–39). New York, NY: Routledge.

Lowe, B. M. (2006). *Emerging moral vocabularies: The creation and establishment of new forms of moral and ethical meanings*. Oxford, England: Lexington Books.

Maher, S. (2013, November 18). Retail giants agree to play fair on food. *The Australian*. Retrieved from http://www.theaustralian.com.au/.

Make it Possible [Facebook]. (n.d.). Make it Possible. [Facebook statistics]. Retrieved from https://www.facebook.com/MakeItPossible/.

Make it Possible [Web]. (n.d.). Make it Possible. Retrieved from http://www.makeitpossible.com/.

Malone, P. (2013, June 9). Farmers face changing world. *Canberra Times*. Retrieved from http://www.canberratimes.com.au/.

Marketing Magazine. (2015, September 21). Pigs can fly: Inside Animals Australia's 'make it possible' campaign. Retrieved from https://www.marketingmag.com.au/.

Marks, J. (2016, July 23–25). *Effective animals advocacy*. Paper presented at EAGx-Australia Conference in Melbourne, Australia.

Marres, N. (2015). Why map issues? On controversy analysis as a digital method. *Science, Technology & Human Values, 40*(5), 655–686.

McAdam, D. (1994). Culture and social movements. In E. Lanaña, H. Johnston & J. R. Gusfield (Eds.), *New social movements: From ideology to identity* (pp. 36–57). Philadelphia, PA: Temple University Press.

McCafferty, D. (2011). Activism vs. slactivism. *Communications of the ACM, 54*(12), 17–19.

Melucci, A. (1994). A strange kind of newness: What's 'new' in new social movements. In E. Lanaña, H. Johnston & J. R. Gusfield (Eds.), *New social movements: From ideology to identity* (pp. 101–132). Philadelphia, PA: Temple University Press.

Melucci, A. (2013). The process of collective identity. In H. Johnston & B. Klandermans (Eds.), *Social movements and culture* (pp. 73–109). Hoboken, NJ: Taylor & Francis.

Mercea, D. (2011). Digital prefigurative participation: The entwinement of online communication and offline participation in protest events. *New Media & Society, 14*(1), 153–169.

Miloni, D. L., & Triga, V. (2012). Web 2.0 and deliberation: An introduction. *International Journal of Electronic Governance, 5*(1), 3–10.

Mortimer, G. (2013, August 12). FactCheck: Is our grocery market one of the most concentrated in the world? *The Conversation*. Retrieved from http://theconversation.com/.

Mummery, J., Rodan, D., Ironside, K. & Nolton, M. (2014). Mediating legal reform: Animal law, livestock welfare and public pressure. In D. Bossio (Ed.), *Refereed Proceedings of the Australian and New Zealand Communication Association conference: The digital and the social: Communication for inclusion and exchange* (pp. 1–16). Swinburne University, Victoria, 9–11 July 2014. Retrieved from http://www.anzca.net/documents/2014-conf-papers/822-anzca14-mummery-rodan-ironside-nolton.html.

Munro, L. (2015). The live animal export controversy in Australia: A moral crusade made for the mass media. *Social Movement Studies*, *14*(2), 214–229.

Nabi, R. L. (2009). The effect of disgust-eliciting visuals on attitudes toward animal experimentation. *Communication Quarterly*, *46*(4), 472–484.

Nabi, R. L., & Green, M. C. (2015). The role of a narrative's emotional flow in promoting persuasive outcomes. *Media Psychology*, *18*(2), 137–162.

Nason, J. (2013, June 27). Coles drops Animals Australia shopping bag. *Beef Central*. Retrieved from https://www.beefcentral.com/news/coles-drops-animals-australia-shopping-bags/.

Neales, S. (2012, October 22). Animals Australia campaigns to end 'factory farming'. *The Australian*. Retrieved from http://www.theaustralian.com.au/.

Neo, H. (2014). Ethical consumption, meaningful substitution and the challenges of vegetarian advocacy. *The Geographical Journal*, *182*(2), 1–12. doi:10.1111/geoj.12130.

O'Sullivan, S. (2015, February 17). New laws could stop revelations of animal abuse. *The Sydney Morning Herald*. Retrieved from http://www.smh.com.au/.

Papacharissi, Z. A. (2010). *A private sphere: Democracy in a digital age*. Cambridge, England: Polity Press.

Permanent Culture Now. (2013). Introduction to activism. [Blog post]. Retrieved from http://www.permanentculturenow.com/what-is-activism/.

Poletta, F., & Jasper, J. M. (2001). Collective identity and social movements. *Annual Review of Sociology*, *27*, 283–305.

Rachels, J. (1986). *The end of life: Euthanasia and morality*. Oxford, England: Oxford University Press.

Rodan, D., & Mummery, J. (2014a). Platforms and activism: Sharing 'My Make It Possible Story' narratives. In D. Bossio (Ed.), *Refereed Proceedings of the Australian and New Zealand Communication Association conference: The digital and the social: Communication for inclusion and exchange* (pp. 1–22). Swinburne University, Victoria 9–11 July 2014. Retrieved http://www.anzca.net/conferences/past-conferences/2014-conf.html.

Rodan, D., & Mummery, J. (2014b). The 'make it possible' multi-media campaign: Generating a new 'everyday' in animal welfare. *Media International Australia Incorporating Culture and Policy*, *153*, 78–87.

Rodan, D., & Mummery, J. (2016). Doing animal welfare activism everyday: Questions of identity. *Continuum: Journal of Media & Cultural Studies*, *30*(4), 381–396.

Roddick, A. (2001). *Take it personally: How globalisation affects you and powerful ways to challenge it*. London, England: Harper Collins.

RSPCA. (2016, December 5). What are Ag-gag laws and how would they affect transparency and trust in animal production? [Information sheet]. Retrieved from http://kb.rspca.org.au/entry/558/.

Sampson, A. (2013, June 4). Animals Australia bag fight heats up. *Weekly Times Now*. Retrieved from http://www.weeklytimesnow.com.au/.

Scammell, M. (2003). Citizen consumers: Towards a new marketing of politics? In J. Corner & D. Pels (Eds.), *Media and the restyling of politics: Consumerism, celebrity and cynicism* (pp. 117–137). London, England: Sage.

Sharman, K. (2009). Farm animals and welfare law: An unhappy union. In P. J. Sankoff & S. W. White (Eds.), *Animal law in Australasia: A new dialogue* (pp. 35–56). Sydney, Australia: Federation Press.

Shaw, D., Newholm, T. & Dickinson, R. A. (2006). Consumption as voting: An exploration of consumer empowerment. *European Journal of Marketing*, *40*(9/10), 1049–1067.

Shotwell, A. (2011). *Knowing otherwise: Race, gender and implicit understanding*. Pennsylvania, PA: Pennsylvania State University Press.

Simone, M. A. (2010). Deliberative democracy online: Bridging networks with digital technologies. *The Communication Review*, *13*(2), 120–139.

Slater, D. (2001). Political discourse and the politics of need. In W. L. Bennett & R. Entman (Eds.), *Mediated politics: Communication in the future of democracy* (pp. 117–140). Cambridge, England: Cambridge University Press.

Smerdon, X. (2015, December 17). Australian charity recognised on world stage. *Pro Bono Australia*. Retrieved from https://probonoaustralia.com.au/news/2015/12/australian-charity-recognised-on-world-stage/.

Snow, D. A., & Benford, R. D. (1988). Ideology, frame resonance and participant mobilization. In B. Klandermans, H. Kriesi & S. Tarrow (Eds.), *From structure to action: Comparing social movement research across cultures* (pp. 197–217). Greenwich, CT: JAI Press.

Theocharis, Y. (2015). The conceptualisation of digitally networked participation. *Social Media + Society*, 1–14. doi:10.1177/2056305115610140.

van Gurp, M. (2012, November 4). Factory farming the musical. *Osocio*. Retrieved from http://osocio.org/message/factory-farming-the-musical/.

Warnke, G. (1995). Communicative rationality and cultural values. In S. K. White (Ed.), *The Cambridge companion to Habermas* (pp. 120–142). Cambridge, England: Cambridge University Press.

Watkins, M. (2010). Desiring recognition, accumulating affect. In M. Gregg & G. J. Seigworth (Eds.), *The affect theory reader* (pp. 250–285). London, England: Duke University Press.

Weisbrot, D. (2007). Comment. *Reform*, *91*, 2–8.

Wrenn, C. L. (2013). Resonance of moral shocks in abolitionist animal rights advocacy: Overcoming contextual constraints. *Society & Animals*, *21*(4), 379–394.

Yeow, P., Dean, A. & Tucker, D. (2014). Bags for life: The embedding of ethical consumerism. *Journal of Business Ethics*, *125*(1), 87–99.

Young, I. M. (2000). *Inclusion and democracy*. Oxford, England: Oxford University Press.

Chapter 4

Social Networking and Activist Action in the Digital Age

As foregrounded in the previous chapters, core issues for activists and advocacy groups in the digital age concern two key components: the dispersal of timely information and events coordination and the ways digital tools and cultures can more broadly facilitate (or hinder) the growth and mobilisation of social justice movements. Digital social networking has been a recognised and effective conduit for such practices, and of particular interest for us have been the way activist and advocacy groups use combinations of digital media platforms in an attempt to gain sympathetic attention – and bypass negative media framing of what may be classed acts of civil disobedience – and the ways digital frameworks can be brought to interact with physical conditions and deliberative processes in support of activist aims. Also of interest – and foregrounded in this chapter – is the growing phenomenon of activists and advocacy groups not just engaging commercially developed digital communications platforms and applications but beginning to build their own digital media architecture to realise goals.

Continuing discussions from the previous chapters regarding the scope and reach of multimodal digital campaigns and various platforms, this chapter examines the take-up of not only existing social media platforms but app development by advocacy groups eager to engage and mobilise large-scale groups. Focusing here on a range of global as well as on Australian examples, with a final focus on some of the innovative app developments taking place within the domains of Australian animal activism, this chapter demonstrates the profound implications of digital social networking for the mobilisation and collaboration of often-disparate activist groups and individuals in direct activist action. Importantly, however, these kinds of developments need to be understood as taking place within the complicated nexus of neoliberalism and consumer capitalism, and their framing and uptakes of digital culture, with regard not just to communications but also to issues of commodification and securitisation. While some of these issues have been introduced in previous chapters, this chapter brings them together explicitly as context for the earlier (and subsequent) considerations of activism in the digital age.

THE NEXUS OF SOCIAL NETWORKING, CONSUMER CAPITALISM AND NEOLIBERALISM

As has been explored in chapter 1, as well as demonstrated throughout other chapters, Australian social movements and activists have seized upon the networking capacities inherent in Web 2.0 tools even as they acknowledge and work around some of the tensions also present with the use of these tools. Here we refer again to the tension between activist aims for social change and the neoliberal assumptions, systems and expectations which inform many, if not all, of the Web 2.0 developments. The development and use of social media platforms is a case in point. Even though, as we have demonstrated, an important part of the activist arsenal these days, social media platforms are commercially oriented. Building and fostering community arguably is a central activist aim, but such community is always built within the framework of commercial interests. This is an issue we have raised but not as yet fully delved into, an omission we need to rectify now. The issue at hand, specifically, can be summed up in terms of what one commentator has called *dubjection* (McCutcheon, 2012, 2014, 2016), by which he refers to the ways the neoliberal contexts and practices of digital media have come to colonise our life-world (the latter meaning, following Habermas [1987], our lived realm of informal, culturally grounded understandings and mutual accommodations). Under such a framework, and specifically because 'everything we do now involves computers' (Schneier, 2013; also see Foshay, 2016), McCutcheon (2012) argues that the subject has effectively been translated from the site of its individual body to the multiple mediated and distributed spaces of digital representation. McCutcheon's theory of the dubject is thus an attempt to name the kind of experience Siemens (2013) has described as 'seeing bits and pieces of yourself all over the Internet'. This is the doubled – tripled, incessantly multiplied – self (both individual and collective), whose work of being is its

> practice of uploading and globally distributing [its] identity; a practice of mediatizing subjectivity itself, transcribing the improvisational experience of corporeal embodiment into the archival fixity of recording media. The dubject is a self recording and recorded, dubbed and doubled; a doppelgänger self whose 'live' presence becomes radically supplemented by its recordings and representations. (McCutcheon, 2011, p. 735)

More than this, however – although this much raises profound issues for ideas of individual and collective ideas of identity and identification, some of which we take note of in other chapters with specific regard to activism – McCutcheon's ideas of the dubject and dubjection also refer to the correlated commodification of the self. As McCutcheon (2016, p. 139) puts this, the enaction of dubjection always 'entails supplying work and product (content) for corporate and state powers' insofar as every click and keystroke in our dubjection generates data for unknown interests to analyse and use. Dubjected, the social media user is in all of its senses always a commodity (McNeill, 2014; van Dijck, 2009).

Dubjection and commodification are not by-products of the affordances of social media platforms (or of other Web 2.0 technologies) but rather part and parcel of their development and functioning. Platforms such as Facebook and Twitter (and others) 'coax life-narratives from . . . users' (Morrison, 2014, p. 119) in the form of multiple identity updates that are themselves most typically expressed 'in fleeting ways through forms of consumption' (Cover, 2014, p. 61). This is an important point. Because of the way they are structured, social media platforms urge us to continually devise and display new demonstrations of our identity, where our identity becomes visible to us and others as a particular kind of recurring problem that can be solved only by replenishing social media's various channels with fresh content (Horning, 2011). And this content not only operates as a kind of self-branding and self-advertising – usually performed, as argued by Hearns (2008, p. 204), in the interests of 'material gain or cultural status', with both in the context of social media tied to ideas of expanding one's visibility, connectedness and influence – but typically marks a further tying together of our identity with what we consume. Thus, dubjectivity stands for the way the individual self is remixed – by ourselves in a manner some have suggested marks an ongoing participation in our own exploitation (e.g., Fuchs, 2010) – as the commodity of a global market, the product of competing property claims and a consumer of media that is simultaneously consumed by media (McCutcheon, 2012).

All this is exacerbated by the ways social media websites share user data with advertisers in order to help them optimise their marketing campaigns. As noted in chapter 1, such platforms are financed not only by advertisement placement within their web pages but also by the sale of information gleaned from their users (Foshay, 2016). This is the point that

> personal information left on sites by users of Web 2.0 platforms . . . eventually becomes metadata that can be used for sophisticated profiling of Web clients. Profiles can then be sold or exchanged between companies, producing increasingly precise targeting of advertising campaigns and marketing strategies. (Proulx, Heaton, Kwok Choon & Millette, 2011, p. 23)

Such data is a valued object of Terms of Service licensing. After all, insofar as the users who so generate content are arguably from a privileged demographic, they comprise an 'attractive demographic to advertisers' (van Dijck, 2009, p. 47). This 'personal information economy' (Lace, 2005, p. 17) is arguably the neoliberal dream insofar as neoliberalism has itself frequently been characterised by two informational trends. These comprise (a) the expansion and commodification of information and communication technologies (ICTs), and (b) the increasingly detailed management of consumption and leisure time (Dyer-Witheford, 1999; Harvey, 2005). These, as Manzerolle and Smeltzer (2011) have argued, are in turn premised on the belief that outward behaviour can be turned into data that, when sufficiently assembled, will embody (as information) the consumer's will. Social media, of course, through their status/identity update mechanisms, their foregrounding of practices of self-branding and the data these deliver, not only cash out this belief but make it mineable by external interests. It is on this basis, then, that the argument has been made that the social media platform ecosystem should be understood as constituting a 'commercial, profit-oriented machine that exploits users by commodifying their personal data and usage behaviour . . . and subjects these data to economic surveillance so that capital is accumulated with the help of targeted personalized advertising' (Fuchs, 2011, p. 304). Our question will be to see whether this argument is compelling, and if so whether it negatively impacts activism from within digital culture.

This is an important question insofar as such data is not only desired by corporate interests; it is also of interest to the state under both of its neoliberal market-oriented and securitisation guises (keeping in mind that these are not separable as such). This market-orientation has already been introduced (although it will be unpacked further later), but the latter focus on securitisation is well exemplified with reference to the desire of governments to construct what has been called the National Surveillance State:

> This National Surveillance State is characterised by a significant increase in government investments in technology and government bureaucracies devoted to promoting domestic security and (as it name implies) gathering intelligence and surveillance using all the devices that the digital revolution allows. (Balkin & Levinson, 2006, p. 131)

According to Balkin and Levinson, the National Surveillance State began its emergence in the aftermath of 9/11, when countries around the world started passing new surveillance legislation with the aim of taking 'action in the online environment' so as to 'secure national interests' (Birnhack & Elkin-Koren, 2003, p. 16). This action, in the majority of cases, was to authorise and employ multiple means of surveillance, including via data drawn from the commercial sector (and from social networking sites). One such program, for example, that has been brought to public attention in the aftermath of Edward Snowden's whistleblowing revelations in 2013 concerning the massive levels of surveillance carried out by the United States National Security Agency, is PRISM. This, it was found, permits officials direct access to the servers of Facebook, Google, Apple and Skype, allowing them 'to collect material, including search history, the content of emails, file transfers, and live chats' (Greenwald, 2013). Another program, X-Keyscore, permits officials to search metadata and the content of almost every action undertaken by a user when online, including the content of every browser search, every website visited and all emails received or sent (Smith, 2016). Other new digitalised surveillance technologies, including biometric and molecular scanning and laser photography, give governments further means to sample their populations en masse (Guertin, 2016). Despite the initial shock of Snowden's revelations, such levels of surveillance have now become almost commonplace throughout states due to the setting and diffusion of common global standards via various international treaties. *The Convention on Cybercrime*, for example, drafted by the Council of Europe in 2001, and ratified by Australia in 2013, incorporates and arguably normalises such actions by the state as:

- Retention of specified computer data of subscribers by Internet service providers
- Requiring ISPs and telecommunications providers to produce subscriber metadata [Article 18(3)]
- The collection of content data by ISPs in real time in certain circumstances.

What is quite clear overall, then, is that along with supporting neoliberal assumptions regarding commodification, consumerism and identity construction, Web 2.0 technologies are affording states nearly limitless capacities for electronic surveillance, data collection and analysis (Rodriguez, 2012; Smith, 2016). These latter capacities – those engaged by all attempts to realise a National Surveillance State – are very clearly demonstrated by the unsettling text message that was received by people who were near a clash between protesters and Ukrainian police in January 2014: 'Dear subscriber, you are registered as a participant in a mass disturbance' (Peterson, 2014). The capacities demonstrated by such a message thus stand as a recognised obstacle for activist activities and not simply in states considered to be more authoritarian than democratic.

ACTIVIST TRAJECTORIES WITHIN NEOLIBERAL CULTURE

> Consumer profiling done by corporate entities for the purpose of selling products, combined with a political discourse that emphasizes security

> over freedom, makes for a toxic mix. . . . What is lost . . . is the expression of a larger common good that is not market- or security-related. (Stefanick & Wall, 2016, p. 232)

While initially framed – perhaps legitimately – in terms of threat abatement, such state surveillance becomes problematic when more and more actions, and more and more cohorts of people, are perceived in terms of risk. This concerns the state's move, analysed in Agamben's (2005, 2007) work, from the targeted or select surveillance of certain persons to the untargeted surveillance of entire populations. Clearly, this is the case with attempts to realise a form of the National Surveillance State. Such an aim, as Australian Internet service provider and telecommunications giant iiNet's Chief Regulatory Officer, Steve Dalby (2014), has put it critically – with specific reference to one of Australia's recent attempts to bring in mandatory data collection and retention – always means, in effect, that the state is 'collecting and storing every single haystack in the country, indexing and filing all the straws, keeping them safe for two years' (two years being the time set in this instance), 'just in case there's a needle, somewhere'. It is the idea that although there may or may not be a needle, it must be better to have all the haystacks than not, just in case there is a needle. As Dalby (2014) stresses, however, speaking here on behalf of iiNet:

> The focus of this data retention proposal is not crooks; it's the 23 million law-abiding men, women and children that will go about their daily lives without ever bothering law enforcement. Those 23 million customers include my 93-year-old mum and my 12-year-old niece. We don't believe that is either necessary or proportionate for law enforcement. . . . I say forget spying on my mother and niece and get on with chasing the crooks.

Also problematic in all of this is the state's capacity – strengthened immeasurably under the framework of the war against terrorism – to designate what should be considered a risk (see Agamben, 2007, for analysis of this capacity). Under this framework, as Lorna Stefanick and Karen Wall (2016) have noted at the beginning of this section, activist aims can easily slide into a perceived category of risk to the state. Such has certainly been the case with activist ideas that challenge market logic and, hence, perceived state interests. This is a trend further illustrated through the term 'domestic terrorist' coming into law and common use within the United States through the US Patriot Act enacted six weeks after 9/11 (Salter, 2011). Following a similar trajectory, Spain introduced a highly oppressive anti-protest law in 2015. Named the Citizen's Security Law – and underpinned and facilitated by the state capture and permanent storage of metadata, registration data of users and generated content for the whole population – four articles in particular look to problematise activism of all kinds excepting state-sanctioned activities (see Nurra, 2015b). First, organising or convening an unauthorised protest, or distributing information about that protest, was made an illegal act. Such activities, as Nurra (2015b) details, include the following:

- Publishing information on a future unauthorised protest
- Creating or signing an online petition to support an unauthorised rally
- Endorsing publicly the reasons of an unauthorised protest
- Urging others to take part in an unauthorised demonstration
- Posting on one's profiles slogans, flags or other symbols that refer to an unauthorised protest

Second, this law presented cyber-activism as synonymous with terrorism. Any viewing of propaganda websites now stands, third, for a terrorist act; and finally photographing or publishing photographs of police officers – no matter their actions or the context (although journalists have a little leeway) – has become a punishable offence (Nurra, 2015b). In outline of the law, the official position has been that such actions – all unsanctioned and hence illegal actions – should be understood as impacting negatively on public safety and that the state must be proactive in the fight against terrorism and criminality (Nurra, 2015a, 2015b). This negative framing of activism in terms of criminality and terrorism has become the norm in a range of states.

Although not all states have gone so far along this line of equating activism with terrorism, we have noted previously that states such as Australia and the United States are linking activist aims that challenge accepted – and economic – environmental or animal welfare standards with criminal activity and terrorism (Potter, 2011). In both cases such connections are typically again being made with reference to public safety and the overarching importance of protecting the state's economic interests. In Australia, for instance, activists striving to overturn accepted state practices with regard to animals and the environment are now being labelled as terrorists. Such, of course, was the case when New South Wales Primary Industries Minister Katrina Hodgkinson said that animal activists who were covertly filming animal abuse in factory farms were carrying out acts 'akin to terrorism' (as cited in Greer, 2013). Similarly, in 2012 Australia's former Resources and Energy Federal Minister Martin Ferguson not only requested increased surveillance of environmental activists who were peacefully protesting at coal-fired power stations and coal export facilities but was being prompted by energy company lobbying to urge harsher criminal penalties against protests that disrupted critical energy infrastructure (Dorling, 2012), or when we saw in 2015 Australia's Attorney-General George Brandis and then Prime Minister Tony Abbott accuse environmental groups of engaging in acts of economic sabotage in their attempts to use public mobilisation and legal challenges to block the going ahead of Adani's Carmichael mega-coalmine in Queensland's Galilee Basin (Balogh & McKenna, 2015; Medhora & Robertson, 2015).

These are framings of activism very clearly in line with the Ag-gag laws introduced in the United States – and which have been proposed by some officials as useful for Australia (one such example being Western Australian Liberal Senator Chris Back's proposed Criminal Code Amendment [Animal Protection] Bill) – which have effectively allowed non-violent civil disobedience to be prosecuted as (domestic) terrorism. More specifically, the 2006 Animal Enterprise Terrorism Act has allowed for the argument that any activists who cause a loss of profits to animal enterprises, or who interfere with the operations of these enterprises, should face prosecution (Potter, as cited in Potter & Eng, 2014). Within such framing the FBI has come to describe environmentalists and animal rights activists as the top domestic terrorist threat in the United States (Greer, 2013; Potter, 2011). And more recently, in the week after Trump was elected president, the Republican state senator from Washington, Doug Ericksen, proposed a bill that would create a new class of felony for what he has called 'economic terrorism'. Such a bill facilitates the criminalising of protests that can be argued as aimed at causing economic damage (Harper, 2017).

The operating context of activism within the twenty-first century is always fraught given that it is also constitutively informed by this neoliberal prioritising of securitisation. Digital platforms current in this period clearly facilitate activist activity while simultaneously also containing capacities to surveil and otherwise constrain it. It is this nexus that we wish to continue to sound out here, but now with specific attention to activist strategies that take advantage of some of the affordances of this complex neoliberally ordered digital domain. These are strategies which strive, in particular, to positively engage with some of the securitisation and/or commodification dimensions of the neoliberal project, alongside their taking advantage of the communicative and mobilising dimensions of digital media. Although there are a variety of activist strategies that we could consider here, the one that we consider best exemplifies this attempt to productively engage not just with the communicative affordances of digital media but with this media's seeming problems for uptake by activist projects – that is, their orientation towards commodification and securitisation – is mobile application (app) development. After all, in many ways, app development and dissemination marks the culmination of the Web 2.0 digital media and neoliberal nexus. That is, apps arguably mark another step in dubjection – in what has also been called 'prosumption', this neologism combining 'consumption' and 'production' so as to suggest the dual nature of contemporary online participation (Beer & Burrows, 2010) – insofar as they (apps) further facilitate the commodification of the self and of everyday life. Is this all they can do?

APPS AND ACTIVISM

Apps are most generally software programs that run on the Internet, on computers or on any mobile digital communications device such as smartphones and tablet computers. These latter, however, are the most commonly understood and used vehicles for apps in the contemporary context. Depending on licence conditions, once downloaded an app is available whenever and wherever its users wish to engage it. More specifically, apps facilitate – and normalise – interactions between their users and relevant networked systems and collective and personal databases. As with social media platforms, apps are typically constructed to facilitate regular engagement and updating of a version of one's personal status or achievements within the app's frame of reference. Once focused around general productivity and information retrieval – including email, calendar, contacts, stock market and weather information – mobile apps have exploded their focus to cover all aspects of personal life. Importantly, however, because mobile devices run on battery and have less powerful processors than personal computers, and also because of the informational trends characteristic of the neoliberal personal information economy – that is, as noted previously, to further expand and commodify ICTs, and increase the detailed management of one's consumption and leisure time – mobile apps tend to have a specific and narrow focus. Apps have specific purposes in other words, and a quick survey of any one of the app stores – Google Play or the Apple App Store – seems to suggest that there is now an app for almost everything for one's lifestyle, including one's productivity, health (physical, psychological or sexual), fitness, travel, not to mention entertainment, creativity and life and home styling. One can now, it seems, measure – and update – every action one takes.

Apps, in other words, have effectively deepened both the personal and portable nature of mobile communication devices, which have themselves already been established as an intimate technology that users take with them wherever they go, carrying or wearing them close to the body and keeping them nearby, even in rest or sleep (Goggin, 2011). Apps are in this sense ubiquitous, and their use is arguably rendering multiple aspects of everyday life, embodiment and identity much more visible, calculable and governable – commodifiable in the ways talked of earlier. Further to this, because apps need to be downloaded, and often require users to sign up to them with an account, they typically engage users within a highly controlled digital environment. Apps, in other words, also make it a lot easier for the reaching and targeting of consumers by advertisers – and for state-based data collection – an ease only enhanced by the location-based technology (and apps) also at work inside mobile devices. In addition, app development and designated app stores clearly support the entrepreneurial activities of individuals and small micro-enterprises associated with software development industries, for whom the political economy of the computing, software and mobile telecommunications industries might otherwise have been difficult to navigate successfully (Goggin). These points together thus suggest that the successful incursion and use of apps across almost all aspects of everyday life effectively marks delivery of that neoliberal dream of combining commodification with personal – and personally facilitated – surveillance.

This all being so, it would seem that apps are always facilitative of neoliberal ends; they are constitutively products both of and delivering outcomes in consumerism and personal commodification. Indeed, it is arguable that app purchase and use can only be a marker of a consumption-oriented and commodified identity. And yet apps are also starting to be developed for more than consumer – and prosumer – oriented ends. Although many activist projects have tended to be understood as problematic and/or as incoherent within the neoliberal paradigm, apps are becoming a new tool for activists, and app development by activists is a growing domain. Apps, for instance, can facilitate the development and publication of non-state sanctioned news, upload fresh footage automatically to a secure server and delete that footage from the device (in case of the activist's arrest), as well as *stamp* that uploaded footage with metadata (e.g., time, date and location) so as to enable its possible use as evidence (O'Carroll, 2013). Apps have furthermore been developed to allow for secure communications and the encryption of Internet traffic (Shieber, 2016), again in the course of circumventing state surveillance of and desired state crackdown on activist activities. They can also provide an alert if the user is under threat, one such example being Amnesty International's Panic Button app, which, according to its creator, turns an activist's mobile phone into an emergency alert system (Rucke, 2014).

Other apps have been designed by and for activists to take a different kind of advantage of the quantities and kinds of data made available in a digital culture. Two such examples in this category are the activist-developed apps iSee and Sukey. The first of these, developed by the technologist activist group the Institute for Applied Autonomy (IAA), is an app that draws on maps of CCTV locations – initially just in Manhattan, but attempts have been made to extend it into other cities (Baard, 2001) – and allows users to create routes of 'least surveillance' (Institute for Applied Autonomy, 2002). As IAA describes the app elsewhere, 'It allows people to play a more active role in choosing when and how they are recorded by CCTV cameras by providing a means for them to avoid surveillance cams if they want' (as cited in

Schienke & IAA, 2002). More specifically, users log on to the iSee website and select their point of departure and their destination, and a dotted line sketches a route around identified CCTV cameras which are marked on the map as red boxes. Although this is, of course, a tool potentially of interest to activists, it is more broadly described by the IAA as turning 'the model of policing that is about centralized authoritarian control of urban space on its ear and instead makes surveillance systems transparent to the general public' (Schienke & IAA, 2002). In this sense it operates more as a pedagogic tool designed to facilitate public discussion of critical public issues, a point stressed by the IAA, who have argued that iSee has

> allowed journalists to talk critically about surveillance. The way journalism works is that there has to be some sort of news angle, and by creating iSee, we provided an opportunity for journalists to address the subject. (Schienke & IAA, 2002)

Although iSee was in some ways less of a practical tool than a pedagogic one – its route of least surveillance 'can be so circuitous it transforms a walk of several blocks into an odyssey of miles' (Baard, 2001) – this is not the case for another app called Sukey. This was created in 2011 in London in response to police tactics in breaking up student protests, specifically with reference to *kettling*, often brutal formations in which dozens of often riot-gear-attired police suffocatingly surround or funnel groups of protesters. Basically this app aims to provide users up-to-the-minute overviews of what is going on at any given demonstration and provide a means for demonstrators to send and receive reports and updates. The app is a concrete instance of Mann's theory of sousveillance as a form of 'counter-surveil' (as cited in Mann, Nolan & Wellman, 2003, p. 333), that is, as providing a tool with which activists can observe and further resist and observe organisations, corporations and governments. The app then confirms reports and sends official information back to users. Information is crowdsourced – mostly via Twitter – but the app also uses a mash-up of Google maps, GPS (Global Positioning System) and encryption to securely and instantaneously monitor police movement so as to allow activists maximum effectiveness – and personal safety – in their protest activities (Reed, 2014). In terms of its use, 'the app provides an in-built compass which gives an indication of the best direction to move. A red marker on the compass could point towards a police cordon or kettle so a protester caught in trouble should follow the green direction to escape' (Hudson & Price, 2011). If Polly puts the kettle on – as the nursery rhyme goes – Sukey always takes it off again.

Other apps also work to increase the effectiveness of activists' individual and collective action, with three further examples – this time within the domain of animal activism – developed within Australia. The first of these, Animal Effect, had a simple premise: many activists and advocates believed that relying on email, Facebook, Twitter, websites, newspapers, word of mouth or notice boards for communication was too unwieldy for achieving maximal effects with actions. Potential participants in actions felt they were missing out on knowing about upcoming events or were overwhelmed by the amount of information they were expected to keep track of. The solution was to create in one app a platform able to work as a dynamic repository of information for animal advocacy groups. An additional challenge was to make this customisable to the subscriber and a strategically useful tool for mobilisation for organisations publishing their events via the app. The result was an app that allowed subscribers to filter a number of categories (advocacy, campaigns, competitions, conferences, education, expos, festivals, fundraisers, meeting, rallies, social, TV/media/film) and access and disseminate comprehensive information about event location (including maps, addresses, access to websites and calendar connectivity). Using a single app as a conduit for multiple interest groups and organisations was considered to work to offset the kind of information fatigue experienced by subscribers receiving information from multiple sources, or from cross-posting (Doherty, 2013; Mann, 2013).

Although this app was short lived, launched in 2013 and shelved in 2015 in response to financial constraint and competition between animal advocacy groups (C. Mann, personal communication, 16 July 2016), its realisation of dynamic content – filtered preferences, live maps, event information, search functionality, an integrated and customisable calendar with GPS-enabled location information – has profound implications for the mobilisation of previously disparate groups and concerned individuals. Such innovation allows users – who would be spread across the spectrum of highly organised, well-established groups through local community groups and interested individuals, as well as across the world – to share content and to mobilise for animal social justice at the push of a button. Explicitly designed as a capacity-builder and mobiliser, such an app arguably facilitates the articulation both of individuals into communities of people with shared interests and of multiple disparate activist organisations into new and powerful configurations (Mummery, Rodan & Nolton, 2016). Dana Campbell, the CEO of the Australian animal advocacy group Voiceless, indeed described the Animal Effect app at the time of its launch in these terms: 'It's a one-stop-shop for everyone interested in animal welfare', going on to say that it would fill a need 'we didn't know we had, and now we're wondering what we did without it' (as cited in Doherty, 2013).

A similar app in its explicit focus on the building of community in advance and support of collective action, and developed by the same group as created Animal Effect, is Vegan Voices. More specifically, this app strives to bring together and facilitate vegans in both identifying as a community united against animal cruelty and effectively communicating their ethical stance with members of the broader community. Tagged a lifestyle app, Vegan Voices connects users with a range of resources, including films, articles, books and websites examining key vegan concerns (social justice, environment, health and speciesism) which users can use to support their discussions and easily share with interlocutors. The app also includes thirty days of personal training (by vegan psychologist Clare Mann, one of the creators of this and the Animal Effect app) in communications (for vegans to use with non-vegans) – including video lessons and personal communications challenges – providing, it is claimed, 'a complete tool-box to skilfully navigate the trickiest of conversations' (Vegan Voices, n.d.). Users can further recommend additional resources – which are checked before inclusion – however, as yet, they cannot interact live through the app with each other. This function is, nevertheless, expected to be included in later iterations of the app (Vegan Voices, 2016). What should be clear is that this app is designed not only to extend individual skills and resilience with regard to communicating vegan ideas and decisions in a non-vegan world (described by Clare Mann as an often-traumatic experience; see Mann, 2014) but to support – and furthermore build – a burgeoning community of effective activists. As the app is described:

> Vegan Voices is about becoming a powerful voice for veganism. This requires a person to be self-aware, manage the anguish of knowing what happens to animals for industrial purposes and then communicate the issues and solutions effectively. Managing your own emotions and channeling your distress into powerful action is part of being a powerful vegan voice. (Vegan Voices, 2016)

A third Australian app – this time an example fitting within the rapidly growing genre of apps designed to facilitate ethical consumerism – was developed by Choice, Australia's leading consumer advocacy organisation. Unlike the apps discussed previously, the app for consideration here works directly to facilitate an individual's ethical purchasing or consumerism at the everyday level (Rodan & Mummery, 2014, 2016). As such it fits within the domain of what should be understood as a form of consumer activism, where consumers are conceived as having the capacity and commitment to 'engage and influence the suppliers of products and services through their actions in the marketplace' (Shaw, Newholm & Dickinson, 2006, p. 1050). Such an app, in other words, strives to bring activism and consumerism into alignment, rejecting the idea that there must be some disconnect between the activist's desire for justice and mainstream consumers' desires for choice and pleasure in consumption (Glickman, 2009; Kozinets & Handelman, 2004). Certainly, there are indications, as discussed previously, that many consumers' everyday practices may not always live up to stated commitments to ethical buying, a discrepancy often summed up as the attitude-intention-behaviour gap. As previously discussed, such a gap has been explained as resting on a lack of information, a lack of appropriate substitutes, dissatisfaction with the quality – variously defined – and the cost of ethically produced items, convenience and, most damningly, apathy (see, e.g., Bray, Johns & Kilburn, 2011; Burke, Eckert & Davis, 2014; Eckhardt, Belk & Devinney, 2010). Nonetheless, as we have noted previously, arguments for ethical consumerism do stress that as long as consumer satisfaction and aesthetic pleasure are equal, and if given relevant information and choice and if this information is attained relatively easily, consumers will choose companies and products that do not pollute, disregard human rights or subject people and animals to inhumane treatments (Scammell, 2003).

The app in focus is Choice's CluckAR app, which was launched in April 2016 and designed to help consumers identify and purchase genuine free-range eggs in the supermarket. More specifically, this app scans the labelling on commercial egg cartons to determine whether the birds producing the eggs are 'fully choice' – using phrasing from the app's assessments – meaning they meet Choice's 1,500 hens per hectare standard (the density also recognised within Australia's voluntary Model Code of Practice for free-range egg production and preferred by animal advocate groups), or are pushing their way through a space where there's 'barely room to swing a chook', or, even worse, whether they are caged 'jailbirds' (representative of the density of 10,000 hens per hectare that was legislated in 2016 as still counting in Australia as free range under certain conditions). The 2016 redefinition of free range has been a contentious issue within Australia, and as one review of the app pointed out, 'CluckAR launched like a rocket, garnering a thousand scans of egg cartons in the first ten minutes of release. Consumers all over Australia have downloaded the app, using it to guide their buying decisions. At a steady 10,000 inquiries a day, that's a lot of decisions, and a lot of dollars on the table' (Pesce, 2016). And, as was noted in early September 2016 by Choice, the app had by then 'been downloaded 42,000 times' and had generated 'over 600,000 scans of egg boxes and counting' (Day & Browne, 2016).

What stands out with regard to these varying forms of app development for activist means is the simultaneous uptake of neoliberal frameworks by app developers and consumers alike. Of interest to us, however, is the more complex relationship of activists with neoliberal trends towards commodification of not only products but identity and everyday life, that is, in addition to the obvious claim that the neoliberal focus with regard to the securitisation and surveillance of digital culture has generated a range of productive digital countermeasures by activists. In, for instance, the domain of activist app development, it is clear that the affordances of neoliberal commodification must underpin these developments. The identification of a narrow-enough need or purpose – to set off a distress beacon in the fact of arrest, to evade kettling, to make vegan communications more effective, to identify which eggs to buy – informs the development of every purpose-built activist app. The relevant activist community, whether narrow (vegans) or broad (ethically oriented egg-buyers), provides the market; the openness of the app market and the pre-existence of app stores as well as the ubiquity of apps throughout everyday life make their promotion and dissemination easy. In addition, while exemplifying and supporting the individualist orientation of neoliberalism, apps can work in effect to align and mobilise collective action (this is an issue we will also be examining in crowdfunding). The app, that is, dictates and facilitates an action, and each action – while indicative of only one individual at one instance – works aggregatively, if not collectively, in the sense usually understood as requisite to activist projects. Finally, we would suggest that it is the very alignments possible between identity, and identity and identification commodification, and purpose-built applications which exemplify the making of forms of activism part of the everyday, and for that matter facilitating citizens' individual and collective identities and practices. If apps are ubiquitous, they can promote activist actions as much as those to do with health or fitness.

Along with noting the way apps might be able to facilitate individualist activist actions in the online domain – clicktivist actions that we argue are still demonstrably activist – a further point for consideration is the potential role of apps in furthering public deliberation regarding activist aims. This is, however, a contested issue insofar as apps as commodities arguably only have a tangential relation to the ideals of public deliberation. First, while they might promote discussion as to their utility with regard to their given cause (an issue we will come back to later), any discussion might also remain limited to price considerations and ease of use. Such discussion too would not obviously meet the kinds of expectations we have noted previously regarding public deliberation. For instance, this is discussion clearly informed by commercial interests and only tangentially related to issues of public concern. In addition, while apps can clearly go viral themselves – that is, their being talked about and shared can go viral in the way of any other online content – it is obvious that such sharing and trending takes place within existing interrelated social networks. This is the homophilousness talked of with reference to the blogosphere (see chapter 2), that apps like blogs would tend to be discussed, shared and used within ideologically constrained networks. And yet it would also appear possible that commodification is the only truly limiting framework for app circulation, with consumerism entailing a broader circulation of app specifics than might otherwise be implied (a possibility supported by the tendency of app stores to profile apps as, among other categories, new or updated, or as trending). If this is so, then the potential visibility of apps as desirable products of commodification within the public sphere may nonetheless also play a role in increasing public deliberation with regard to activist causes. This would particularly be the case with regard to apps related to causes that the securitisation and surveillance dimensions of neoliberalism have problematised. For example, while animal activists are being increasingly vilified for their actions in exposing animal abuse within institutionalised factory farming (and other systemic engagements of animals in the economy) – and being thereby framed as criminal, deviant and extremist within the public sphere – apps promoting ethical consumerism such as CluckAR can be visible and debatable, and may indeed bring about some of the public discussion and shifts in consumer attitude desired by animal activists. Indeed, the app may facilitate the discussion of the problematic of factory farming for eggs in a broader community than an animal activist campaign might achieve, and – insofar as the app promotes an easy action for consumers to take against factory farming – may be more effective than a conventional awareness-raising campaign. Apps in other words, while unlikely proponents of public deliberation and activist action, may provide a framework and space that facilitates such deliberation and action, bringing activist causes further into the patterns of everyday life.

REFERENCES

Agamben, G. (2005, December 5). No to biometrics. *Le Monde*. Retrieved from http://www.notbored.org/agamben-on-biometrics.html.

Agamben, G. (2007). *State of exception* (K. Attell, Trans.). Chicago, IL: University of Chicago Press.

Baard, E. (2001, November 28). Routes of least surveillance. *Wired* magazine. Retrieved from http://archive.wired.com/politics/security/news/2001/11/48664?currentPage=all.

Balkin, J. M., & Levinson, S. (2006). *The processes of constitutional change: From partisan entrenchment to the National Surveillance State*. Faculty Scholarship Series 231. Yale Law School. [Series paper]. Retrieved from http://digitalcommons.law.yale.edu/cgi/viewcontent.cgi?article=1230&context=fss_papers.

Balogh, S., & McKenna, M. (2015, August 17). Green gaming: George Brandis says economy 'threatened by lawfare'. *The Australian*. Retrieved from http://www.theaustralian.com.au/.

Beer, D., & Burrows, R. (2010). Consumption, prosumption and participatory web cultures: An introduction. *Journal of Consumer Culture*, *10*(1), 3–12.

Birnhack, M. D., & Elkin-Koren, N. (2003). The invisible handshake: The re-emergence of the state in the digital environment. *Virginia Journal of Law and Technology*, *8*(2), 1–48.

Bray, J., Johns, N. & Kilburn, D. (2011). An exploratory study into the factors impeding ethical consumption. *Journal of Business Ethics*, *98*(4), 597–608.

Burke, P., Eckert, C. & Davis, S. (2014). Segmenting consumers' reasons for and against ethical consumption. *European Journal of Marketing*, *48*(11/12), 2237–2261.

Council of Europe. (2001, November 23). *Convention on cybercrime*. Retrieved from http://www.refworld.org/docid/47fdfb202.html.

Cover, R. (2014). Becoming and belonging: Performativity, subjectivity, and the cultural purposes of social networking. In A. Poletti & J. Rak (Eds.), *Identity technologies: Constructing the self online* (pp. 55–69). Madison, WI: University of Wisconsin Press.

Dalby, S. (2014, July 21). Protecting your privacy: Our stand against 'mandatory data retention'. [Blog post]. Retrieved from http://blog.iinet.net.au/protecting-your-privacy/.

Day, K., & Browne, K. (2016, September 7). CluckAR is here to help! *Choice*. Retrieved from https://www.choice.com.au.

Doherty, P. (2013, October 13). Apps for animal lovers. *The Sydney Morning Herald*. Retrieved from http://www.smh.com.au/.

Dorling, P. (2012, January 7). Spies eye green protesters. *The Sydney Morning Herald*. Retrieved from http://www.smh.com.au/.

Dyer-Witheford, N. (1999). *Cyber-Marx: Cycles and circuits of struggle in high-technology capitalism*. Urbana, IL: University of Illinois Press.

Eckhardt, G., Belk, R. & Devinney, T. (2010). Why don't consumers consume ethically? *Journal of Consumer Behaviour*, *9*(6), 426–436.

Foshay, R. (2016). Introduction: The computational turn and the digital network. In R. Foshay (Ed.), *The digital nexus: Identity, agency, and political engagement* (pp. 1–22). Edmonton, Canada: Athabasca University Press.

Fuchs, C. (2010). Labor in informational capitalism and on the Internet. *The Information Society: An International Journal*, *26*(3), 179–196.

Fuchs, C. (2011). Web 2.0, prosumption, and surveillance. *Surveillance & Society*, *8*(3), 288–309.

Glickman, L. B. (2009). *Buying power: A history of consumer activism in America*. Chicago, IL: University of Chicago Press.

Goggin, G. (2011). Ubiquitous apps: Politics of openness in global mobile communities. *Digital Creativity*, *22*(3), 148–159.

Greenwald, G. (2013, June 6). NSA PRISM program taps in to user data of Apple, Google and others. *The Guardian*. Retrieved from http://www.theguardian.com/.

Greer, A. (2013, August 9). 'Akin to terrorism': The war on animal activists. *Overland*. Retrieved from https://overland.org.au/2013/08/akin-to-terrorism-the-war-on-animal-activists/.

Guertin, C. (2016). Hacktivist (pre)occupations: Self-surveillance, participation, and public space. In R. Foshay (Ed.), *The digital nexus: Identity, agency, and political engagement* (pp. 109–125). Edmonton, Canada: Athabasca University Press.

Habermas, J. (1987). *The theory of communicative action*: *Lifeworld and system, 2*. (T. A. McCarthy, Trans.). Boston, MA: Beacon Press.

Harper, J. (2017, January 7). This Republican just launched a bill to charge Trump protesters as 'terrorists'. Occupy democrats. [Web log post]. Retrieved from http://occupydemocrats. com/2017/01/07/republican-just-launched-bill-charge-trump-protesters-terrorists/.

Harvey, D. (2005). *A brief history of neoliberalism*. Oxford, England: Oxford University Press.

Hearns, A. (2008). 'Meat, mask, burden': Probing the contours of the branded 'self'. *Journal of Consumer Culture*, *8*(2), 197–217.

Horning, R. (2011, July 29). Social media, social factory. *The New Inquiry*. Retrieved from https://thenewinquiry.com/.

Hudson, A., & Price, P. (2011, April 12). How is technology changing protests? *Click: The World of Technology across the BBC*. Retrieved from http://news.bbc.co.uk/2/hi/programmes/click_online/9451521.stm.

Institute for Applied Autonomy. (2002). iSee. In T. Y. Levin, U. Frohne & P. Weibel (Eds.), *CTRL [space]: Rhetorics of surveillance from Bentham to Big Brother* (pp. 606–607). Karlsruhe, Germany: ZKM Center for Art and Media.

Kozinets, R. V., & Handelman, J. M. (2004). Adversaries of consumption: Consumer movements, activism, and ideology. *Journal of Consumer Research*, *31*(3), 691–704.

Lace, S. (2005). *The glass consumer: Life in a surveillance society*. Bristol, England: Policy.

Mann, C. (2013, October). *Communicating animal social justice*. Paper presented at the Animal Activists Forum, Melbourne, Australia.

Mann, C. (2014, June 12). Should vegans be issued with a mental health warning? *The Scavenger*. Retrieved from http://www.thescavenger.net/social-justice-to-all/social-justice-for-animals/943-should-vegans-be-issued-with-a-mental-health-warning.html.

Mann, S., Nolan, J. & Wellman, B. (2003). *Surveillance & Society*, *1*(3), 331–355. Retrieved from http://www.surveillance-and-society.org.

Manzerolle, V., & Smeltzer, S. (2011). Consumer databases and the commercial mediation of identity: A medium theory analysis. *Surveillance & Society*, *8*(3), 323–337.

McCutcheon, M. A. (2011). Frankenstein as a figure of globalization in Canada's postcolonial popular culture. *Continuum: Journal of Media and Cultural Studies*, *25*(5), 731–742.

McCutcheon, M. A. (2012). Towards a theory of the dubject: Doubling and spacing the self in Canadian media culture. In M. Mannani and V. Thompson (Eds.), *Selves and subjectivities: Reflections on Canadian arts and culture* (pp. 235–264). Edmonton, Canada: Athabasca University Press.

McCutcheon, M. A. (2014). Dubjection: A node. In M. Kuester (Ed.), *McLuhan's global village today* (pp. 59–73). London, England: Pickering and Chatto.

McCutcheon, M. A. (2016). Institutions and interpellations of the dubject, the doubled and spaced self. In R. Foshay (Ed.), *The digital nexus: Identity, agency, and political engagement* (pp. 127–150). Edmonton, Canada: Athabasca University Press.

McNeill, L. (2014). Life bytes: Six-word memoir and the exigencies of auto/tweetographies. In A. Poletti & J. Rak (Eds.), *Identity technologies: Constructing the self online* (pp. 144–166). Madison, WI: University of Wisconsin Press.

Medhora, S., & Robertson, J. (2015, August 17). George Brandis: Vigilante green groups destroying thousands of mining jobs. *The Guardian*. Retrieved from https://www.theguardian.com/.

Morrison, A. (2014). Facebook and coaxed affordances. In A. Poletti & J. Rak (Eds.), *Identity technologies: Constructing the self online* (pp. 112–131). Madison, WI: University of Wisconsin Press.

Mummery, J., Rodan, D. & Nolton, M. (2016). Making change: Digital activism and public pressure on livestock welfare. *Ctrl-Z New Media Philosophy*, *6*. Retrieved from http://www.ctrl-z.net.au/articles/issue-6/mummery-rodan-nolton-making-change/.

Nurra, M. (2015a, March 26). Spain approves the most repressive anti-protest law in Europe. (R. Aiello, Trans.). *Valigia Blu*. Retrieved from http://www.valigiablu.it/anti-protest-law-spain/.

Nurra, M. (2015b, July 3). Repressive new law in Spain: Digital surveillance against activism and freedom of speech (R. Aiello, Trans.). *Valigia Blu*. Retrieved from http://www.valigiablu.it/repressive-new-law-in-spain-digital-surveillance-against-activism-and-freedom-of-speech/.

O'Carroll, T. (2013, December). Apps helping activists and human rights defenders. *Ethical Consumer*. Retrieved from http://www.ethicalconsumer.org/ethicalreports/mobilesreport/activism.aspx.

Pesce, M. (2016, April 20). Clucking hell! Farcical free-range egg standard pecked apart by app. *The Register*. Retrieved from http://www.theregister.co.uk/2016/04/20/clucking_hell_farcical_freerange_egg_standard_pecked_apart_by_app/.

Peterson, A. (2014, January 21). Ukraine's 1984 moment: Government using cellphones to track protesters. *The Washington Post*. Retrieved from https://www.washingtonpost.com/.

Potter, W. (2011). *Green is the new red: An insider's account of a social movement under siege*. San Francisco, CA: City Lights Books.

Potter, W., & Eng, K. (2014, January 31). Green is the new red: Will Potter on the problem of treating environmentalists like terrorists [Web log post]. Retrieved from http://blog.ted.com/will-potter-on-of-treating-environmentalists-like-terrorists/.

Proulx, S., Heaton, L., Kwok Choon, M. J. & Millette, M. (2011). Paradoxical empowerment of produsers in the context of informational capitalism. *New Review of Hypermedia and Multimedia*, *17*(1), 9–29.

Reed, T. V. (2014). *Digitized lives: Culture, power, and social change in the Internet era*. London, England, and New York, NY: Routledge.

Rodan, D., & Mummery, J. (2014). The 'make it possible' multi-media campaign: Generating a new 'everyday' in animal welfare. *Media International Australia*, *153*, 78–87.

Rodan, D., & Mummery, J. (2016). Doing animal welfare activism everyday: Questions of identity. *Continuum: Journal of Media & Cultural Studies*, *30*(4), 381–396.

Rodriguez, K. (2012, December 31). 2012 in review: State surveillance around the globe. Electronic Frontier Foundation. [Web log post]. Retrieved from http://www.eff.org/deeplinks/2012/12/2012-in-review-state-surveillance-around-globe.

Rucke, K. (2014, March 13). Protecting human rights activists? There's an app for that. *Mint Press News*. Retrieved from http://www.mintpressnews.com.

Salter, C. (2011). Activism as terrorism: The green scare, radical environmentalism and governmentality. *Anarchist Developments in Cultural Studies*, *1*, 211–238.

Scammell, M. (2003). Citizen consumers: Towards a new marketing of politics? In J. Corner & D. Pels (Eds.), *Media and the restyling of politics: Consumerism, celebrity and cynicism* (pp. 117–137). London, England: Sage.

Schienke, E. W., & IAA. (2002). On the outside looking out: An interview with the Institute for Applied Autonomy (IAA). *Surveillance & Society*, *1*(1), 102–119.

Schneier, B. (2013, March 16). The Internet is a surveillance state. *CNN Opinion*. Retrieved from http://www.cnn.com/2013/03/16/opinion/schneier-internet-surveillance.

Shaw, D., Newholm, T. & Dickinson, R. (2006). Consumption as voting: An exploration of consumer empowerment. *European Journal of Marketing*, *40*(9/10), 1049–1067.

Shieber, J. (2016, May 23). Wickr Foundation invests in Whistler, an app dedicated to helping activists and citizen reporters. *Tech Crunch*. Retrieved from https://techcrunch.com/2016/05/23/wickr-foundation-invests-in-whistler-an-app-dedicated-to-helping-activists-and-citizen-reporters/.

Siemens, G. (2013, April 5). *Identity formation in distributed networks and social spaces*. Paper presented at Identity, Agency, and the Digital Nexus: An International Symposium. Athabasca University, Athabasca, Canada.

Smith, P. J. (2016). The rise of the national surveillance state in comparative perspective. In R. Foshay (Ed.), *The digital nexus: Identity, agency, and political engagement* (pp. 207–230). Edmonton, Canada: Athabasca University Press.

Stefanick, L., & Wall, K. (2016). Democracy and identity in the digital age. In R. Foshay (Ed.), *The digital nexus: Identity, agency, and political engagement* (pp. 231–247). Edmonton, Canada: Athabasca University Press.

Van Dijck, J. (2009). Users like you? Theorizing agency in user-generated content. *Media, Culture & Society*, *31*(1), 41–58.

Vegan Voices. (2016). Vegan Voices FAQ. Communicate31 Pty Ltd Australia. Retrieved from http://vegan-voices.com/.

Vegan Voices. (n.d.). Vegan Voices description. [App].Retrieved from https://itunes.apple.com/au/app/vegan-voices/id1027717064?mt=8.

Chapter 5

GetUp! and Participatory Activism

In late 1997, 122 countries signed an international treaty to ban landmines, and, at the same time, the People's Treaty endorsing this ban treaty was signed by thousands of people around the world. One of the key facilitators of this achievement was the International Campaign to Ban Landmines (ICBL), which, along with Jody Williams, its inaugural coordinator, was awarded the Nobel Peace Prize for its work in starting a process that 'in the space of a few years changed a ban on antipersonnel mines from a vision to a feasible reality' (The Nobel Peace Prize 1997, 1997). Not only is the ICBL still touted as one of the most successful international efforts to promote and achieve humanitarian goals, but its success has been related to its use of Internet technologies and computer-mediated communications (see Williams, Goose & Wareham, 2008). Just over a decade later, the International Red Cross launched a campaign in 2010 for donations to help relief efforts in the aftermath of the catastrophic earthquake that devastated Haiti. The campaign raised $7 million within four days. Its success too was attributed to computer-mediated communications, with one spokesperson noting that the affordances of text messaging for facilitating awareness and donation have 'opened up a whole new world for philanthropy' (Pepitone, 2010). This is a world in which transnational progressive campaigning movements such as AVAAZ, MoveOn and GetUp! have thrived, able to engage and mobilise substantial numbers of people through both online and offline mechanisms. It is a world in which an issue can be posted and shared and mobilise broad-scale public response from across the world within comparative moments. It is a world in which people can become aware of social problems and make a response to them – even take part in a global action – without having to leave their house, their armchair, their bed, even without having to give their own actions in so doing their full attention. It is this world of activism made easy that has also, of course, been critically dubbed that of clicktivism or slacktivism, with Malcolm Gladwell publishing in 2010 that provocative article in *The New Yorker* in which he argued that carrying out such actions are nothing like what it means to participate in the 'practical activism' of Tiananmen Square or the civil rights movement in the United States. Clearly, this is true; the question however concerns whether this matters. That is, are the practical effects of online activism when carried out on a global scale more important than the fact that most participants may be only weakly or briefly caught up with an issue? Does the type of participation really impact on the efficacy of the action? Do some types of participation support only some outcomes?

Addressing these questions, this chapter examines in more detail the issue of online activist participation through consideration of the progressive movement GetUp!, which began campaigning using digital culture in 2005. An Australian not-for-profit movement similar in approach to MoveOn (n.d.), and drawing on multiple forms of digital media to mobilise public opinion on key social issues, GetUp! (n.d.) presents itself as providing the tools and the potential to inform, educate and engage people's participation in the public and political spheres, and to facilitate their engagement in the striving for progressive social change. Examining the affordances of GetUp! for what we are calling participatory activism, our further question is whether the resources GetUp! provides for members to develop and participate in grassroots activist campaigns also promote, support and facilitate broadly understood deliberative practices and exchanges. Although these are definitely not the ideal forms often proposed in democratic deliberative theory, this chapter assesses whether GetUp!'s campaigning is effective in not only (a) galvanising public engagement and participation, both online and offline, as well as considering the extent to which its effectiveness is dependent on a deliberate mobilisation of affect, but (b) supporting at least some aspects of deliberative practices. In our examination of GetUp! in these terms of the capacities and work of online participatory activism, we will explore one of GetUp!'s current but long-running national campaigns: 'Protecting the Great Barrier Reef'. As a campaign engaging multiple yet seemingly irreconcilable viewpoints and stakeholders – including contestation between the federal and state governments and broader community groups – this campaign has needed a range of strategically oriented and responsive actions across both the online and offline domains. Furthermore, it has been underpinned – tasked even – by the need to achieve increases in civic engagement insofar as it is an issue which is arguably calling for broad-ranging social change.

CLICKTIVISM, SLACKTIVISM OR PARTICIPATORY ACTIVISM?

> In promoting the illusion that surfing the web can change the world, clicktivism is to activism as McDonalds is to a slow-cooked meal. It may look like food, but the life-giving nutrients are long gone. (White, 2010)

In chapter 1 we started with a definition of activism as meaning the taking of action 'to effect social change' (Permanent Culture Now, 2013), and this definition has informed our subsequent discussions. Now, however, we need to draw this definition out further to better foreground the interrelation of the idea of activism with associated ideas of civic engagement (this latter an important idea for deliberation as we will discuss later), and the kinds of engagements typically associated with so-called Internet or online participatory activism. Until recently, social movement theory had demarcated collective action and individual action, as if they were two different things, and as will be discussed later – and has been noted in other chapters in various ways – this distinction has been significant for many of the dismissals of online participation as not being proper activism. In response, however, to what has been named the 'Internet turn', contemporary social movement theory is coming to recognise the increasingly important role of the anonymous individual – both together with and independent from groups of people – in social movements and calls for social change. Here Rheingold's (2002, p. xii) idea of the 'smart mob' is pertinent insofar as it stands for a bringing together of 'people who are able to act in concert even if they don't know each other'. More specifically, smart mobs are comprised of anonymous individuals who become linked by pervasive digital devices, such as phones and computers, which connect them – and their actions – via the Internet and locative technology. As Rheingold notes, it is because of this anonymity and autonomy that smart mob activism is arguably less about the group or organisation and more about the individual. Under such a conception of activism, diverse people with overlapping interests can join alliances and come together in solidarity and action without having to negotiate requirements around collective identity, or acknowledge who they are beyond what they support. As a result of such possibilities, what it means to be an activist has become less certain and less able to be distinguished from the general idea of the civically minded and engaged citizen.

At the same time, as has been discussed throughout this book, the question of what counts as political participation has become fuzzy in the digital universe, with a range of thinkers asking whether online participation can be considered participation at all. In considering this issue, the Pew Charitable Trusts defines civic engagement, a basic concept of public participation, as

> individual and collective actions designed to identify and address issues of public concern. Civic Engagement can take many forms, from individual volunteerism to organizational involvement to electoral participation. It can include efforts to directly address an issue, work with others in a community to solve a problem or interact with the institutions of representative democracy. (Delli Carpini, 2010)

Online activities, particularly identifying issues of concern and organising and mobilising people to address issues, certainly fulfil this definition. Is this participatory activism, however? If the nature of new social movements is taken into consideration, then arguably 'yes'. On the one hand, the emergence of new social movements – which are constitutively issue based – has led to individuals understanding activism as itself needing to be issue based, and thus as expecting to be able to use activism pursue their own issues-based interests (Tranter, 1996). On the other hand, the affordances of a digital participatory culture are not only providing mechanisms for networked participation but have led to individuals 'increasingly expecting to be able to engage online' (Lundy, 2009). Participatory activism, then, has come to mean an activism that not only is 'rooted in community organizing' and 'focused on building popular support' for issues 'through effective education' (Hartford, 2008) but strategically engages both online and offline mechanisms for participation. After all, if participatory activism stands in the twenty-first century for 'the potential and actual magnitude of individual and group participation in civic life, interest group activities, voting and elections' (Petrova & Tarrow, 2007, p. 79), then it cannot afford to reject any means of civic engagement.

And yet, when issues-based movements engaging online tools such as GetUp! are discussed, descriptions of their actions and claimed effects tend to fall into one of two camps. On the one hand, movements such as GetUp! are often described in Gladwellian terms, as slacktivist in nature, meaning – as defined by *Oxford Dictionaries* – that while they may facilitate actions in 'support of a political or social cause', these actions are regarded as 'requiring little time or involvement'. More critically, *UrbanDictionary* ("Slacktivism," n.d.) defines slacktivism as

> the act of participating in obviously pointless activities as an expedient alternative to actually expending effort to fix a problem. Signing an email petition to stop rampant crime is slacktivism. Want to really make your community safer? Get off your ass and start a neighborhood watch!

Similarly, the *Boston Herald*'s Beckham Falcone wrote of a Facebook child abuse campaign: 'Armchair activism only goes so far. Changing your status does not change anything' (Beckham Falcone, 2010; cf. Rhimes, 2014). White goes even further, 'Exchanging the substance of activism for reformist platitudes that do well in market tests, clicktivists damage every genuine political movement they touch' (White, 2010; cf. Shulman, 2009). This is the view that activism, to be real and truly effective, requires not just the aggregation of easy online micro-actions – such as adding your name to a petition, sharing a petition with your social networks or changing your status in social media – which arguably crowd out well-thought-out public commentary and fit too comfortably within a marketplace economy (an issue we return to throughout this book), but strong social bonds, organisation and sacrifice. In Gladwell's framing, for instance, activism is not simply about attempted system change – which arguably at least some online campaigns and actions are also striving for – but is constitutively hard to accomplish and assumes a willingness to sacrifice life and liberty.[1] The kinds of actions typically promoted by such organisations as GetUP!, when considered under this view, would rarely fit this bill.

Counter-positions vary. Some positions have heralded the digital turn with revolutionising all social organisations, including activist organisations. This is the overblown 'cyber-utopian' argument that Internet technologies have the capacity to not just 'spread participatory democracy' but forge 'a new era of Athenian democracy' (Gore, 1995) and that the 'Internet is possibly one of the biggest tools for democratisation and political freedom that we have ever seen before' (Rice, as cited in Dobriansky, 2008). According to this kind of view, because these new technologies are so effective in enabling and promoting the circulation of information and the participation of the subjects in political issues, collective action can be facilitated even within societies lacking in freedom. There are also positions that accept that many of those who do sign online petitions and share campaign messages with their social networks are only minimally engaged in and committed to that campaign. However, their argument is that using the Internet as a channel for participation in activism in effect lowers the cost of involvement because it allows for the aggregation of 'micro-contributions' (Garrett, 2006), stressing the point that even weak ties among a campaign's members can be sufficient for its promotion (Hampton, 2003). This is the view that 'instead of convincing people who care a little to do more', online social movements allow for the engaging of people 'who care a little to do a little' (Shirky, 2008, p. 181). This is an important point because the cost of participation (Olson, 1968) in activist movements has been generally accepted as a motivator – or demotivator – of potential activists, to the point that lower participation in collective action has been tied to participant unwillingness or inability to manage large time and financial commitments. The Internet, however, has dramatically lowered such participation costs, further allowing for individuals to make smaller contributions that, when aggregated, can still account for a much larger whole. Given that backing by large numbers of people is widely considered to be at the heart of any campaign's influence and ultimate success, online social networks are highly effective in enabling individuals to quickly and without cost *click* their support, and in essence vouch for a cause, and in so doing implicitly – and sometimes explicitly – ask others within their networks to do the same.

This kind of framing of the Internet's affordances for activism can also present online activism as a highly productive supplement to the traditional conceptions of activism lauded by Gladwell. In one commentator's phrasing it can support, amplify and inspire traditional face-to-face activism (Jackson, 2011). More specifically, activists might use social networking sites to build online communities, which can be mobilised to participate in online and offline activities from fundraising to protesting. They blog and create videos to raise awareness of campaigns and causes; and they circulate electronic petitions and mass emails. DigiActive.org, a volunteer-run organisation that helps grassroots activists everywhere use the Internet and mobile phones to increase their reach, indeed lists eighteen digital activist tools with corresponding case studies as the potential and efficacy of their use. Regardless, the hope tends to be that far from online involvement being its own end, it might facilitate an individual's progression into fuller offline investments in a movement or campaign (this is a hope we discussed with reference to Animals Australia campaigning in chapter 3). At the same time, as Franklin (2014) has pointed out, 'in Internet-dependent contexts, any sort of serious political or social form of action now has to include an online dimension, and a sustained one at that'. Campaigns and social change movements, in other words, need both offline and online forms of mobilisation. As Franklin goes on,

> It is a sign of our age that sociopolitical action needs to know how to combine age-old, pre-digital age techniques to mobilize others with those that can speak in the 24/7, mobile, and user-generated idioms of online solidarity that can engage people close to home as well as those living far away.

It is this need and the subsequent entanglement of offline with online activist campaigning that drive, we propose, not only the idea and practice of participatory activism but the development and work of such organisations as GetUp! Examining the affordances of these practices is the focus of the next sections of this chapter.

GETUP!

> GetUp is an independent movement of more than a million people working to build a progressive Australia and bring participation back into our democracy. We campaign on human rights, democratic participation,

economic fairness and environmental sustainability. (GetUp! Media Room, n.d.)

GetUp! began in 2005 as an Australian not-for-profit, 'grassroots community advocacy organization', with the aims of facilitating the involvement of 'everyday Australians' in developing Australia as a progressive society and to 'hold politicians accountable on important issues' (Huijser & Little, 2008, p. 2). Given this was in the later part of the Howard government in Australia (1996–2007), it should be noted that mainstream public discourse at this time – informed by the Howard government's combination of neoliberalism and neoconservatism – typically foregrounded 'nationalism, moral righteousness' and 'family values' (Maddison & Martin, 2010, p. 104; cf. Burgmann, 2008). Such attitudes, as discussed earlier, are generally unfriendly to the work of activists and new social movements. Indeed Howard, particularly during his prime ministership, was in explicit conflict with two social movements around 'family values' – the women's and the gay, lesbian and transgender movement (as cited in Maddison & Martin, 2010, pp. 104–105). However, despite this mainstream discursive framing of Australia and Australianness as 'predominately white, heterosexual, patriotic, self-interested, and acquisitive' (p. 109), there were indications that 'a growing sector of the Australian public' was becoming less and less tolerant of the Howard government's 'official talk on everything from trees to terror' (Huijser & Little, 2008, p. 7). It is within this context that GetUp! was conceived.

The organisation was established by two young Australians, Jeremy Heimans and Dave Madden, who had worked on MoveOn's Internet-based campaigns in the United States (Huijser & Little, 2008). Modelled on MoveOn, GetUp! has been described in several ways. As an online activist and campaigning organisation, it has been described as an independent 'grassroots community advocacy' group (Rodan & Balnaves, 2010), a 'political advocacy group' (Bruns & Wilson, 2009) and an 'online civil society' campaign organisation (Chen & Walsh, 2010, p. 51). Importantly, it presents itself as driven by values – specifically those of 'fairness, compassion and courage' (GetUp!, n.d.) – rather than by party politics, although this has been debated with various accusations of political partisanship being levelled at the organisation (see, e.g., Vromen, 2008, 2015; Vromen & Coleman, 2011). Like MoveOn (and Animals Australia), GetUp! is best described as a hybrid campaigning body. It uses both online and offline tactics to engage citizens, and it functions as both an insider-oriented interest group that lobbies politicians and an outsider-focused social movement organisation able to engage and coordinate mass-based political participation (Vromen, 2015). In summation, GetUp! maintains its role as a rigorous watchdog of the Australian Parliament, while striving to enable broader participatory activism by providing the infrastructure for members and potential members to engage with the organisation, each other and the broader public and political spheres, and take political action both online and offline.

With regard to its internal organisation, GetUp! depends on its board, a small 'core of paid staff', and a volunteer program through which individual members are enlisted to work on selected campaigns (Vromen, 2008, p. 111). The board sets the movement's strategy as well as manages financial, legal and compliance requirements (GetUp Board, n.d.), but organisational decisions, choice of campaigns and decisions regarding strategic action are made by the board along with the small team of staff. Finally, there are the organisation's members and sponsors (see tables 5.1 and 5.2).

Although GetUp! overall has more members than the combined membership of Australian political parties in Australia (Gauja, 2015), becoming a member only requires an individual to respond to an email campaign petition or agree to receive emails. In other words, membership does not include any joining fees, and member participation has 'a very low threshold' (Vromen, 2008, p. 115). Members can be involved in any campaign on an 'ad hoc and informal basis' (p. 115), meaning that they are 'free to act on the campaigns they feel passionate about' (Hill, 2010, p. 11). Individuals who have an email account and consider that their 'issue-based interests' might be of public

Table 5.1. GetUp! state membership 2015–2016.

Australian State/Territory	*Number of Members*	*Percentage of Membership*
ACT	22,129	2.2
NSW	314,669	31.0
NT	5,591	0.6
QLD	165,318	16.3
SA	60,656	6.0
TAS	22,601	2.2
VIC	210,638	20.7
WA	74,514	7.3

Source: Figures from the GetUp! Annual Report 2015–2016 (2016).

Table 5.2. GetUp! total membership 2013–2016.

	2013–2014	*2014–2015*	*2015–2016*
Membership	677,500	948,000	1,015,140
Core members*	9,142	11,684	15,006
Core member contributions	2,447,476 AUD	3,251,167 AUD	3,585,608 AUD

*Core members give small donations on a regular basis.

Source: Figures from GetUp! Annual Report 2015–2016 (2016); GetUp! Annual Report 2014–2015 (2015); GetUp! Annual Report 2013–2014 (2014).

concern are thus likely contenders to join GetUp! (Huijser & Little, 2008, p. 9). Members also, in effect, sponsor the organisation through fundraising and donations, with further funding coming from the union movement and actions in coalition with other 'progressive NGOs' (Vromen, 2008, p. 110). Fundraising campaigns, however, are nearly always focused towards achieving campaign actions and outcomes as opposed to covering the organisation's administrative costs (Hill, 2010, p. 9).

While GetUp!'s primary methodology to date has been to encourage its membership to lobby their elected representatives (Vromen, 2008), the organisation has also employed a range of other campaigning techniques. These include taking out advertisements in major daily newspapers (both Australian and international), developing and organising the screening of television commercials and holding and facilitating a range of face-to-face events. These have included GetUp! forums, rallies, media stunts aiming to garner mainstream media attention, public Q&A events with politicians, the presence of volunteers at polling booths on election day and post-election community get-togethers (Huijser & Little, 2008; Rodan & Balnaves, 2009). GetUp! also supplies members with a downloadable Host Pack, which is a guide on how to facilitate a meeting and connect to the community media (Rodan & Balnaves, 2010).

RAISING AWARENESS AND MOBILISING ACTION

In utilising similar campaigning tactics to MoveOn, AVAAZ and other like organisations, GetUp!'s aim, like that of these similar organisations, is to supplement its website presence – which is arguably still 'core to the network governance of the group' (Rodan & Balnaves, 2009, p. 178) – with Web 2.0 technologies so as to build a socially networked 'progressive activism' able to operate well beyond the scope and scale of conventional political party organisation and action (Bruns & Wilson, 2009). As campaigns and campaign messages are to go viral, the GetUp! team scrupulously craft and test every part of their outgoing communication 'from subject lines (to maximise opens) to length and style of communication to maximise "follow through"' (Hill, 2010, p. 8; cf. Vromen & Coleman, 2013), the latter including here signing petitions, communicating directly with political representatives, volunteering and donating. With regard, for instance, to the organisation's use of email – GetUp!'s primary mechanism for instigating a campaign and sustaining its trajectory – the key element always concerns 'how the moral urgency of member action is articulated' (Vromen & Colemen, 2013, p. 87). That is, the aim is to 'create a moral urgency to the grievances' informing the campaign (p. 80). Email campaigns are therefore primarily driven by narrative storytelling, insofar as such a structure supports the layering in of emotionally laden and/or morally driven values, stories and messages (similar structures are to be found in crowdfunding pitches; see chapter 6 for this discussion). A campaign email would thus typically start with a story about the campaign aims and focus – an *us* story – but would then move to the members' interests – the *self* story – so that members make the transition to what should be called a 'driven conclusion' (pp. 80, 87). These emails are thus calls to action which aim to facilitate what Vromen and Coleman (2011, pp. 80, 85) have called 'a rapid response' model of civic engagement in campaigns and to use this towards achieving both campaign momentum and social and legislative change.

GetUp! also draws on a number of other communicative strategies in order to connect with and engage the broader Australian society as well as work to influence decision-makers. For instance, it uses strategically timed 'media-stunts'[2] to increase campaign awareness (Hill, 2010, p. 9), a key aim being to get campaigns and campaign objectives into the mainstream news so as to increase its public exposure. Another related strategy is the use of promotional video clips, with one study finding that GetUp! videos – eight of them in total – released during the 2010 Australian election campaign received nearly 550,000 views, more views than received by the 100 videos released in total by Australia's three major political parties (Chen, 2012). One such video was the GetUp! Spoof Trailer, Election (2010), which, replete with in-jokes from contemporary popular culture and politics (Rodan, 2010), was developed to encourage young Australians to enrol to vote. This video, which also introduced the key election issues of the time – those of carbon pollution and refugees – received 400,000 hits on YouTube in 2010 and was further shown on national television (during *Q&A*, for example).[3] GetUp! members were also encouraged to disseminate the video, sharing it across My Space, Facebook, YouTube and Twitter. With regard to video release, while the organisation does develop and release television advertisements, it heavily utilises YouTube as a more durable and much less ephemeral communicative space. GetUp!, for instance, currently has 405 videos archived and available through this platform (GetUp! Australia Channel, n.d.). In addition, to increase its opportunities to influence decision-makers, GetUp! provides online tools with which members can identify and contact their local MPs (member of Parliament) on campaign issues. Finally, GetUp!, as noted previously, does encourage members to participate in offline as well as online activities, promoting the joining of local action groups in particular.

Vromen and Coleman (2013) contend that the success of online campaigning is best measured with reference to two criteria: (a) how well the organisation mobilises citizens and (b) how much political influence is held and can be exercised by the organisation. With reference to GetUp!, both of these would appear to be well met. GetUp! can, for example, demonstrate achievement of legislative outcomes such as bills being shelved, successful court actions – one such being GetUp!'s successful challenge in 2010 to the Australian Electoral Commission with regard to instigating the online enrolment of voters (see Black, 2011) – and government spending being redirected (Vromen, 2008). It can also point to increases in its profile and public traction from when MPs mention GetUp! campaigns in their speeches (see Brandzel, as cited in Rodan & Balnaves, 2009), from positive mention in the mainstream media and simply to the sheer numbers of people joining, mobilising for and participating in its campaigns.

As has been noted already, some have considered GetUp!'s style of civic campaigning and participatory engagement little more than clicktivism (Norman, 2013), as encouraging at best 'talk at the expense of action' (Hill, 2010, p. 7). Under this view, clicking in support of a cause or to sign a petition is simply always too low a threshold to be considered political activism. And yet it has also been argued that within GetUp!'s online campaigning, the online petition 'functions as the political Object' and the Like and Share social networking buttons do enable an individual to be part of a political action without having, in effect, to invest high levels of resources (Halupka, 2014, pp. 127–128). This brings two issues into the foreground. First is the idea of the anonymous individual as activist, with Huijser and Little (2008, p. 7) claiming that this kind of participation appeals to people who do not see themselves as doing grassroots activism in any strong conventional sense, although they would see themselves as interested in and concerned with political matters and, further, as participants in such matters (Lundy, 2009; Zuckerman, 2014). A second issue is that in its engagement of people's online social networks, GetUp! enables individuals to find 'like-minded people' (Huijser & Little, 2008, p. 9). It is arguably in drawing on both of these aspects of online campaigning that GetUp! is able to create 'a space for community concern' and foster precisely the kind of 'talk' that enables 'engagement and deliberation' in political issues (Hill, 2010, p. 7) and has 'an effect on governance' (Rodan & Balnaves, 2009, pp. 178–182). Such work, we would argue, fulfils the criteria of participatory activism, and perhaps even of deliberation, in further examination of which we turn now to an elaboration of one of GetUp!'s current, multifaceted, long-running and expansive campaigns: 'Protection of the Great Barrier Reef'. This, as noted previously, marks a call for significant social change with regard to the weighting Australia should be giving to environmental and economic interests, arguing that Australia's long-standing prioritisation of primary industries and their economic interests over environmental protection must change. This campaign will be examined in detail with the aim of teasing apart the combination of online and offline strategies in use by GetUp! to encourage people's take-up of participatory activism.

PROTECTING AUSTRALIA'S GREAT BARRIER REEF

In 1981, the Great Barrier Reef (GBR) in Australia was listed on the World Heritage List as one of the Seven Wonders of the World. UNESCO (United Nations Education, Scientific and Cultural Organisation) selected the GBR as a World Heritage site due to its meeting of four criteria. These comprise its (a) outstanding universal value relating to its natural beauty, (b) extreme vastness, (c) scientific significance to ecology and (d) extensive biodiversity (as cited in Markham, Osipova, Lafrenz Samuels & Caldas, 2016). Estimated to be 8,000 years old and covering an area of 348,000 square kilometres off the coast of Queensland, the GBR is the worlds 'most extensive coral reef ecosystem' and is one of the few Earth sites that can be seen from space (United Nations Educational Scientific Cultural Organisation World Heritage Centre, n.d.).

In 1975 the Great Barrier Reef Marine Park Act was passed by the Australian Parliament (Australian Government, 2016). Every five years the Great Barrier Reef Marine Park Authority (GBRMPA), an independent government agency, is responsible for protecting and managing the GBR, and produces a report identifying any long-term challenges the reef might face (2009, 2014). Since 2009 the authority has noted a variety of emerging challenges for the reef, such as proposed port expansions, increased shipping, intensified and changed land use, increased population, the impact of marine debris, illegal fishing, extreme weather such as floods and cyclones and Climate Change.[4] To ensure the GBR continues to meet and improve on its 'outstanding universal value', the *Reef 2050 Long-Term Sustainability Plan* was developed with input from 'scientists, communities, Traditional Owners, industry and non-governmental organisations' (Department of Environment and Energy, 2015, p. 3). The Turnbull coalition government cemented how important the GBR is to the Australian national interest for current and future generations by committing $1 billion in June 2016 to ensure its protection (Hunt & Turnbull, 2016). At the same time, however, the challenges faced by the reef have only intensified, with a range of coastal and marine developments still being proposed and in some cases passed, and the reef already showing clear signs of damage. The Australian Government has in fact requested that UNESCO not include the GBR as a case study in the UNESCO report on 'World Heritage and Tourism in a Changing Climate' (Markham, 2016; Markham et al., 2016), as it anticipates such a report will impact negatively on the tourism industry in the area (Readfern, 2016; Slezak, 2016a).

One main threat is to do with mining development. In 2010 Adani Mining Pty Ltd and the then Queensland state government began a series of negotiations and approvals to establish two mines and a railway line in the

Galilee Basin in North Queensland. The premier at the time declared that the Carmichael Coal Mine and rail project would create significant jobs for Queenslanders (Chang, 2016). Approval of the Carmichael Coal Mine and Rail Infrastructure Project to the Abbot Point Coal Port was given by the state's coordinator general and received eventual approval from the federal Environment Minister Greg Hunt in July 2014 (Department of Environment, 2014). Activists in Australia have contested, campaigned and conducted legal challenges against this project since its proposal, contending that the opening of a coal mine, the building of a rail line and the increase in shipping to service the mine so close to the GBR are simply too dangerous (Chang, 2016). Major campaigns and challenges have been mounted by Mackay Conservation Group, Australia Marine Conservation Society, World Wildlife Fund, Greenpeace, GetUp!, Greens Party, Labour Party, Wangan & Jugalingou Traditional Owners Council and other supporters such as the Commonwealth Bank and Sunrise Project. Specific contentious issues include

(a) the impact of dredging – deepening the sea bed – to develop a harbour; action with the potential to smother parts of the reef and ultimately add another layer of threat to the health of the reef floor;
(b) the bleaching of coral due to 'heat stress' from sea temperature rising even by one degree due to Climate Change (Great Barrier Reef Marine Park Authority, n.d.; Climate Council, 2016);
(c) the increased risk of shipping accidents on the reef (Queensland Government, 2016);
(d) the clearing and development of land with potential to cause increased run-off such as 'flow of nitrogen, pesticides, and sediments of the Reef' (Department of Environment and Energy, 2015, p. 25);
(e) the increased direct use of the reef for marine tourism, fishing, ports and so on (Department of Environment and Energy, 2015).

While the Queensland Government (2016) outlined its proposed address of a number of these issues in a report dated 31 August 2016, what is clear is that with consideration of reef health, competing interest claims are pitted against each other. On the one hand is the environmental impact of new and expanded development on the reef itself and the run-on effect of potential loss of jobs in the tourism industry (Slezak, 2016b). On the other hand is the fossil fuel industries' economic interests and the flow on effect of increased wealth (mining royalties) and increased jobs in the state of Queensland (Department of State Development, Infrastructure and Planning, 2014). The protracted challenges to such developments by activists and their supporters are due to their belief that the GBR – as a natural wonder – is itself a priceless asset. Adani conversely offers Australia increased inward investment with the Carmichael Coal Mine and Abbot Point Coal Port project approvals; these have been estimated to generate approximately 6,000 new jobs and earn the government $22 billion in taxes and royalties into the future (Department of Environment and Energy, 2015; Queensland Government, 2016).

Activists and their supporters in mainstream and social media have disputed and debunked the economic gains from the Adani mine project, especially with regard to the increased jobs for Queensland. Alongside the environmental facts stated earlier, they have also proffered revised economic facts to contest the Queensland Government's claims of the number of new jobs to be created, drawing in particular on recent reports noting that Adani's economist has in fact stated that there will be only '1464 net jobs' created from Adani's Carmichael mine (Chang, 2016; Eltham, 2016). Activists are also stressing that the GBR tourism industry already employs an estimated 70,000 people – overall equivalent of full-time workers – annually (a figure of 68,978 also estimated by Deloitte Access Economics, 2013; Eltham, 2016; Hunt & Turnbull, 2016) and the potential use of 457 visas to import labour (Dempster, 2016). These jobs will be under threat should the reef be adversely affected by these proposed developments. This, then, is the context of GetUp!'s GBR campaigns – and it should be noted that GetUp! has been one of the major campaigners within Australia in the ongoing efforts to block Adani – and of our first detailed examination of GetUp!'s campaigning with regard to its meeting the criteria of both participatory activism and deliberation.

Campaigns and Tactics

Each of the GBR-oriented campaigns conducted by GetUp! has used multiple tactics to promote collective action, to support and facilitate participatory activism. In table 5.3 we outline the six campaigns to date and their major campaign tactics, each of which will also be unpacked in some detail later.

Abbot Point Expansion

Prior to the Environment Minister Greg Hunt's approval of the Abbot Point coal terminal expansion (on 31 January 2014), GetUp! members lobbied the government throughout 2013 and into 2014 by funding full-page advertisements, signing and sharing petitions and attending rallies. GetUp! members also participated in the following actions:

(a) The crowdfunding of two legal challenges relating to the approval of dredging and dumping inside the reef

Table 5.3. GetUp!'s GBR campaigns and tactics.

Great Barrier Reef Campaign	*Social Media*	*Engage Stakeholders*	*Legal/Policy Challenge*	*Donate*	*Advertisement Billboards*	*Rallies*	*Rapid Response*	*Volunteers*	*Petition*
Abbot Point Expansion	✓	✓	✓	✓	✓	✓			✓
Banks	✓	✓		✓	✓				
Expose Adani	✓	✓	✓	✓	✓				✓
Queensland Election Reef	✓		✓	✓	✓		✓	✓	
Reef Reels	✓		✓		✓			✓	✓

Sources: Table 5.3 collates information about GetUp!'s GBR campaigns gathered from GetUp!'s Annual Reports (2013–2014, 2014–2015, 2015–2016) and from GetUp! [Web] (n.d.).

(b) The lobbying of major banks to persuade them that financing the reef's destruction would damage the banks reputation with its customers
(c) The sharing of the results of investigations exposing the environmental track record of Indian-owned mining company Adani

Exemplifying how activists can harness participatory activism in a highly practical way, 17,500 GetUp! members contributed over $300,000 to a Citizen's Reef Fighting Fund. A first challenge questioned the legality of the Environmental Minister's approval of the Adani proposal on two grounds: (a) the decision to allow the dredge spoil dumping in World Heritage Area was unlawful because the environmental assessment carried out was improper, and (b) the Environmental Minister failed in his obligation to protect a World Heritage Area. GetUp! also funded the North Queensland Conservation Council to legally challenge and fight dumping, as well as the Mackay Conservation Group to legally challenge and fight dredging. Although these actions have not been able to deter government interest in the project, they have delayed development and instigated extensive public debate regarding the project. Such attention has arguably brought more Australians into debate about the pros and cons of the project, and increased GetUp!'s membership.

Targeting the Banks

In addition to such systemic challenges, GetUp! created the opportunity and provided the infrastructure for a range of individual civic engagements and actions. For example, GetUp! members were encouraged to petition banks directly by saturating their Facebook and Twitter feeds, the overriding tactic being to undermine the ability of the Adani mining company to attract bank investment.[5] Working alongside its German counterpart, Campact, and other activist groups, GetUp! campaigned to persuade Deutsche Bank (and others) to walk away from the Adani mining project (Saunders, 2014). According to GetUp!, Campact reprocessed GetUp!'s (Save the Reef, n.d.) campaign materials in May 2014 to persuade thousands of Deutsche Bank customers to swamp the bank's Facebook, Twitter and email accounts, urging them in each instance not to fund Abbot Point. When it appeared that Deutsche Bank was still likely to fund Abbot Point, around 4,000 GetUp! members raised $140,000 to fund a full-page advertisement in the mainstream media *Financial Times* across Europe. The advertisement featured in a leading German newspaper and generated international coverage (GetUp! Save the Reef, n.d.). Due, at least partially, to this orchestration of consumer pressure, Deutsche, HSBC, Barclays, and Royal Bank of Scotland all eventually backed away from funding the project (McCarthy, 2015). Such campaigning is still being carried out within Australia.

Expose Adani

In its Expose Adani campaign, GetUp! again made extensive use of social media, such as Facebook and YouTube, specifically to educate and mobilise members (and potential members given that these platforms' encouragement of sharing and liking can translate into the connection of friends and friends of friends with civic matters). In this campaign GetUp! hired documentary film-makers to produce the short video *Don't Trust This Company with Our Great Barrier Reef.* This video appears on GetUp!'s campaign website as well as in YouTube (published 2 March 2015), and features an exposé of the Adani Mundra–based coal mine in India, highlighting in particular the company's record of environmental destruction, corruption and human rights abuses (GetUp! Don't Trust This Company with Our Great Barrier Reef, n.d.). Although the video was blocked by YouTube for a perceived copyright breach after only 70,000 views (Hannam, 2014), GetUp! successfully raised additional funds (over 4,000 members donated) to take legal action to have it reinstated. As of February 2017, this video – appearing in YouTube as *Can We Trust Adani with the Great Barrier Reef?* – has received over 600,000 views (GetUp! Australia, n.d.). In addition, GetUp! developed a targeted online advertising campaign so that potential investors in the company would also come to see the video.

The overall success of this kind of participatory activism can be noted through the following outcomes. As well as the number of views of the YouTube video, the video on GetUp!'s Facebook page has reached 1.5 million views (n.d.). The copyright breach story was published in mainstream media, the *Sydney Morning Herald* (Hannam, 2014), and was the most popular article on the website at the time. The story was also featured on the current affairs program *The Project*. Also available on GetUp!'s Facebook campaign website, The Juice Media's video *Carmichael Coal Mine Honest Government Advertisement* has been shared from YouTube 1,544,257 views (December 2016). With an aim of supporting increased public engagement with the campaign, when viewers click onto any of GetUp!'s campaign videos they are asked to share it, tweet it, email it and add it to Google+. For GetUp!, then, these videos on YouTube work to alert and educate members about issues (Poell, 2014), but more to the point is their spreadability. They have been published so that they can be easily recirculated, repurposed and re-watched many times over, meaning that they not only promote enhanced awareness of issues but support civic engagement and participatory activism.

Queensland Election: Reef Protection

Another element informing participatory activism concerns the capacity of individuals and groups to participate in advocating for issue-based interests, volunteering at elections and voting (Petrova & Tarrow, 2007). Each of these is a crucial part of civic life in a democracy. For instance, GetUp!'s actions around the Queensland election (31 January 2015) demonstrate how movements can enable individuals to participate in civic life both online and offline. In this instance, GetUp! worked with political strategists to create and produce a 'series of hard-hitting' advertisements that would inform and educate people about the Queensland Liberal National Party's (LNP) track record on the protection of the GBR (GetUp! Save the Reef, n.d.). Members also donated funds to pay for a series of mainstream television advertisements to be shown during prime time in significant marginal electorates around Queensland. (GetUp! does not state when and which stations the advertisements were aired in the lead-up to the election.) Following the advertisement campaign, on Election Day 600 members volunteered to hand out 'How-to-Vote' Reef cards at polling booths across Queensland (GetUp! Save the Reef, n.d.).

In a last-minute effort to gag this civic campaign, Queensland's Newman government attempted to silence GetUp! by filing a Supreme Court injunction against the How-to-Vote cards. Members once again donated funds to fight the court case and GetUp! won based on the judge's verdict that 'there was no real question to be tried' (GetUp! Save the Reef, n.d.). Campbell Newman and the LNP lost the election and, according to GetUp!, polling revealed that for Queenslanders saving the reef was a major vote-changing issue. Certainly, the campaign made a significant contribution to the Newman government losing the election; however, it was not the only reason, with other major factors comprising the premier's leadership style and ongoing bitter disputes with the judiciary, public servants, doctors and same-sex individuals (Lewis, 2015).

#ReefReels

GetUp's style of offline campaigning clearly works hand in hand with online campaigning. Both, after all, are tasked with the same three objectives. These are to (a) mobilise support through online and offline petitions; (b) engage volunteers in civic participation; and (c) continue to reach new audiences and garner potential members. This triad of objectives thus saw GetUp! also partner with TropFest and Upworthy to launch a short film competition about the environmental threats to GBR. Using the hashtag #ReefReels, this competition received over seventy entries, with five chosen to be screened at the TropFest film festival (see GetUp! ReefReels, n.d.). To ensure the broadest exposure of these materials and of the campaign's key issues, GetUp! volunteers also sold 1,000 seats to the TropFest film festival – tickets included an advertisement for GetUp!'s reef campaign – and over fifty GetUp! volunteers then attended TropFest during which they collected 800 new signatures on a 'Save the Reef' petition. The #ReefReels competition and videos exposed the GetUp! campaign to an entirely new audience not only at the TropFest but also via Facebook and Twitter as viewers could easily share videos of their choice. Once again this sees videos – in this instance community-developed videos – in use to educate and inform people who might be ignorant about the dangers to the GBR. As community-developed materials, they arguably also pack a strong affective punch; once individuals know the 'truth', they cannot but care.

Dump Dumping

GetUp! members are encouraged and supported to engage in participatory activism whether it is to mount legal challenges or to address and respond to state government submissions. Achievement of legislative outcomes (Vromen, 2008, p. 111), such as the successful legal challenge to stop dumping at Abbot Point, are then celebrated by GetUp! as a means of further strengthening members' commitment to the broader campaign and, in turn, reinforcing the power of participatory action. This circularity of campaign action, member support, success and affirmation is important, as campaigns such as reef protection are in effect endless. There are always new threats, and campaign work and support thus needs to be long-term, multifaceted and highly strategic. Hence, although the stopping of Abbot Point dumping was successful, the proposal of a new dumping site meant that GetUp! needed to mobilise members for additional stages of campaign work. In late October 2015 Environment Minister Greg Hunt attempted to fast track approval, quickly and quietly, and without a full Environmental Impact Statement, a new dumping site at the Caley Valley wetlands. The Queensland public was given only ten days to make submissions. GetUp! immediately released this information on Facebook, from which point the post was shared by 20,000 people and viewed by 2 million (GetUp! Save the Reef, n.d.). Within the short time frame given, GetUp! members responded to the 2,000-page document, sending in 25,000 submissions. The state government ultimately abandoned its plans as a result of participatory activism by GetUp! members and other publics.

CAMPAIGNING TOWARDS PUBLIC DELIBERATION

It seems clear that GetUp!'s campaigning strategies have been effective in gaining public support and what we have called civic engagement. (A further issue, and one to be discussed in the following chapter, is that neoliberally oriented governments have a tendency to 'lean on the "successes"' [Hamman, 2015, pp. 172–173] of civic engagements rather than meeting their own public interest responsibilities.[6]) It also seems evident that GetUp! is being successful in its calls for and facilitation of participatory activism and that such activism requires the strategic engagement of both online and offline actions and networking. The remaining question, however, concerns the relation of GetUp!'s formula for participatory activism and deliberation insofar as deliberation has often been framed as integral for the development of long-lasting social change. After all, deliberation – as we set out in chapter 2 – in facilitating the development of reciprocal understanding and of at least some form of a desired consensus, helps a community determine what issues and values are of communal concern and even what the nature of that community should be given past, current and future challenges. As we have discussed previously, however, there are tensions between conventional understandings and practices of deliberation and activism. Advocates of the former see direct activist action as extremist, disconnected from broader community concerns and values, while advocates of the latter consider models of deliberation as tending too easily towards conservatism and as far too easily manipulated by those with institutional power. And certainly, if deliberation is conceived in a strictly rational way with required practices constraining how it is carried out and who can be heard, then activist disavowal of such practices is not surprising. Indeed, this is Young's (2003) point against deliberation. As she puts it, an activist prioritisation of practices of direct confrontation – of striving to cause moral shock in the way of many social movements – may appear substantially more effective than trying to facilitate and then participate in a deliberation where the vested interests of powerful adversaries would seem to hold sway. This is particularly the case when stakes are considered to be high and when the broader public is considered most likely to side with the status quo.

And yet we would see this as a very limited view of deliberation. Deliberation in our view should not be constrained to a procedurally legitimated discussion. While we would agree that it is about the process of coming to recognise a better argument – or position, set of values or proposed action – in which case it must also be about keeping the process of debate open to the multiple viewpoints which inform the various positions under debate, it is also reliant on participants gaining an understanding of the positions of these various viewpoints. This, of course, is where a lot of activism fits – it is the work of striving to get specific, usually non-conservative, viewpoints into the public domain for consideration and to gain traction for them (see Marks, 2010). Like all progressive activist campaigners, GetUp! can be seen as operating within this domain, but it is also striving to increase public participation within this debate. Indeed, this is where it should be remembered that GetUp! was formed with an explicit aim of broadening the Australian public's democratic engagement, of becoming a 'broad based movement' able to shape progressive Australian politics (Vromen, 2008, p. 118). In this sense, perhaps GetUp!, and organisations of its ilk, should be understood as a facilitator of deliberation.

This is to say that along with providing a range of tools to support deliberative exchanges, GetUp! works to bring specific topics – and specific positions with regard to these topics – into public deliberation and to draw increasing numbers of Australians into participating within deliberations concerning these topics. Individual actions and exchanges carried out within the GetUp! remit may not be deliberative in any strong sense – and clearly many of them are not, such as those occurring as media stunts – yet we would suggest that these same actions and exchanges promote deliberative responses.

Of final concern is the question, raised also in previous chapters, as to whether any activist or campaigning organisation can be supportive of deliberation insofar as it is not in fact value neutral. This is the challenge – often levelled against GetUp!, as it is against all activist organisations – that because the organisation is irremediably partisan, it cannot in fact facilitate deliberation. This concerns the idea that deliberation – and its various participants – must be constitutively neutral as to the various positions and arguments under debate, able to rationally debate various options and accept whichever one of these is considered to gain majority support. As we have already stressed, however, this is always going to be a problematic point for activist campaigning insofar as while such campaigns are certainly aiming to gain a majority support for their causes, they are never neutral as to their preferences. They cannot afford to be; as we noted in chapter 2, there 'are no reasons to expect the right decision to emerge automatically from a deliberative procedure' (Arias-Maldonado, 2007, p. 247). Given these issues, then, perhaps what should be underscored with regard to the activist engagements of deliberation is that such engagements are always affectively informed, striving to inspire both care and solidarity – even if built on weak links – with regard to specific affectively presented issues.

NOTES

1 Activist Tammy Tibbets, founder of 'She's the First', a not-for-profit that supports girls' education in the developing world, pushed back against the very notion that all activist efforts fall into categories that must involve risk. In her blog post about Gladwell's article, she wrote: 'My activism is peaceful and a lot of the time it involves the color pink. But you know what, it's working. . . . No kidnappings, no killings, no houses burning down, no bomb scares, no beating of volunteers, no arrests, no sit-ins. My question to Mr. Gladwell is, "When did violence become barometer for the strength of activism?"' (Tibbetts, 2010).

2 One such media stunt was carried out in support of GetUp!'s 'Marriage Equality' campaign. In this instance, GetUp! members were encouraged to donate to win the chance to have a 'sit down dinner with the then Prime Minister Julia Gillard' in 2012. With $31,000 received in donations, three same-sex couples (one family was

featured in the GetUp!-sponsored documentary *Gayby Baby*) were selected to make their case for marriage equality. The event made headlines in the national newspaper *The Australian* (Australian Associated Press, 2012). GetUp! members also rallied at Tony Abbott's electoral office in Warringah (NSW) with a 'bold proposal', petition, 'a bunch or rainbow balloons and a giant engagement ring'; the rally included a stunt in which GetUp! members 'popped the question', with the Prime Minister asked if he would permit liberal MPs to have a conscience vote on marriage equality (GetUp! Marriage Equality in Australia, n.d.).

3 Another of GetUp!'s highly successful campaign videos has been *It's Time*. Part of GetUp!'s 'Marriage Equality' campaign, another long-running multifaceted national campaign, this video was uploaded on YouTube on 24 November 2011. Highly affectively charged, the video depicts the story of romantic love from the first date to building a shared life, with emphasis – regardless of whether individuals are in a heterosexual or homosexual relationship – on the similarity of feelings and emotions. So far the video has received 16,175,533 views, 122,979 likes (compared to 7,047 dislikes) and 34,947 comments – significantly more views than the total of the other fourteen videos on Marriage Equality also uploaded by GetUp! on YouTube. In another example, also part of the Marriage Equality campaign, GetUp! teamed with the film-makers of *Gayby Baby* (2015), a documentary from the perspective of four Australian children raised by same-sex couples. Funding for the project was raised by crowdfunding (Gayby Baby, n.d.), and to coincide with the documentary's release, GetUp! sent packages of the documentary including glitter to MPs and conducted protests outside their electoral offices (GetUp! Marriage Equality in Australia, n.d.). The aim was to influence MPs into calling for a 'Free Vote' on marriage equality (GetUp! Call for a Liberal Free Vote on Marriage Equality, n.d).

4 Activist communication regarding the reef in Australia has a long history starting with the 'Save the Reef' protest campaign in the 1960s and now with the 'Fight for the Reef' protest campaign (post-Internet). The earlier campaign was fostered through mainstream media such as radio, print and television as well as alternative media (Foxwell-Norton & Lester, 2017, p. 573). Over a fifty-year period environmentalists have developed a 'sophisticated media strategy' (p. 574).

5 Banks in Australia are being targeted by both activists and politicians. For instance, Westpac was targeted by the Resources Minister Matthew Canavan, who denigrated and disparaged Westpac for deciding to not finance the Adani mega mine in Queensland's Galilee Basin (Baxendale, 2017). The Minister claims Westpac was listening to 'noisy activists in Sydney' rather than 'job-seekers in north Queensland' (Baxendale).

6 Hamman (2015) here considers the civic crowdfunding carried out for the *Sea Dumping Case* – a legal challenge in which GetUp! was a major partner.

REFERENCES

Arias-Maldonado, M. (2007). An imaginary solution? The green defence of deliberative democracy. *Environmental Values*, *16*(2), 233–252.

Australian Associated Press. (2012, February 22). Julia Gillard says gay marriage inevitable: Couples. *The Australian*. Retrieved from http://www.theaustralian.com.au/.

Australian Government. (2016, March 10). *Great Barrier Reef Marine Act 1975.* Retrieved from https://www.legislation.gov.au/Details/C2017C00279.

Baxendale, R. (2017, April 28). Westpac 'more interested in noisy activists'. *The Australian*. Retrieved from http://www.theaustralian.com.au/.

Beckham Falcone, L. (2010, December 7). To be charitable, online activism not worth much. *The Boston Herald*. Retrieved from www.pressreader.com/usa/boston-herald/20101207/285834369663438.

Black, P. (2011). Elections 2.0: Reflections on the 2010 federal election and the future of Australian electoral law. *Alternative Law Journal*, *36*(3), 149–152.

Bruns, A., & Wilson, J. (2009). Citizen consultation from above and below: The Australian perspective. In A. Prosser & P. Parycek (Eds.), *Proceedings of EDEM 2009 – Conference on Electronic Democracy*. Vienna, Austria: Austrian Computer Society. Retrieved from http://eprints.qut.edu.au/27368/2/27368.pdf.

Burgmann, V. (2008). Aspirational authoritarianism: Howard governments v. new social movements. *Social Alternatives*, *27*(1), 10–16.

Chang, C. (2016, December 6). Why Adani's $21 billion Carmichael mine could be unstoppable. *News com.au*. Retrieved from http://www.news.com.au/.

Chen, P. (2012). The new Media and the campaign. In M. Simms & J. Wanna (Eds.), *Julia 2010: The caretaker election* (pp. 65–84). Retrieved from https://press.anu.edu.au/publications/julia-2010-caretaker-election/download.

Chen, P., & Walsh, L. (2010). E-Election 2007? Political competition online. *Australian Cultural History*, *28*(1), 47–54.

Climate Council. (2016). *Climate Council alert: Climate change and coral bleaching*. Retrieved from https://www.climatecouncil.org.au.

Delli Carpini, M. X. (2010). Defining civic engagement. [Blog post] Retrieved from http://alliance1.org/ce/defining-civic-engagement.

Deloitte Access Economics. (2013, March). *Economic contribution of the Great Barrier Reef.* Townsville, Australia: Great Barrier Reef Marine Park Authority.

Dempster, Q. (2016, December 9). Adani/Carmichael mega coal mine: The mother of all our fears. *The New Daily*. Retrieved from http://thenewdaily.com.au/.

Department of Environment. (2014). *Carmichael coal mine and rail infrastructure project, Queensland (EPBC 2010/5736)*. Canberra, Australia: AGPS. Retrieved from http://www.environment.gov.au/epbc/notices/assessments/2010/5736/2010-5736-approval-decision.pdf.

Department of Environment and Energy. (2015). *Reef 2050 long-term sustainability plan*. Canberra, Australia: AGPS. Retrieved from https://www.environment.gov.au/marine/gbr/publications/reef-2050-long-term-sustainability-plan.

Department of State Development, Infrastructure and Planning. (2014, May). *Carmichael coal mine and rail project: Coordinator-General's evaluation report on the environmental impact statement*. Brisbane, Australia: State of Queensland. Retrieved from www.dsdip.qld.gov.au.

Dobriansky, P. (2008, September 10). New media vs. new censorship: The authoritarian assault on information. [Remarks to Broadcasting Board of Governors]. Retrieved from https://2001-2009.state.gov/r/pa/ei/speeches/2008/.

Eltham, B. (2016, December 7). Is the rush to approve one of the world's biggest coal mines delusion or corruption? *Newmatilda.com*. Retrieved from https://newmatilda.com/.

Foxwell-Norton, K., & Lester, L. (2017). Saving the Great Barrier Reef from disaster: Media then and now. *Media, Culture & Society*, *39*(4), 568–581.

Franklin, M. I. (2014, November 19). Slacktivism, clicktivism, and 'real' social change. Oxford University Press blog [Web log post]. Retrieved from https://blog.oup.com/2014/11/slacktivism-clicktivism-real-social-change/.

Garrett, R. K. (2006). Protest in an information society: A review of literature on social movements and new ICTs. *Information, Communication & Society*, *9*, 202–224.

Gauja, A. (2015). The state of democracy and representation in Australia. *Representation*, *51*(1), 23–34.

Gayby Baby. (n.d.). Supporters. Retrieved from http://thegaybyproject.com/supporters/.

GetUp! (n.d.). About us. Retrieved from https://www.getup.org.au/about.

GetUp! Australia. (n.d.). Can we trust Adani with the Great Barrier Reef? [Video file]. Retrieved from https://www.youtube.com/user/getupaustralia.

GetUp! Australia Channel. (n.d.). GetUp! Australia YouTube channel [Video file]. Retrieved from https://www.youtube.com/results?search_query=GetUp%21+Australia+GetUp%21+Australia++GetUp%21+Australia+.

GetUp Board. (n.d.). The GetUp board. Retrieved from https://www.getup.org.au/campaigns/board/the-getup-board/the-getup-board#openings-list.

GetUp! Call for a Liberal Free Vote on Marriage Equality. (n.d.). Retrieved from https://www.getup.org.au/campaigns/marriage-equality/conscience-vote/call-for-a-liberal-free-vote-on-marriage-equality.

GetUp! Don't Trust This Company with Our Great Barrier Reef. (n.d.). Retrieved from https://www.getup.org.au/campaigns/great-barrier-reef-3/adani/dont-trust-this-company-with-our-great-barrier-reef.

GetUp! Facebook. (n.d.). GetUp! Facebook. [Facebook page]. Retrieved from https://www.facebook.com/GetUpAustralia/.

GetUp! Marriage Equality in Australia. (n.d.). Retrieved from https://www.getup.org.au/campaigns/marriage-equality/marriage-equality-static-page/marriage-equality-in-australia.

GetUp! Media Room. (n.d.). Retrieved from https://www.getup.org.au/about/media-room.

GetUp! ReefReels. (n.d.). Retrieved from https://www.getup.org.au/campaigns/reef-reels/reefreels/reefreels.

GetUp! Save the Reef. (n.d.). Save the Reef. Retrieved from https://www.getup.org.au/campaigns/great-barrier-reef–3/save-the-reef/save-the-reef?t=4QtnteW.

GetUp! Spoof Trailer, Election. (2010). Spoof Trailer, Election 2010. [Video File]. Retrieved from https://www.youtube.com/watch?v=Qub4lWT6GNk.

GetUp! [Web]. (n.d.). GetUp! Retrieved from https://www.getup.org.au/

GetUp! (2014). GetUp! Annual Report 2013-2014. Retrieved from http://annualreport2013-14.getup.org.au/.

GetUp! (2015). GetUp! Annual Report 2014-2015. Retrieved from https://d68ej2dhhub09.cloudfront.net/1329-GetUp_Annual_Report_2015_V1_(1).pdf.

GetUp! (2016). GetUp! Annual Report 2015-2016. Retrieved from https://d68ej2dhhub09.cloudfront.net/2039-Annual_report_2015-16withdesign.pdf.

Gladwell, M. (2010). Small change: Why the revolution will not be tweeted. *The New Yorker*. Retrieved from http://www.newyorker.com/.

Gore, A. (1995). Forging a new Athenian age of democracy. *Intermedia*, *22*(2), 4–6.

Great Barrier Reef Marine Park Authority. (2009). *Great Barrier Reef outlook report*. Retrieved from http://elibrary.gbrmpa.gov.au/jspui/handle/11017/429.

Great Barrier Reef Marine Park Authority. (2014). *Great Barrier Reef outlook report*. Retrieved from http://elibrary.gbrmpa.gov.au/jspui/handle/11017/2856.

Great Barrier Reef Marine Park Authority. (n.d.). Coral bleaching. [Web log post] Retrieved from http://www.gbrmpa.gov.au/managing-the-reef/threats-to-the-reef/climate-change/what-does-this-mean-for-species/corals/what-is-coral-bleaching.

Halupka, M. (2014). Clicktivism: A systematic heuristic. *Policy & Internet*, *6*(2), 115–132.

Hamman, E. (2015). Save the reef! Civic crowdfunding and public interest environmental litigation. *QUT Law Review*, *15*(1), 159–173.

Hampton, K. (2003). Grieving for a lost network: Collective action in a networked suburb. *The Information Society*, *19*, 417–428.

Hannam, P. (2014, July 28). GetUp! Fears 'dirty tricks' after YouTube pulls video. *The Sydney Morning Herald*. Retrieved from http://www.smh.com.au/.

Hartford, B. (2008). Activists and activism [Presentation 'Civil Rights Movement and Social Justice' panel at San Francisco State College in 1968]. Retrieved from Civil Rights Movement Veterans website http://www.crmvet.org/comm/activist.htm.

Hill, S. (2010). *Models of online activism and their implications for democracy and climate change*. Unpublished discussion paper, Foundation for democracy and sustainable development, London, England. Retrieved from http://www.fdsd.org/site/wp-content/uploads/2014/11/Online-activism-democracy-and-climate-change.pdf.

Huijser, H., & Little, J. (2008). GetUp! For what? Issues driven democracy in a transforming public sphere. *Transformations*, 16. Retrieved from http://www.transformationsjournal.org/wp-content/uploads/2017/01/Huijser-Little_Transformations16.pdf.

Hunt, G., & Turnbull, M. (2016, June 13). Coalition to deliver $1 billion boost to protect Great Barrier Reef. Liberal Party of Australia. [Web log post]. Retrieved from https://www.liberal.org.au/.

Jackson, J. (2011, May 25). The hype about online activism, or 'clicktivism'. *The Huffington Post*. Retrieved from http://www.huffingtonpost.com/john-jackson/the-hype-about-online-act_b_749670.html.

Lewis, D. (2015, February 1). Queensland election 2015: What led to Campbell Newman's political demise? *ABC news*. Retrieved from http://www.abc.net.au/news/2015-02-01/queensland-election-2015-what-led-to-campbell-newman's-demise/6060934.

Lundy, K. (2009). Public sphere 2: Government 2.0. *A briefing paper*. Retrieved from http://www.katelundy.com.au/.

Maddison, S., & Martin, G. (2010). Introduction to 'surviving neoliberalism: The persistence of Australian social movements'. *Social Movement Studies*, *9*(2), 101–120.

Markham, A. (2016, May 26). Australia's iconic Great Barrier Reef world heritage site at risk from global warming. Union of Concerned Scientists. [Blog post]. Retrieved from http://blog.ucsusa.org/adam-markham/australias-iconic-great-barrier-reef-worldheritage-site-at-risk-from-global-warming.

Markham, A., Osipova, E., Lafrenz Samuels, K. & Caldas, A. (2016). *World heritage and tourism in a changing climate*. Retrieved from http://whc.unesco.org/document/139944.

Marks, K. (2010). Exclamation politics: GetUp! *The Monthly*. Retrieved from https://www.themonthly.com.au/.

McCarthy, J. (2015, April 9). Eleven international banks rule out funding Adani's Galilee coal project. *The Courier Mail*. Retrieved from http://www.couriermail.com.au/.

MoveOn. (n.d.). About. Retrieved from http://front.moveon.org/about/.

The Nobel Peace Prize 1997. (1997). Nobelprize.org. [Web log post] Retrieved from https://www.nobelprize.org/nobel_prizes/peace/laureates/1997/.

Norman, J. (2013, June 8). 'Cashed-up sheep' need to get their activism together. *The Sydney Morning Herald*. Retrieved from http://www.smh.com.au/.

Olson, M. (1968). *The logic of collective action*. New York, NY: Schocken.

Pepitone, J. (2010, January 16). Text donations raise $7m for Red Cross Haiti effort. *CNN Money*. Retrieved from http://money.cnn.com/2010/01/14/technology/haiti_text_donation/.

Permanent Culture Now. (2013). Introduction to activism. [Bog post]. Retrieved from http://www.permanentculturenow.com/what-is-activism/.

Petrova, T., & Tarrow, S. (2007). Transactional and participatory activism in the emerging European polity: The puzzle of East-Central Europe. *Comparative Political Studies*, *40*(1), 74–94.

Poell, T. (2014). Social media and the transformation of activist communication: Exploring the social media ecology of the 2010 Toronto G20 protests. *Information, Communication & Society*, *77*(6), 716–731.

Queensland Government. (2016, August 31). *Great Barrier Reef: Government priorities*. Retrieved from http://www.gbr.qld.gov.au/priorities/.

Readfern, G. (2016, May 30). Australia's censorship of UNESCO climate report is like a Shakespearean tragedy. *The Guardian*. Retrieved from https://www.theguardian.com.

Rheingold, H. (2002). *Smart Mobs: The next social revolution*. Cambridge, MA: Basic Books.

Rhimes, S. (2014). Shonda Rhimes '91, Commencement address.[Speech]. Retrieved from http://www.dartmouth.edu/~commence/news/speeches/2014/rhimes-address.html.

Rodan, D. (2010). Tactics for mobilizing participation and action: GetUp! A case study of communicative spaces. *Proceedings of CPRF Annual Conference* (pp. 29–40). Sydney, Australia: Network Insight Institute.

Rodan, D., & Balnaves, M. (2009). Democracy to come: Active forums as indicator suites for e-participation and e-governance. In A. Macintosh & E. Tambouris (Eds.), *Proceedings of First International Conference*, ePart 2009 (pp. 175–185). Berlin, Heidelberg: Springer-Verlag.

Rodan, D., & Balnaves, M. (2010). Media activist websites: The nature of e-participation spaces. *Australian Journalism Review*, *32*(1), 27–39.

Saunders, A. (2014, July 10). Australian banks face more pressure over support for coal projects. *The Sydney Morning Herald*. Retrieved from http://www.smh.com.au/business/

mining-and-resources/australian-banks-face-more-pressure-over-support-for-coal-projects-20140709-zt14p.html.

Shirky, C. (2008). *Here comes everybody: The power of organizing without organizations*. New York, NY: Penguin Press.

Shulman, S. W. (2009). The case against mass e-mails: Perverse incentives and low quality public participation in the U.S. federal rulemaking. *Policy & Internet 1*(1). doi:10.2202/1944-2866.1010.

Slacktivism. (n.d.). In *UrbanDictionary online dictionary*. Retrieved from http://www.urbandictionary.com/.

Slezak, M. (2016a, May 27). Australia scrubbed from UN climate change report after government intervention. *The Guardian*. Retrieved from https://www.theguardian.com.

Slezak, M. (2016b, May 7). Great Barrier Reef: Tourism operators urge Australian Government to tackle climate change. *The Guardian*. Retrieved from https://www.theguardian.com.

Tibbetts, T. (2010, September 27). Letter to the editor: 'Small Change' by Malcolm Gladwell [Blog post]. Retrieved from http://shesthefirst.org/blog/2010/09/27/letter-to-the-editor-small-change-by-malcolm-gladwell/.

Tranter, B. (1996). The social bases of environmentalism in Australia. *ANZJS*, *32*(2), 61–85.

United Nations Educational Scientific Cultural Organisation World Heritage Centre. (n.d.). *Great Barrier Reef*. Retrieved from http://whc.unesco.org/en/search/?criteria=Great+Barrier+Reef.

Vromen, A. (2008). Political change and the internet in Australia: Introducing GetUp. In T. Häyhtiö & J. Rinne (Eds.), *NetWorking/networking: Citizen initiated internet politics* (pp. 103–126). Tampere, Finland: Tampere University Press.

Vromen, A. (2015). Campaign entrepreneurs in online collective action: GetUp! In Australia. *Social Movement Studies*, *14*(2), 195–213.

Vromen, A., & Coleman, W. (2011). Online movement mobilisation and electoral politics: The case of GetUp! *Communication, Politics & Culture*, *44*(2), 76–94.

Vromen, A., & Coleman, W. (2013). Online campaigning organizations and storytelling strategies: GetUp! In Australia. *Policy & Internet*, *5*(1), 76–100.

White, M. (2010, August 12). Clicktivism is ruining leftist activism. *The Guardian*. Retrieved from https://www.theguardian.com/.

Williams, J., Goose, S. D. & Wareham, M. (Eds). (2008). *Banning landmines: Disarmament, citizen diplomacy, and human security*. Lanham, MD: Rowman & Littlefield.

Young, I. M. (2003). Activist challenges to deliberative democracy. In J. Fishkin & P. Laslett (Eds.), *Debating deliberative democracy* (pp. 102–120). New York, NY: Blackwell.

Zuckerman, E. (2014). New media, new civics? *Policy & Internet*, *6*(2), 151–168.

Chapter 6

Crowdfunding Initiatives for Social Movements

According to the Charities Aid Foundation (CAF) *2016 World Giving Index*, Australia was the third most *giving* country in that year (following Myanmar and the United States, in that order) (CAF, 2016). This index, billed as 'the world's leading study of generosity' (CAF, 2016), rates 140 countries in three categories: helping a stranger, donating money and volunteering time. According to CAF's data, Australia ranked highly with regard to the first two criteria although – despite its final status in the index – it does not rank in the top ten 'giving' countries with regard to the third criterion of volunteering time. Australia's own recent research into its record of giving – *Giving Australia 2016*, funded by the government through the Prime Minister's Community Business Partnership and drawing on the expertise of the Australian Centre for Philanthropy and Nonprofit Studies – in turn concluded that 14.9 million Australian adults (80.8 percent of the population) gave $12.5 billion in Australian dollars to charities and not-for-profit organisations in 2015–2016. Compared with a total of $10.1 billion (in 2015 dollar terms) given by Australians to charities and not-for-profit organisations in 2005, this looks like an increase; however, the *Giving Australia 2016* report concluded that, in comparison with 2005, what is actually happening is that fewer Australians are now giving larger amounts (see table 6.1).

Australians have a history of being big supporters of one-off appeals that fundraise to support victims of fires, floods and natural disasters, or to support such initiatives as keeping a children's hospital at the front edge of medicine or maintaining an air rescue service. A key example is the Australian response to the 2004 Boxing Day tsunami, in the face of which the Australian Government pledged $500 million, while World Vision of Australia, the country's largest international non-governmental organisation (NGO), raised over $100 million in public donations in less than two months following

Table 6.1. Comparative rates of giving in Australia, 2005 versus 2016.

	2005 (in 2016 Australian Dollar Terms)	*2016*
Total donations from individuals	$10.1 billion	$12.5 billion
Donors		
Number	13.4 m	14.9 m
Percentage	87	81
Average donation	$553.92	$764.08
Median donation	$130.64	$200

Source: Table 6.1 adapted from Giving Australia 2016 (2016).

the tragedy (Feeny & Clarke, 2007, p. 24). In total, $313 million was raised within five months by Australian businesses, community groups and ordinary citizens to assist affected countries (The Parliament of the Commonwealth of Australia, 2006). Such responses are a well-recognised phenomenon. As Good2Give CEO Lisa Grinham has noted, 'Australia has a strong culture of helping a stranger, helping a mate. It's no surprise that when natural disasters hits, like the Earthquake in Nepal, we see heightened levels of giving from Australians' (as cited in Good2Give, 2016). Or, as Red Cross Head of Fundraising David Armstrong has stated, 'There's a whole cohort of people who don't normally give to charity who step up and start donating in response to a disaster' (as cited in Gibbs, 2013).

Natural disasters are not the only disasters that appeal to generosity within the Australian public. In 2013, when the Climate Commission was abolished by the incoming conservative Federal Government of Australia, the Australian public responded to appeals from its former Chief Commissioner, Tim Flannery, and supported – funded – its re-establishment as the community-funded independent Climate Council (*ABC News*, 2013). Given that the Climate Commission had been receiving '$1.6m in annual taxpayer funding' (Australian Associated Press, 2013) to 'provide independent, authoritative climate information to the Australian public' (Climate Council, n.d.) – a service based on the belief that Australia's response to climate change 'should be based on the best science available' – and given that the anticipated challenges from Climate Change were only increasing (one such challenge being a conservative government suspicious of strong climate commitments), this work was recognisably clearly still imperative despite the lack of political support. It was this imperative that underpinned the call for public support. On the basis of this call, and subsequent massive public support, the proposed Climate Council raised over one million Australian dollars in one week, with 20,000 Australians donating an average of $50 (McKenzie, as cited in Australian Associated Press, 2013).

It is this pattern of generous response to one-off appeals that has been engaged not just by telethons and disaster appeals but underpins the development and increasing uptake of what has come to be called crowdfunding. This refers to, according to the *Oxford Dictionary* ("Crowdfunding," n.d.), 'the practice of funding a project or venture by raising many small amounts of money from a large number of people'. Although this model arguably refers to all versions of public fundraising tailored in response to a specific call for help, or as concerning the achievement of a specific goal, our focus in this chapter is on digitally enabled crowdfunding, and specifically on its engagement by activists and social movements for the advocacy and achievement of social change. In particular, given our overarching focus throughout this book on the affordances of digital culture for the work of activists and the achievement of progressive social change, our interest in crowdfunding is with its facilitation of the intersection of specifically developed Web 2.0 platforms with an individual's or organisation's desire to contribute to something they feel is important as well as being, possibly, much neglected by regular institutional financing, governance or society. As should be no surprise, however, while crowdfunding has over a decade's history of being used to fund a variety of individual and collective projects – most usually artistic or entrepreneurial – our major interest is with its more recent uptake by individuals and groups wishing to effect social change.

There are many different digital crowdfunding platforms in operation throughout the world, most supporting diverse projects and calls. Such platforms have been presented in a variety of ways as paradigm-shifters in their addressing and engaging of already-networked communities and individuals for the funding of projects, and in utilising game-like formats to promote fundraising, including the offering of variously levelled rewards for action or support. Given our focus is, however, specifically on the promotion and achievement of social change, after a broad examination of the crowdfunding phenomenon, this chapter will consider the context and practices of the successful Australian social change crowdfunding platform, Chuffed.org (henceforth Chuffed). More specifically, we examine within this platform the framing and development of the category refugee and asylum seeker which was initiated in 2014, as well as touching on a variety of the projects contained therein. Our overall interest with this chapter lies in both examining the utility of a mechanism that is fully reliant on digital networks and culture for the achievement of sociopolitical objectives, as well as its role in broader calls for collective action and social change.

CROWDFUNDING AND CROWDFUNDERS

From its development in 2006, crowdfunding was initially a domain for the funding of art, music, film, games, design and technology through the likes of Sellaband (2006), Indiegogo (2008) and Kickstarter (2009). Crowdfunding has grown exponentially from this beginning and has expanded to fund initiatives in journalism, medicine, civic public works, fashion, design and outer space, as well as school projects, scientific research, software development, academic research and projects for social change (Belleflamme, Lambert & Schwienbacher, 2011; Bennett, Chin & Jones, 2015; Macht & Weatherston, 2015). This latter expansion of focus is not without controversy, however, with two conflicting perspectives being aired regarding the use of crowdfunding for social change. On the one hand, supporters argue that crowdfunding offers both founders and funders a democratising approach (Golić, 2014), especially in the achievement of social change insofar as crowdfunding means, by definition, that there are no gatekeepers such as government or corporate policy makers able to direct or constrain public vision of the social good. As remarked by Cathy Henkel (personal communication, 10 February 2017), a successful crowdfunder and film-maker, crowdfunding is important because there is such little chance – given the prevalence and traction of neoliberal assumptions – that the government will support and facilitate all important social change causes. The crowdfunded Climate Council (discussed earlier) exemplifies this position and demonstrates the power and efficacy of social cause–oriented community action.

On the other hand, others have exclaimed that crowdfunding is itself just another neoliberal manoeuvre to ensure that the individual user pays for services – in this case public goods – that should be, and would previously have been, funded by the state (in the case of public interest services, see Hamman, 2015). According to this perspective, it is a problem that working towards achieving the public good has shifted from being the responsibility of states to being that of individual consumers. While the actions of individuals in such cases are clearly well-meaning and potentially very efficacious, their actions play a part in normalising the neoliberal rejection of responsibility for the public good by the government. The launching of the community-funded Climate Council is a case in point, and this problematic is well exemplified by Environment Minister Greg Hunt's satisfaction in telling *Lateline* that strength of public support for the Climate Council proves the government does not have to pay for the work of its previous incarnation. In his words: 'That's the great thing about democracy, it's a free country and it proves our point that the commission didn't have to be a taxpayer funded body' (Hunt, as cited in *ABC News*, 2013). Also pertinent to this perspective, it is worth noting that crowdfunding has itself become a billion-dollar business for the digital platforms that enable it. Platforms make millions of dollars from fees and the production of research statistics, as well as through industry experts being invited guest speakers at a variety of events. Certainly ordinary people would not be able to pledge or donate funds securely without platform infrastructure, but payment processing fees, paid either by the founder or by funders, all go to the credit card companies, PayPal and ultimately the banks. To give some insight into the scope of the industry's finances, the Massolution Crowdfunding Industry 2015 report estimated that the global crowdfunding industry will raise US$34 billion industry worldwide (CrowdExpert, 2015–2016a).

In further emphasis of the financial side of the industry, entrepreneurial studies researchers have claimed that crowdfunding developed out of microfinancing and crowdsourcing practices (Belleflamme et al., 2011; Mollick, 2014). Modern microfinancing practices date back to the 1970s and the work of Muhammad Yunus in Bangladesh (see, e.g., Perkins, 2008), with 'microfinance' defined as referring to the delivery of an 'array of financial services', including microloans, savings and insurance schemes, that are made 'available to entrepreneurs and small business owners who have no collateral and wouldn't otherwise qualify for a standard bank loan' (Brooks, 2013). The term 'crowdsourcing' was first used in 2006 in *Wired*, an American technology magazine, by Jeff Howe and Mark Robinson (as cited in Kleemann, Voß & Rieder, 2008). It rested on the assumption that a sizeable volunteer team of individuals – both online and offline – would always be more 'effective' at 'mobilizing' and 'problem-solving' than any single expert or consultant (Amtzis, 2014, p. 128). According to this view, if the 'wisdom of the crowd' is always going to be more 'efficient' than teams or a few equity investors at solving corporate challenges or dilemmas (Schwienbacher & Larralde, 2012, p. 380), then making use of the 'crowd to obtain ideas, feedback and solutions' for business and corporate undertakings makes good commercial sense (Belleflamme, Lambert & Schwienbacher, 2014, p. 586).

Although 'crowdfunding' was itself first recorded as a term also in 2006, on the now-defunct website fundalog (Stiver, Barroca, Minocha, Richards & Roberts, 2015, p. 251), and again in 2008 (Davies, 2015, p. 342), it was not popularised until the development of the global crowdfunding platforms Indiegogo (2008) and Kickstarter (2009) which inaugurated 'reward based crowdfunding' (Stiver et al., 2015). Arguably – again in line with the second perspective referred to previously – its early use referred to little more than the idea of sourcing and facilitating consumers for the provision of financial assistance to companies (and prospective companies), seeing it thereby as simply a more specialised category of fundraising (Mollick, 2014; Schwienbacher & Larralde, 2012). So conceived its key focus was to procure funds by tapping into the crowd or general public. In simple terms, then, harking back to our earlier definition, crowdfunding is the 'financing of a project or venture' by a large number of individuals who may each contribute only small fiscal amounts. This is in contradistinction to initiative support by institutions such as banks, or professional bodies such as venture capitalists, and business angels (Mollick, 2014; Schwienbacher & Larralde, 2012). While these starting definitions of crowdfunding make no necessary distinction between the various modes of mass appeal and support – and thus between telethons and web-based platform-supported appeals – understandings of crowdfunding have come to be more closely connected with Web 2.0 technologies. Thus, Belleflamme, Lambert and Schwienbacher (2014, p. 588, original emphasis) have come to define crowdfunding as involving an '*open call, mostly through the Internet, for the provision of financial resources either in the form of donation or in exchange for the future product or some form of reward to support initiatives for specific purposes*'. Other researchers also see the now-typical mode for procuring funds as the Internet-based crowdfunding platforms (Schwienbacher & Larralde, 2012). A further stress in these later definitions is that the aim of such funding is 'to convert an idea into a project or business' (Best & Ness, 2014, p. 3) and for consumers to 'self-select into one group according to their personal preferences' (Belleflamme et al., 2014, p. 587). Such an aim thus constitutively shows a strong neoliberal allegiance, with consumers – investors – being given the opportunity to provide input into the development of a project in the form of financial help as well as ideas, advice and support.

Although, as noted, the main feature of crowdfunding is to raise financial backing, crowdfunding can also provide information about consumer preferences and create interest in and promote new products and/or projects at an early development stage (Belleflamme et al., 2011; Mollick, 2014). According to this view, individual investors are not always motivated by financial gains; often they want to be participants in 'innovative projects' and by so doing gain 'recognition' as well as 'personal satisfaction' (Schwienbacher & Larralde, 2012, p. 386). This is to say that groups or individuals may invest in crowdfunding because they want to donate funds to a not-for-profit cause – the patronage model – or impart funds 'in return for interest payments', or obtain rewards (non-financial) or equity (Mollick, as cited in Macht & Weatherston, 2015, p. 197). Or they may want to play a part in history, to have a role in a venture, cause or innovation which is greater than their individual self (Best & Ness, 2014).

Such interests, once met only on the basis of several contingencies, are now – with crowdfunding's intersection with Web 2.0 social networking – easily supported. More specifically, the rise of Web 2.0 participatory culture has been fundamental to numerous individuals and groups getting involved in projects, as well as making it easy for those individuals to spread the message to family and friends about projects they believe in via their personal as well as public social networking sites (Golić, 2014; Maguire, 2012). In addition, it is through their indirect linking into these personal and social networks that crowdfunders can gain access to communities who are likely to share their goals and viewpoints and thus likely to support them (Borst,

Moser & Ferguson, 2017). On this point, studies (Belleflamme et al., 2011, p. 9) show that the most widely used platforms used by crowdfunders to reach personal social networks were crowdfunding platforms such as Kickstarter, community blogs, Facebook and Twitter. The reach of these platforms does not need re-emphasising. Overall, what is important to stress is that this capacity to tap into personal networks via social media networks is crucial to the success of most crowdfunding campaigns today. One key reason for this is that family and friends tend to be the early investors in funding calls; distant relations, friends of friends and unfamiliar persons tend to invest later, often only once the campaign has already started to boom (Agrawal, Catalini & Goldfarb, 2011; Mollick, 2014). Another is that for any crowdfunding proposal to succeed, trust needs to be invested in the individual, group, company and/or not-for-profit seeking crowdfunding (Macht & Weatherston, 2015). Social networks have, of course, already established at least some levels of inter-member trust. Finally, the size of the social network founders are able to tap into plays a role in how successful their fundraising is, alongside the promoter's ability to 'mobilize their social networks' (Díaz & Cacheda, 2016; cf. Mollick, 2014). Unsurprisingly, it is the large vibrant social networks that often lead to successful fundraising (Borst et al., 2017).

It is also unsurprising that the common criticisms of the crowdfunding model revolve around funding arrangements and networks. According to Bennett, Chin and Jones (2015, p. 142), some of the most common accusations are that media conglomerates use crowdfunding to 'exploit their fan bases', that independent producers procuring 'seed money' from crowdfunding have little control over how those funds are spent (Pebler, 2013) and that providing and delivering rewards to funders or donors takes time and money away from the project. A further criticism, introduced previously, is that civic crowdfunding campaigning sets up that problematic expectation that community and individuals will – and should – provide funds for public works and assets, instead of this being a responsibility of the state (see, e.g., Davies, 2015; Stiver et al., 2015). Additional concerns have been raised concerning the length and detail of platform disclaimers which have the potential to mislead participants, and the often-opaque nature of service as well as transaction fees (Kollmorgen, 2016). Crowdfunding has also been criticised for being just another form of clicktivism and slacktivism, an issue that is, of course, under debate within this chapter (and throughout the book). One preliminary comment on this issue is that research does seem to show that funds raised/won through crowdfunding, especially for causes or towards an aim of social change, are 'meaningful to the organizations, communities and people who benefit from' them (Amtzis, 2014, p. 140). These are issues we will come back to.

If the preceding discussion has provided a clear picture of the development and focus of crowdfunding practices, who are the typical participants in crowdfunding? Most generally, and unsurprisingly, Davies (2015, p. 345) notes three factors that enable an individual's ability to participate in crowdfunding: (a) having access to technology as well as crowdfunding platforms; (b) having the skills to organise, plan and/or support a crowdfunding campaign; and (c) having the finances to execute and/or participate in a campaign. Citing *The American Dream Composite Index* (2012), Calic and Mosakowski (2016, p. 742), in their turn, report that crowdfunders are most likely to fall into the 25–34 age group. Most are male on sites like Kickstarter and usually invest in start-ups ("Art of Kickstarter", 2016). Conversely, on non-profit crowdfunding sites such as Chuffed, females appear to be the ones more likely to donate to cause-based campaigns (Paramanathan, 2016). Considered globally, investors in crowdfunding come primarily from North America and Europe and tend to earn over $100,000 per year, and finally, many of these investors, as Calic and Mosakowski (2016) found in their analysis of Kickstarter, also tend to see themselves in terms of an ideological orientation towards sustainability, with the result being that this group is arguably already oriented towards social good–oriented projects. This is an interesting finding given that it presents crowdfunding in the light of not only endorsing neoliberal preferences for individualised over collective action and for economic answers to sociopolitical problems but also challenging the neoliberal tendency to prioritise economic over other interests. These tensions, of course, underpin the growing trend of using crowdfunding to support campaigns for social change, a trend that will become our focus later in the chapter as we discuss the Australian crowdfunding context and experience.

CROWDFUNDING PLATFORMS AND THE CHARACTERISTICS OF CAMPAIGNS

The Deal Index: Democratizing Finance Report estimates from June 2015 that there were 1,250 crowdfunding platforms worldwide (CrowdExpert, 2015–2016b), although noting also that many of these were specific to countries or regions (Agrawal et al., 2011; Mollick, 2014). Although a range of these platforms focus specifically on raising funds for civic public works – with some of the major English-language platforms being IOBY (2009), Spacehive (2011), Citizinvestor (2012) and Neighborly (2012) (Davies, 2015; Stiver et al., 2015) – the major global crowdfunding platforms used by ordinary individuals and groups (i.e., not purely aimed at industry entrepreneurs wanting equity funding) are listed in table 6.2.

Table 6.2. Platform comparisons.

Funding Platform	*Year Established*	*Funding and Fee Structures*	*Project Types*	*Estimated Total Funded*
Kickstarter (largest)	2009	All-or-nothing fixed funding: 5 percent fee from a project's funding total only if a project is successfully funded plus a payment processing fee of 3–5 percent	Range of creative arts, design, fashion, food, games, journalism, publishing and technology	Over US$2 billion
Indiegogo (second)	2008	Fixed or flexible funding: 5 percent fee from a project's funding total only if a project is successfully funded, plus 3 percent + .30c third-party credit fees. Non-profits and socially minded campaigns have 0 percent platform fee	Range of creative arts, animals, community, design, education, fashion, food, gaming politics, religion, small business and technology (some of the twenty-four categories)	Over US$1 billon
GoFundMe (fifth)	2010	Flexible funding: 5 percent plus a small processing fee of 3 percent. Campaigner keeps every donation received so is not required to reach set goal	Non-profit charities, medical, emergencies, sports, animals, individual 'wishes' and personal expenses such as funerals, weddings and IVF treatment are some of the twenty categories	Over US$130 million

Source: Statistics from Statistic Brain (2016), GoFundMe (2010), Kickstarter (2009) and Indiegogo (2008).

What is also evident from table 6.2 is the variety of funding arrangements which, as shown, include fixed or flexible models. This fixed or flexible distinction refers to whether campaigns need to achieve a target figure – often within a specified time period – in order for the campaign founder to receive funding. As explained in the Indiegogo site (n.d.), flexible funding arrangements suit projects in which 'any amount of money will help you reach your campaign objective'. Under this arrangement, you 'keep all your funds even when your campaign does not reach its goal'. Fixed funding arrangements conversely mean that

> you only keep the funds you raise if you meet your funding goal. If your campaign does not meet its goal by its deadline, all contributions will be refunded back to the contributors by Indiegogo, typically within 5–7 business days.

As the Indiegogo site further explains, a campaign founder would choose only fixed funding 'if your campaign objective requires a minimum amount of money to be accomplished'. Arguably, social cause–based campaigns would tend to choose a flexible funding model, as this would allow their campaigns to still be facilitative of change even if campaign targets were either not met or not met in the initially specified time.

Another pertinent distinction between platforms pertains to what crowdfunders may receive in return for their support of a project. This concerns what are conventionally called 'rewards' or 'perks', which the Indiegogo site (n.d.) defines as the 'incentives offered to contributors in exchange for their support'. As noted by Indiegogo, their experience has been that

> campaigns offering perks raise 143% more money than those that do not. Perks help you attract a larger audience, make people feel more valued for their contributions, and help you spread the word about your campaign.

Perks can take a variety of forms of course. Indiegogo, for instance, suggests that they can be material, personal or experiential. Kickstarter's CEO, Yancey Strickler (2011), in his turn also breaks down Kickstarter rewards into these three different categories. First is a copy of the 'thing', with the campaign reward working like a pre-order for the product and importantly providing the capital to finance its production. A second category is to 'share the story' by which he means to make one's backers insiders to the creative process and the project development. Under this system crowdfunders are further engaged with the project through receiving updates, videos, blogs, photos or even credits in the finished film or book. Small items such as props or spare/broken parts and simple tokens may also be sent to funders as part of the development story. Third are actual experiences. Here funders may receive actual access to and/or participation in the project. Experiential forms may include visits to the set or office, or going out for coffee or a meal with the development team. Such experiences are often reserved for premium backers who are prepared to buy a story they can tell their friends. Within entrepreneurial crowdfunding, reward- and equity-based models for perks are also distinguished. In the former instance, what is often the case is that entrepreneurs presell a product or service to launch a business concept without incurring debt or sacrificing equity/shares. With equity crowdfunding, the backer receives shares of a company, usually in its early stages, in exchange for the money pledged; often this is purely speculative. The broad idea of the role of perks is well summed up by Strickler (2011) when he states that 'every project should benefit its backers just as much as its creator, and it's up to you [the project founder] to define how'.

As well as advice about possible and effective perks, general advice about how to carry out a successful crowdfunding campaign is freely available. 'How to . . .' sheets and other resources are made available from crowdfunding platforms, and blogs such as CrowdCrux and published books such as *Crowdfund It!* (Maguire, 2014) all share basic pointers along with an array of tips and tricks to guarantee success. Despite some variation, most of these materials agree that there are several criteria that must be met for a founder's success in crowdfunding. The first is preparedness, which, according to Mollick (2014, p. 8), is assessable and evident in terms of how well 'project pitches' follow the standard of winning pitches on platform sites. A compelling video that is produced in the pre-launch stage is the minimum requirement (Maguire, 2014; Mollick, 2014). According to the Kickstarter platform, 'skipping this step will do a serious disservice' to the founder's project (as cited in Mollick, 2014, p. 8). Following the pre-launch stage, providing updates 'within three days of the launch' about the progress of the fundraising is crucial to keeping investors interested (Maguire, 2014; Mollick, 2014). A second criterion concerns network size. The initial network for most projects will be the founder's own network of friends and family; this network must then extend to '*their network*' on social network, this being made up of friends of friends, distant relations, acquaintances and some unknown persons (Mollick, 2014, p. 8; cf. Schwienbacher & Larralde, 2012). The third is geography, which can also play an important role in how successful the campaign is (Mollick, 2014). Henkel (personal communication, 10 February 2017), who has successfully crowdfunded many films and social change initiatives using the Pozible platform in Australia, reiterates and expands these points in her outline of the ten most important factors to address when starting a crowdfunding campaign:

1. Preparation – the founder must have a clear understanding of who their audience is for the specific campaign.
2. Have a smart-looking 'teaser' with a video of 2 to 3 minutes.

3. The video should include a sequence on 'meet the team' and include something 'edgy' as well as comedy.
4. The campaign should be outcomes based and focus on solutions.
5. Set a realistic target.
6. Source the initial third of the funding from family and friends up front (before day one) and ask them to pledge on opening day of the campaign.
7. Make the launch a fanfare and fun.
8. Campaigns that trend on the home page attract more and go wider.
9. A celebrity featured in the 'teaser' will help send the campaign call wider.
10. Be crystal clear about what you – the founder – want the funds for.

As is also outlined on the Pozible (2015) platform, Henkel (personal communication, 10 February 2017) confirms that by the end of the first day of the campaign, the founders need to have raised at least a third of the funds in order to have a chance of successfully raising the balance by the end of the campaign. With crowdfunding, Henkel stresses, there is almost always a dip in interest in the middle of the campaign.

As only about 42–55 percent of submitted projects are typically funded on crowdfunding platforms (Mollick, 2014; Wade, 2014), high levels of exposure for the project are fundamental. Thus, as Henkel (personal communication, 10 February 2017) has noted earlier, another important factor that can increase exposure – and the chances of success – of a crowdfunding project concerns public positive 'endorsements' of project aims (also see Calic & Mosakowski, 2016). Once attained, endorsement effect can also be intensified through public exposure via interviews, press releases and having the project showcased in mainstream media. According to Calic and Mosakowski (2016, p. 749), endorsements from technology media websites and well-known blogs such as 'CNET, PCMag, Wired or Gizmodo' for technology projects can assist in marketing and can potentially add to the quality of the project. Similarly, for film and video projects, endorsements from newspaper websites such as the *Huffington Post* and blogs such as *Timeout* greatly increase exposure (p. 749). Celebrity endorsements, if they can be gained, not only increase exposure but can drastically expand the founder's social media network.

Apart from not gaining enough exposure, the major problem affecting crowdfunding projects is delivering the project on time, with even well-developed projects often struggling to meet their project deadline. Mollick (2014, p. 11) claims there are far more examples of projects not meeting their deadline, being delayed or failing to deliver, than of projects succeeding, with only about 25 percent of founders delivering their project on time. In their study, Manning and Berjarno (2017, p. 211) also noted that campaigns failed when they did not 'show a clear narrative pattern' in their videos, something successful projects in the same category do effectively. Or, they add, failed projects may have left out elements of narrative style expected by viewers. Or they may fail because their narrative overemphasised future ideals 'while neglecting the past' aspects that were integral to the campaign's development (p. 211). These latter points draw attention to the significance of the project's narrative arc – usually the basis for the project video – emphasising that it needs to be not only compelling in its appeal but clear from the outset.

CROWDFUNDING FOR SOCIAL CHANGE

In their analysis of the video styles most utilised for crowdfunding projects, Manning and Berjarno (2017) reveal the prevalence of two narrative styles: one clearly addressing the commercial camp and the other a social change one. Of these, a 'results-in-progress' narrative is typical of projects with commercial orientation, while projects with a 'strong social orientation' tend to present their pitch in the form of an 'ongoing journey' (Manning & Berjarno, 2017, pp. 203, 210). This latter pitch is furthermore often 'highly emotional' (pp. 210–211) in an effort to engage not only a viewer's reasoned commitment but affective investment. As previous chapters have shown, this double focus is de rigueur for activists and social movements in both online and offline domains, a preference we have particularly exemplified with reference to Animals Australia's skilful creation of campaigns that draw on both reasoned and affective modes of expression. Interestingly, and also demonstrated by Animals Australia in its own campaigning, social change–focused crowdfunding further stresses the importance of orienting a campaign's affective hooks not simply to negative emotions of shock, guilt and anxiety but to positive emotions connected to the sense of being able to make a difference. For instance, non-profit campaigners are instructed by Chuffed (n.d.-b) when developing the visual elements of their campaigns, to create images that induce supporters to 'feel inspired, entertained or curious'. Chuffed states this explicitly on its 'Create your page':

> For clarity, Chuffed.org is a guilt-free site. We reject campaigns that use guilt-imagery like dehumanizing photos of starving children to get donations, or graphic, disturbing images of animals.

This attitude is also supported by Henkel (personal communication, 10 February 2017), who claims that 'people will turn off if it is going to make them depressed'. A common mode of presentation in this manner is thus to show the cause or social change to be personally important to the originator as well as clearly marking a significant issue for others, with the plan given to tackle the issue being 'practical, specific and neither overly simplistic nor complex' (Amtzis, 2014, p. 144). Finally, there is research showing that not-for-profit organisations tend to achieve more success in fundraising than profit-based projects (Schwienbacher & Larralde, 2012). While this has been explained away as being to do with not-for-profits tending to commit to `high quality products and services' (Belleflamme et al., as cited in Schwienbacher & Larralde, 2012, p. 378; also see Therriault, 2015), and to transparency in funding use (Amtzis, 2014), success may also arguably be attributed to social change crowdfunding campaigns being driven, by definition, by relatively strong ideological commitments on the part of both founders and funders. In a link with our starting consideration of the trends in Australians' generosity, Pozible project advisor Elliot Chapple comments that 'crowdfunding in Australia is still more about giving than getting', something that is particularly the case 'when there's a really compelling story involved' (as cited in Therriault, 2015).

This is an important point insofar as social cause crowdfunding needs to engage not simply someone's self-interest – contributing to a campaign for specified and perceived personal benefits – but also what could be called their social good or philanthropic interest. This need, of course, relates to a point that all activists and social movements would seem to agree upon: that all of us should consider not only one's individual interest but the common good, and sometimes also be prepared to extend one's idea of the common good – and perhaps override one's individual interest – to take account of interests that had hitherto received short shrift, not to mention, of course, the underpinning imperative to act in alignment with these extended beliefs. The point is often made, however, that prevailing neoliberal assumptions have led to an over-prioritising of individual interests at the expense of the common good (Brown, 2005; Giroux, 2014; Mummery, 2017). This is the view that neoliberalism is unfriendly towards collective interests for social change that would run counter to the actions and outcomes of a market logic. And yet it is this same weighting towards individual interests – weighting presumed to run counter to attempts to achieve social change – that is arguably being eroded – in many cases very consciously – through the neoliberally inspired crowdfunding model, or, better, that the distinction typically positioned between individual interests and collective interests can be and is being collapsed through the operation of the crowdfunding model. This, for instance, is a view held very strongly by Chuffed founder Prashan Paramanathan, who contends – with reference to conventional models of activist and cause-based appeal – that people do want to be generous beyond their individual interests but that it is the model for appeal that turns them off. In Paramanathan's words, people 'are not stingy, they want to contribute, they just don't like the way that charities interact with them, particularly the big ones, we wanted to find a different way to link them . . . and that's how we started Chuffed' (as cited in Chang, 2015).

This is the view mentioned earlier, that crowdfunding is a paradigm-changer, that 'the big charity model is broken, and the trust too', and that crowdfunders 'have a wonderful set of ideas of how it might work differently in the future' (Scevak, n.d.). According to this view, then, the idea that one needs to be motivated either to step beyond the scope of one's individual interests or to align one's individual interests with the common good – such motivation often described as needing to be delivered by moral shock – can be revised to one of seeing individual and common good interests as able to work reciprocally in what Paramanathan calls a win-win scenario, or of specifically appealing to individual interests to support collective interests. This is Paramanathan's point that while it might be easy to see altruistic motivations and selfish motivations as opposing forces, this need not be the case. In his words: 'If you tap into both altruistic motivations and selfish motivations, you get a multiplier effect. People always think one subtracts from the other but it's not true' (as cited in Swan, 2016). This possibility, of course, is best exemplified through the crowdfunding use of perks. After all, as Paramanathan points out, providing a reward for donating means a cause can tap into people's 'spending purse' and thereby into money that would not normally go towards charity (as cited in Chang, 2015). Perks, Paramanathan (2016) stresses, as attendant on readily achievable actions with clearly visible outcomes, can make the process of donating enjoyable and inspirational rather than one of having been made to feel guilty. And indeed, as he has noted, 'campaigns that gave donors something back in return were often the most successful for chuffed.org' (as cited in Chang, 2015). This allows the following description of this purported paradigm shift:

> New models of fundraising are now focusing less on making potential donors feel bad, and more on promoting the benefits of giving and making the transaction win-win, including the possibility of playing the stockmarket to make money for yourself, as well as charity. (Chang, 2015)

Although the strength of this paradigm shift is debatable, in some ways at least its presence is easily identifiable in the Australian context. There are multiple crowdfunding platforms in operation within Australia that support not-for-profit, social enterprise and/or social change campaigns – the main platforms being Mycause (from 2007), Pozible (from 2010), StartSomeGood (from 2011), *i*Pledg (from 2011), Chuffed.org (from 2013), OzCrowd (from 2014) and the Funding Network (from 2014). Each of these has facilitated extensive fundraising for a variety of non-profit, cause-based projects. By 2016, for instance, Chuffed collected $10 million in donations towards socially oriented projects (as cited in Swan, 2016). It should also be noted that of these various crowdfunding platforms, Chuffed is the only platform fully dedicated to non-profit campaigning. As stated in the site, 'On Chuffed.org your project won't get lost amongst tech gadgets and design projects' (Chuffed, n.d.-d). Also stressed by that platform is that it is zero fee (apart from payment processing fees paid by funders) and that all funds donated via the Chuffed interface are received by the campaigner, even if the specified target is not achieved. Given these points, and given our aim of delving still more deeply into the nexus of social change activist campaigning and the digitalised platforms of crowdfunding, it behoves us, in this final part to the chapter, to take Chuffed as our exemplar. As such, and in order to examine the potential utility of crowdfunding in broader calls for collective action and social change, we turn now to a more detailed examination of Chuffed achievements, in this instance with respect to another topical issue for Australians, the reception of asylum seekers.

CHUFFED.ORG AND THE AUSTRALIAN RECEPTION OF ASYLUM SEEKERS

> We know that [the days of] dropping your money into a charity and never knowing or hearing where it goes are numbered. And we know that even though people are generous and they want to give, it's hard to know who's actually going to make a difference with your hard earned cash. . . . We've built Chuffed to make sure that even if you're only able to give $1 of your money or a minute of your time, you know that you, along with hundreds of other generous people are building a more awesome world. (Chuffed, n.d.-a)

Chuffed was founded by CEO Prashan Paramanathan in 2013 through the '$1.1 million seed funding round led by Blackbird Ventures, Bevan Clark, and the Telstra Foundation' (Startupdaily, n.d.), and as we have already noted, it by design only crowdfunds non-profit and social enterprise projects. Campaigns are grouped into eight overlapping searchable categories: social enterprise, social welfare, international development, environmental protection, refugees and asylum seekers, health and medical, animal rights and community (a ninth category of 'all' is also searchable). While all of these, of course, are used to generate interest and funding around cause-based projects, the category we intend to make our focus is that of refugees and asylum seekers, an issue that has been politically and publicly sensitive within Australia for many years (for early examinations of Australian attitudes to asylum seekers, see Mummery & Rodan, 2003, 2007; Rodan & Mummery, 2005).

Of this issue, it must be noted that at this time within Australia – we are writing in early 2017 – there are still strong public beliefs that asylum seekers pose a threat to the nation's material well-being, and to Australian values, culture and national security (McHugh-Dillon, 2015; McKay, Thomas & Kneebone, 2012; Suhnan, Pedersen & Hartley, 2012). In this vein, asylum seekers are often condemned for their supposedly un-Australian attitudes and values, attempting to *cheat the system*, taking advantage of Australia's generosity and *exploiting* the country's legitimate processes, systems and resources (see, e.g., Hartley & Pedersen, 2015; McKay et al., 2012). Analysis of public opinion polls from 2012 showed, for instance, that those voters who held strongly negative views on asylum seekers outnumbered those who held strongly positive views, probably by at least two to one (Markus, 2012). Other surveys have also shown that the Australian public by and large supports a tough policy approach to unauthorised arrivals, including support for the turning back of boats and mandatory detention (Markus, 2014; Oliver, 2014; UMR Research, 2013).

These beliefs are not, of course, uncontested within the Australian public sphere, and it is in a humanitarian-inspired challenge to them – and with a focus of welcoming refugees into Australia and supporting them – that many of the projects Chuffed supports in the refugees and asylum seekers category are framed. Projects, for instance, include gifting asylum seekers held in offshore mandatory detention on the Pacific Islands of Manus (PNG) and Nauru with phone credit ('Gifts for Manus and Nauru', in process and has raised $20,510 as of mid-March 2017), helping asylum seekers access legal support for submitting their refugee claim ('Seeking Refuge WA', in process and has raised $44,601 as of mid-March 2017) and developing and rolling out a national poster advertising campaign showing that asylum seekers are people with courage and humanity and that they can contribute greatly to Australian society ('I Came by Boat', campaign completed and has raised $84,336). Other projects coalesce around the provision of legal support, to improve refugees' employment prospects; the provision of accommodation, material goods and social opportunities for refugees once they are in Australia; and the provision of games, toys and other care items for children held in offshore detention. What is key in all cases is that funds are raised and expended in ways that will benefit asylum seekers and refugees directly. This does not mean that funds are necessarily expended directly on these groups; successful campaigns have, for instance, achieved covering salary costs for lawyers and administrators to enable not just better support for asylum seekers and refugees but the more efficient and effective delivery of support programs.

Of completed Chuffed campaigns included in this category (as of the end of 2016), the largest amount raised has been $103,665 by the Mums for Refugees campaign for legal costs for rape survivors and health costs for four women with breast lumps, with the smallest amount raised in a campaign being $625. Campaigns listed were also not all successful in the sense of achieving their set funding goals, but Chuffed regulations meant that founders nevertheless received all funds raised to use towards their campaign goals. Of these various campaigns and their relative successes in fundraising, it is also interesting to note that despite Chuffed's instructions and the tenor of our previous discussions on the important role of rewards in crowdfunding, few of these social cause–oriented campaigns actually offered perks, rather seeming to expect that 'making a difference in people's lives' should be the main reward desired by funders (Henkel, personal communication, 10 February 2017). Arguably, then, the expectation seems to be that campaigners and funders will join forces and invest in a campaign on ideological grounds, or, in other words, that – as we have discussed in previous chapters – funders' personal beliefs, values and identification will already coincide with the cause at hand and this will be the motivation for their participation in the campaign. Finally, it is worth stressing that the Chuffed campaigns in this category have been instigated by a mix of organisations – mostly not-for-profits – as well as by individuals, as indicated in tables 6.3 and 6.4, with these campaigns working across a range of geographical locations and able to raise a range of funds for their activities.

This variety in campaign founders is an important point to take note of insofar as many of the listed organisation-based campaign stories do appear to give weight to the idea that the social change work of not-for-profits is now needing to be funded – partially or wholly – by the broader community of concerned citizens in order to make up the shortfall from reduced or otherwise constrained state funding, or from limited funding from other sectors, or, in other cases, to override or mitigate some of the impacts of state decision-making. Such is the case with many of the campaigns developed to fund asylum-seeker access to legal advice and medical services, particularly when asylum seekers are located in offshore detention centres. Such is also the case with campaigns striving to provide services – such as access to English-language tuition, affordable housing, training and education – for asylum seekers on bridging visas who are ineligible to access state-provided services such as Medicare, Centrelink allowances or government-sponsored English classes.

IMPLICATIONS OF CROWDFUNDING FOR SOCIAL CHANGE

> Chuffed doesn't just raise money. It raises communities. I realised that I was creating a community of people who have bought into my cause. An invaluable resource of future soldiers to fight in the battles that undoubtably lie ahead. (Caslick, as cited in Chuffed, n.d.)

Table 6.3. Selection of the successful campaigns run by organisations 2014–2016 in the Chuffed category refugees and asylum seekers.

Organisation	*Cause*	*Location of Funds Expenditure*	*Funds Raised (and Target Funds)*
Mums for Refugees	Lawyers and access to health system	Nauru	$103,665 ($100,000)
Lentara Uniting Care	Housing	Melbourne	$20,287 ($20,000)
Green Connect	Training	Victoria	$20,090 ($20,000)
Network of Churches in Western Sydney	Purchase a ute to deliver furniture to refugee families	Western Sydney	$19,290 ($18,500)
Refugee Action Coalition	Administrative costs for producing court statements	Manus Island	$15,275 ($15,000)
	Legal challenge	Manus Island	$12,670 ($12,000)
	Court challenge	Manus Island	$10,350 ($10,000)
We Care Nauru	Postage for children's Christmas list	Nauru	$13,232 ($500)
	Supplies for babies and children	Nauru	$5,162 ($5,000)
	Postage to send gifts	Nauru	$1,230 ($1,000)
	Bright colourful bedding	Nauru	$1,029 ($1,000)
Gifts for Manus and Nauru Inc.	Phone credit (multiple short-term campaigns)	Nauru	$12,670 ($12,000)
		Manus Island	$11,910 ($10,000)
			$3,265 ($3,000)
Rise Foundation	Film to raise winter appeal funds	Syria	$12,333 ($10,000)
Foundation Australia	Personal delivery of aid to Syrian refugees	Syria	$10,001 ($10,000)
Stern Media for ASRC	Raise funds for the Asylum Seeker Resource Centre by participating in the Darwin Beer Can Regatta	Detention centres in Indonesia and Malaysia	$6,150 ($5,000)
Road to Refugees	Comedy debate about border policy *The Fence* to raise awareness	Refugees in Australia	$4,695 ($4,000)
Rural Australians for Refugees	Legal representation for a detainee	Manus Island	$4,500 ($4.500)
Love Makes a Way Ltd	Court and legal costs for seven church leaders arrested	Western Australia	$4,110 ($3,723)
Save the Children Fund Asylum Centre Newtown	Fundraiser to raise awareness and funds for refugee crisis	Syria	$2,173 ($2,000)
Epping Church of Christ	To distribute essential supplies and Christmas presents, educational programs	Burma and Thailand orphanages	$2,075 ($2,000)
Tomorrow Foundation	Social enterprise café to train and mentor refugee employees	Victoria	$1,250 ($1.000)
I Am a Boat Person Inc.	To buy young refugees a laptop	New South Wales	$625 ($600)

Source: Table 6.3 collates information about successful Chuffed campaigns in the category Refugees and asylum seekers gathered from Discover Chuffed (n.d.).

Table 6.4. Selection of the successful campaigns run by individuals 2014–2016 in the Chuffed category refugees and asylum seekers.

Individuals	*Cause*	*Location of Funds Expenditure*	*Funds Raised*
Rob Caslick	Build a rooftop garden to give refugees work who are waiting for accommodation	Sydney, New South Wales	$29,607 ($15,000)
Jane and Joan from Darwin	Reunite family	Hagadera Refugee Camp Kenya	$20,016 ($15,000)
David Faulks Lyndall Harris	Printing cost for children's books for refugee families	New South Wales	$11,285 ($10,000)
Jasmine Pilbrow	Legal funds for protesting rights of refugees	Victoria	$11,125 ($10,290)
Holly Wild	Volunteer nutritionist in refugee camp around Athens	Greece	$4,170 ($3,000)
Rosemary Tonkin	Printing of refugee poetry and drawings in book	Western Australia	$3,500 ($3,500)
Julia D'Orazio	Raising funds for small NGO educational project for Syrian refugees	Turkey	$3,195 ($3,000)
Felicity Johns	Transit costs for driving refugee participants to vegetable garden property	Victoria	$3,100 ($3,000)
Shane Bazzi (Advocate)	Phone credit	Nauru Manus Island	$2,535 ($2,000)
Hannah Patchett	A non-violent action to deliver a message to decision-makers	Victoria	$1,530 ($1,500)
Jes Meacham	Disposable cameras developing images and exhibiting photo story to counter media images	Queensland	$1,040 ($600)

Source: Table 6.4 collates information about successful Chuffed campaigns in the category Refugees and asylum seekers gathered from Discover Chuffed (n.d.-c.)

As we noted previously, Chuffed collected $10 million in donations towards socially oriented projects by 2016 (Swan, 2016). Pozible and StartSomeGood have similarly raised multiple millions, with portions going to fund social change projects. Similar stories abound with all crowdfunding platforms. Such results certainly indicate that crowdfunding is successfully carrying out its remit of bringing people together with projects that matter to them, and allowing ease and convenience in one's donations, a point also made by Rob Caslick – and cited earlier – in discussion of his project funding experience with Chuffed. Crowdfunding, as Chuffed stresses, also saves us all from having to deal with charity muggers (*chuggers*) face to face (Chuffed, n.d.-a); more broadly it enables the win-win scenario outlined by Paramanathan where our personal interests are able to coincide exactly and easily with our philanthropic interests.

It also, as noted, facilitates the easy connection of activists and their causes with broad social networks. And, in achieving these connections, Paramanathan is also at pains to stress the potential of crowdfunding to make the entire process of supporting a cause as easy and guilt-free as possible, with campaign or cause supporters not being judged on their commitments or investments or their identifications. Crowdfunding is, in many ways, the absolute culmination of clicktivism, if clicktivism is understood in positive terms.

Is this however a paradigm shift in the giving sector? Does ease of commitment count as a paradigm shift? Is it a paradigm shift to have one's affectively driven individual interests – and indeed one's consumerism – acting as the foremost driver and barometer of one's altruism and one's commitment to social change? These are complex questions taking us into issues of what may be considered worthy motivations for social cause support, and whether 'right' action is somehow better when difficult and seen in opposition to our selfish individual interests, but the point we want to draw forth here concerns the nexus platform-based crowdfunding builds between activism and social change and neoliberalism, a nexus also considered in chapter 4 with reference to the capacities of apps to support social change. And here our question concerns whether crowdfunding marks a model in which what is a fundamentally neoliberal paradigm can effectively take up the work of social change. Our answer is both 'yes' and 'no'. On the one hand, crowdfunding clearly can be brought to the purposes of social change. Arguably, each campaign striving to provide support for Australia's asylum seekers is working also to inculcate more positive responses to asylum seekers across the public sphere. Campaign stories, after all, are educative in alerting audiences to specific issues and are arguably also successful in humanising the people and situations at stake. And, on this front at least, crowdfunding's digitalised platforms are extremely effective insofar as the criteria for a successful campaign – personalised stories, a focus on affect as well as reason, a use of images (video and still) as well as text and the asking for very little while still offering a perk for contribution – match well with the affordances of digital communications and networking and with the requirements of successful activism.

On the other hand, crowdfunding runs in accordance with a neoliberal logic of market success informed by popular support. Projects succeed only if they appeal to potential funders, meaning that the action or social change being looked for needs to already have attained a high level of popular support. This is exacerbated with platforms that require founders to achieve their stated funding goal before they receive any donations. Added to this is that crowdfunding can be pertinent and successful only if the action or social change desired can be detailed and is deliverable in monetary terms. This is an important but problematic point insofar as it requires ideas of social change to be transformed into very specific kinds of goals which can be given a financial footing and which will appear personable and thereby significant to funders. Another problematic relates back to points made in earlier chapters concerning the tendency of Web 2.0 technologies to facilitate the development of what has been called echo chambers, meaning that appeals for support may not often be shared outside of *safe* networks. This, of course, is what entails the win-win situation Paramanathan alludes to, but it is a restriction of the potential educative and deliberative effects of social change–oriented campaigns if they are shared only with those already ideologically predisposed to support them. This is Sauter's (2014) point once again that an activist working within the affordances of Web 2.0 technologies has few chances of having his or her message read except by the already like-minded. These points together – despite the generic Web 2.0 promise of expanded networks – deliver a much-reduced domain in which to strive for ideals of social change. At the same time, and arguably even more problematically, they proffer a redefinition of social change away from broad ideals encompassing systemic change to small-scale practical projects, with one result being most likely that ideals of social change – as manifest within and supported by crowdfunding – take on the work of 'fixing' in-system problems rather than reconceiving systems themselves.

REFERENCES

ABC News. (2013, September 24). Tim Flannery relaunches scrapped Climate Commission as community-funded body. Retrieved from http://www.abc.net.au/news/2013-09-24/tim-flannery-to-relaunch-climate-commission/4976608.

Amtzis, R. (2014). Crowdsourcing from the ground up: How a new generation of Nepali nonprofits uses social media to successfully promote its initiatives. *Journal of Creative Communications*, *9*(2), 127–146.

Agrawal, A., Catalini, C. & Goldfarb, A. (2011). *The geography of crowdfunding*. NBER No. w16820. [Working Paper].Retrieved from https://papers.ssrn.com/sol3/papers.cfm?abstract_id=1770375.

Art of Kickstarter. (2016, June 15). Crowdfunding demographics and statistics. Retrieved from http://artofthekickstart.com/crowdfunding-demographics-statistics-infographic/.

Australian Associated Press. (2013, October 5). Climate council raises $1m through its Obama-style fundraising drive. *The Guardian*. Retrieved from https://www.theguardian.com/.

Belleflamme, P., Lambert, T., & Schwienbacher, A. (2011). *Crowdfunding: Tapping the right crowd*. [Working paper]. Retrieved from http://innovation-regulation2.telecom-paristech.fr/wp-content/uploads/2012/10/Belleflamme-CROWD-2012-06-20_SMJ.pdf.

Belleflamme, P., Lambert, T. & Schwienbacher, A. (2014). Crowdfunding: Tapping the right crowd. *Journal of Business Venturing*, *29*(5), 585–609.

Bennett, L., Chin, B. & Jones, B. (2015). Crowdfunding: A *New Media & Society* special issue. *New Media & Society*, *17*(2), 141–148.

Best, J., & Ness, S. (2014). Crowdfunding: A historical perspective. In S. Dresner (Ed.), *Crowdfunding: A guide to raising capital on the internet* (pp. 3–14). Somerset, NJ: John Wiley & Sons.

Borst, I., Moser, C. & Ferguson, J. (2017). From friendfunding to crowdfunding: Relevance of relationships, social media, and platform activities to crowdfunding performance. *New Media & Society*, 1–9. doi:10.1177/1461444817694599.

Brooks, C. (2013, April 4). What is microfinance? *Business News Daily*. Retrieved from http://www.businessnewsdaily.com/.

Brown, W. (2005). *Edgework: Critical essays on knowledge and politics*. Princeton, NJ: Princeton University Press.

CAF. (2016). *CAF world giving index 2016*. Retrieved from https://www.cafonline.org/about-us/publications/2016-publications/download-the-caf-world-giving-index-2016.

Calic, G., & Mosakowski, E. (2016). Kicking off social entrepreneurship: How a sustainability orientation influences crowdfunding success. *Journal of Management Studies*, *53*(5), 738–767.

Chang, C. (2015, October 17). Could charity muggers become a thing of the past as the focus turns to win-win transactions? *News.com.au*. Retrieved from http://www.news.com.au/finance/could-charity-muggers-become-a-thing-of-the-past-as-the-focus-turns-to-winwin-transactions/news-story/c7cb901af3ae8eb38f7f73f05329d586.

Chang, C. (2015, October 17). Could charity muggers become a thing of the past as the focus turns to win-win transactions? *News.com.au*. Retrieved from http://www.news.com.au/.

Chuffed. (n.d.-a). About Chuffed. Retrieved from https://chuffed.org/about.

Chuffed. (n.d.-b). Create your page. Retrieved from https://chuffed.org/how-it-workscrowdfunding/create-your-page.

Chuffed. (n.d.-c). Discover. Retrieved from https://chuffed.org/discover.

Chuffed. (n.d.-d). Start a crowdfunding campaign. Retrieved from https://chuffed.org/start.

Climate Council. (n.d.). About. Retrieved from https://www.climatecouncil.org.au/about-us.

CrowdExpert. (2015–2016a). *Crowdfunding industry statistics 2015 2016: The MassolutionCrowdfunding Industry 2015 Report*. Retrieved from http://crowdexpert.com/crowdfunding-industry-statistics/.

CrowdExpert. (2015–2016b). *Deal index: Democratizing finance report*. Retrieved from http://crowdexpert.com/crowdfunding-industry-statistics/.

Crowdfunding. (n.d.) In *Oxford online dictionary*. Retreived from https://en.oxforddictionaries.com/definition/crowdfunding.

Davies, R. (2015). Three provocations for civic crowdfunding. *Information, Communication & Society*, *18*(3), 342–355.

Díaz, J. D., & Cacheda, B. G. (2016). Financing social activism: Crowdfunding and advocatory social movement in Spain in times of crisis. In J. Bertot, E. Estevez, & S. Mellouli (Eds.), *Proceedings of ICEGOV 9th International Conference on Theory and Practice of Electronic Governance* (pp. 139–148). Hammamet,Tunisia: Association for Computing Machinery. Retreived from http://dl.acm.org/citation.cfm?id=2910019&picked=prox.

Feeny, S., & Clarke, M. (2007). What determines Australia's response to emergencies and natural disasters? *The Australian Economic Review*, *40*(1), 24–36.

Gibbs, S. (2013, November 27). The Butterfly Effect: Typhoon Haiyan's silver lining. *Generosity*. Retrieved from http://www.generositymag.com.au/.

Giroux, H. A. (2014, April 26). Neoliberalism's war on democracy. *Truthout*. Retrieved from http://www.truth-out.org/opinion/item/23306-neoliberalisms-war-on-democracy.

Giving Australia 2016. (2016). Giving Australia 2016 fact sheet - individual giving. [Fact sheet]. Retrieved from http://www.communitybusinesspartnership.gov.au/wp-content/uploads/2017/04/giving_australia_2016_fact_sheet_-_individual_giving_accessible.pdf.

GoFundMe. (2010). Common questions. Retrieved from https://www.gofundme.com/questions.

Golić, Z. (2014). Advantages of crowdfunding as an alternative source of financing of small and medium-sized enterprises. In *Proceedings of the Faculty of Economics in East Sarajevo 8* (pp.39–48). East Sarajevo, Bosnia and Herzegovina: University East Sarajevo University. Retrieved from http://doisrpska.nub.rs/index.php/zrefis/article/viewFile/1440/1342.

Good2Give. (2016, October 26). *World becomes more generous than ever*. Retrieved from https://good2give.ngo/2016/10/26/world-becomes-generous-ever-worldgiving-index-reports/.

Hamman, E. (2015). Save the reef! Civic crowdfunding and public interest environmental litigation. *QUT Law Review*, *15*(1), 159–173.

Hartley, L. K., & Pedersen, A. (2015). Asylum seekers and resettled refugees in Australia: Predicting social policy attitude from prejudice versus emotion. *Journal of Social and Political Psychology*, *3*(1), 179–197.

Indiegogo (n.d.). Indiegogo. Retrieved from https://www.indiegogo.com.

Indiegogo. (2008). Frequently asked questions. Retrieved from https://www.indiegogo.com/#/picks_for_you.

Kickstarter. (2009). Most importantly, Kickstarter works. Retrieved from https://www.kickstarter.com/learn?ref=nav.

Kleemann, F., Voß, G. G. & Rieder, K. (2008). Un(der)paid innovators: The commercial utilization of consumer work through crowdsourcing. *Science, Technology & Innovation Studies*, *4*(1), 5–26.

Kollmorgen, A. (2016, February). Are crowdfunding sites the real winners? *Choice*. Retrieved from https://www.choice.com.au/.

Macht, S. & Weatherston, J. (2015). Academic research on crowdfunders: What's been done and what's to come? *Strategic Change*, *24*(2), 191–205.

Maguire, A. (2012, December 18). Crowdfunding platforms in Australia & New Zealand. Crowdfund it. [Web log post]. Retrieved from http://www.crowdfundit.com.au/2012/12/18/crowdfunding-platforms-in-australian-and-new-zealand/.

Maguire, A. (2014). *Crowdfund it!* (3rd ed.). Canberra, Australia: Editia.

Manning, S., & Bejarano, T. A. (2017). Convincing the crowd: Entrepreneurial storytelling in crowdfunding campaigns. *Strategic Organization, 15*(2), 194–219.

Markus, A. (2012). *Mapping social cohesion: The Scanlon Foundation Surveys Summary Report*. Melbourne, Australia: Monash University. Retrieved from http://monash.edu/mapping-population/public-opinion/surveys/scanlon-foundation-surveys/.

Markus, A. (2014). *Mapping social cohesion: The Scanlon Foundation Surveys 2014*. Melbourne, Australia: Monash University. Retrieved from http://monash.edu/mapping-population/public-opinion/surveys/scanlon-foundation-surveys/.

McHugh-Dillon, H. (2015). *'If they are genuine refugees, why?' Public attitudes to unauthorised arrivals in Australia*. Melbourne, Australia: Victorian Foundation for Survivors of Torture.

McKay, F. H., Thomas, S. L. & Kneebone, S. (2012). 'It would be okay if they came through proper channels': Community perceptions and attitudes towards asylum seekers in Australia. *Journal of Refugee Studies, 25*, 113–133.

Mollick, E. (2014). The dynamics of crowdfunding: An exploratory study. *Journal of Business Venturing, 29*(1), 1–16.

Mummery, J. (2017). *Radicalizing democracy for the twenty-first century*. Oxon and New York, NY: Routledge.

Mummery, J., & Rodan, D. (2003). Discourses of democracy in the aftermath of 9/11 and other events: Protectivism versus humanitarianism. *Continuum: Journal of Media & Cultural Studies, 17*(4), 433–443.

Mummery, J., & Rodan, D. (2007). Discursive Australia: Refugees, Australianness, and the Australian public sphere. *Continuum: Journal of Media & Cultural Studies, 21*(3), 347–360.

Oliver, A. (2014). *Lowy institute poll 2014*. Lowy Institute. Retrieved from https://www.lowyinstitute.org/publications/lowy-institute-poll-2014.

Paramanathan, P. (2016, September 7). What we've learnt from over 100,000 donations on Chuffed.org [Web log post]. Retrieved from https://chuffed.org/blog/what-weve-learnt-from-over-100000-donations-on-chuffedorg?signupModal=true.

The Parliament of the Commonwealth of Australia. (2006, June). *Australia's response to the Indian Ocean Tsunami*. Joint Standing Committee on Foreign Affairs, Defence and Trade. Commonwealth of Australia. Retrieved from https://knowledge.aidr.org.au/media/3766/fullreport_pdf.pdf.

Pebler, L. (2013, March 15). Guest post: My gigantic issue with the Veronica Mars Kickstarter. *Revenge of the Fans* [Web log post]. Retrieved from http://www.suzanne-scott.com/2013/03/15/guest-post-my-gigantic-issue-with-the-veronica-mars-kickstarter/.

Perkins, A. (2008, June 3). A short history of microfinance. *The Guardian*. Retrieved from https://www.theguardian.com/katine/2008/jun/03/livelihoods.projectgoals1.

Pozible. (2015, September 30). 10,000 projects later [Web log post]. Retrieved from https://blog.pozible.com/10-000-projects-later-9021d1f7153b#.knzqhsnh9.

Rodan, D., & Mummery, J. (2005). Discursive Australia: Public discussion of refugees in the early twenty-first century. In *Mobile Boundaries Rigid Worlds: Refereed Conference Proceedings*. Sydney, Australia: Centre for Research on Social Inclusion, Macquarie University. Retrieved from http://www.crsi.mq.edu.au/mobileboundaries.htm.

Sauter, M. (2014). *The coming swarm: DdoS actions, hacktivism, and civil disobedience on the internet*. New York, NY: Bloomsbury.

Scevak, N. (n.d.). Non-profit crowdfunding platform Chuffed.org raises $1.1 million seed round led by Blackbird Ventures. *Startupdaily*. Retrieved from http://www.startupdaily.net/2016/03/non-profit-crowdfunding-platform-chuffed-org-raises-1-1-million-seed-round-led-blackbird-ventures/.

Schwienbacher, A., & Larralde, B. (2012). Crowdfunding of small entrepreneurial ventures. In D. Cumming (Ed.), *The Oxford Handbook of Entrepreneurial Finance* (pp. 369–391). New York, NY: Oxford University Press.

StartSomeGood. (n.d.). About us and FAQ. Retrieved from https://startsomegood.com/about?view=what_we_do.

Startupdaily. (n.d.). Non-profit crowdfunding platform Chuffed.org raises $1.1 million seed round led by Blackbird Ventures. *Startupdaily*. Retrieved from http://www.startupdaily.net/2016/03/non-profit-crowdfunding-platform-chuffed-org-raises-1-1-million-seed-round-led-blackbird-ventures/.

Statistic Brain. (2016). Crowdfunding industry statistics. [Web log statistics]. Retrieved from http://www.statisticbrain.com/crowdfunding-platform-statistics/.

Stiver, A., Barroca, L., Minocha, S., Richards, M. & Roberts, D. (2015). Civic crowdfunding research: Challenges, opportunities, and future agenda. *New, Media & Society*, *17*(2), 249–271.

Strickler, Y. (2011, February 9). What are some unique rewards for a kickstarter project? *Quora*. Retrieved from https://www.quora.com/What-are-some-unique-rewards-for-a-Kickstarter-project.

Suhnan, A., Pedersen, A. & Hartley, L. K. (2012). Re-examining prejudice against asylum seekers in Australia: The role of people smugglers, the perception of threat, and acceptance of false beliefs. *The Australian Community Psychologist*, *24*, 79–97.

Swan, D. (2016, August 30). Chuffed.org passes $10 million in step towards social good economy. *The Australian*. Retrieved from http://www.theaustralian.com.au.

Therriault, K. (2015, October 15). 15 Pozible statistics from 5 years and 10,000 projects. *CrowdfundingPR*. Retrieved from http://www.crowdfundingpr.org/15-pozible-statistics-5-years-10000-projects/.

UMR Research. (2013, December). *Australian perspective: Insight into asylum seekers and mining*. Sydney, Australia: UMR Pty Ltd.

Wade, E. (2014, February 9). Pozible or kickstarter? Picking the right crowdfunding experience. *Techly*. Retrieved from http://www.techly.com.au/2014/02/10/pozible-kickstarter-picking-right-crowdfunding-crowd/.

Chapter 7

Future Possibilities

Julie Pagano, a self-proclaimed queer cisgender middle-class white woman who works as a software engineer, makes the point in one of her blog posts focused on the fight for marginalised people in tech that there is no one right way to be an activist and to participate in the struggle for social change. As she puts this,

> Everyone is in a different situation. Everyone has different energy, availability, safety concerns, health, etc. to consider. Pick the approach that works for you. You don't have to pick only one approach or stay with it forever. You can mix and match and ebb and flow. There is no one 'right' way. (Pagano, 2014)

Furthermore, as she stresses in this same post, 'let people choose the tactics they want to use and the battles they want to fight. You probably don't know their situation, and it's crappy and presumptuous to tell them what to do. Not everyone can fight every battle, not even those with lots of energy' (Pagano, 2014). In many ways, this is a point that sits at the heart of the digital activism debate and is at stake every time a digital action which arguably has sociopolitical implications is derided as not really being activism (this is the clicktivism taunt). Activism, as any attempt at a definition shows, has no limited suite of actions, an action rather is activist oriented if it is taken to effect social change. (Note, however, that an authentic *activist* intentionality cannot be insisted upon as integral for an act to be recognised as activist; acts may be counted as activist no matter the individual's orienting motivation.) This being so, the simple act of adding one's name to an online petition against whaling or fracking or live export or for marriage equality or the stopping of Adani's mining access in northern Queensland – no matter the motivation – is arguably as much an activist act as participating in a demonstration outside a civic building on one of these same matters. We also want to stress that actions are not definable as activist only if they achieve their specified change. This is a point Pagano makes too when she reminds readers of another activist's setting of an analogy between activism and a chorus:

> Let's say that fighting sexism is like a chorus of people singing a continuous tone. If enough people sing, the tone will be continuous even though each of the singers will be stopping singing to take a breath every now and then. The way to change things is for more people to sing rather than for the same small group of people to try to sing louder and never breathe. (firecat, 2006)

It is joining in the singing, in other words, that matters, not the mode of that joining in or even if you have to take a break to breathe. It is, to continue the chorus analogy further, the chorus not the individual singer that will facilitate change – particularly insofar as both choirs and digital campaigning may be relying on only weakly linked participants. And yet, of course, without the participation of multiple individuals (and actions) there can be neither chorus nor change.

Digital culture, then, which as we have shown from the beginning is all about social connectivity and networking, offers multiple modes not just of joining into a chorus but of alerting others to the chorus. It can be extremely effective with regard to the visibility of a social cause insofar as it is ultimately informed by the capacity of produsers – even dubjected ones – to tag, appropriate, remix and recirculate material from public many-to-many accounts to private accounts and back to public accounts again. After all, it is through this recirculating, retweeting, sharing and liking of material that activists and social change organisations can connect with – and mobilise – the private feelings, beliefs and actions of individuals as well as other activist groups, as well as keep issues visible in a public agenda. Social networking sites, Internet and email, in other words, can make it easy for individuals to identify – and identify and connect with – issue-based causes that are personal to them, further facilitating activist groups in their quests for new members, supporters and advocates. Furthermore, with 'issue-ified' campaigns (Marres, 2015), and the capacities of Web 2.0 multimedia communications, activists can keep topics continually foregrounded in multiple public spheres. As an activist with the Black Lives Matter movement, DeRay McKesson, has noted:

> I'm mindful that we aren't born woke, something wakes us up, and for so many people, what woke them up was a tweet or a Facebook post, an Instagram post, a picture. (McKesson & Opam, 2016)

This book, then, has been an exploration and illustration of some of the opportunities possible for this waking up and singing within digital culture.

More specifically, our task has been to examine how digital culture can offer productive mechanisms and spaces for the shaping of interested and involved citizens, public attitudes and society itself, to allow, in other words, for the progression of activist-sponsored progressive social change. In particular, our aims have been to examine the use of digital multi-platform tools by activist organisations and advocates for social change to (a) disseminate information and raise public awareness; (b) invoke, inform and shape public debate through the provision of information, spaces and mechanisms for public deliberation, and the invocation of affect to support mobilisation; and (c) garner public support (including funding) for social issues and for associated social change.

This has also been a book primarily set within the context of Australian activism. This seemed necessary insofar as we are both Australian academics and, according to the frames we have just set up, activists. The Australian context, in other words, is that which we know best. And Australia – as a neoliberally inflected democratic state but one with a strong tradition in social welfare, and a state that is currently convulsing around the need to shift its economy from being fundamentally informed by fossil fuels, with a range of correlated public debates to do with the value given to the environment and non-human species – provides a very rich source, indeed, of activist case studies. There are, of course, many other case studies and issues we could have chosen to examine – there always are – and we are by no means suggesting that this has been a complete account of (digital) activism within the Australian context. Case studies and examples have, however, been chosen by us because we think they provide interesting and useful insights into the domain under question and because we have attempted to at least touch on the bulk of the major issues currently under debate by activists and social change advocates within the Australian (digital) public sphere. Our striving to give voice to Australian issues and movements has necessarily curtailed our engagement with transnational activist organisations. Certainly, many of these do have Australian arms or projects – the World Wildlife Fund, for instance, has been a substantial player in the struggle around protecting the Great Barrier Reef against the impacts of mining development – but Australia is also currently the site of rancorous political disputes around who should be driving calls for change. Indeed, attempts have been made in Australia, particularly with regard to environmental issues, to place limits around who would have the right to speak up for a specific cause. Such attempts are underpinned by a range of bitter criticisms by state officials of offshore activist organisations *interfering* with domestic politics. Although we do not hold to the same position as these critiques – rather finding the interactions and alignments of transnational organisations with local ones vibrant and significant in establishing that stronger chorus needed for effective activism and social change – we did decide to prioritise Australian-based organisations, partially also with the aim of giving additional visibility to the work of these smaller groups. Although we hold to this focus in this chapter too, it is important to keep in mind that Australian activisms are interconnected with broader social change movements, and transnational bodies and connections do a lot in informing and vitalising Australian-specific movements.

There is one further point to make here, before we turn to examine for the last time the themes and issues explored throughout this book. This concerns Australia's own assumptions regarding activism. As we have noted, Australia – as with the vast majority of states in the twenty-first century – is currently giving a high status to ideas and practices arguably supporting national and public security, a move which is having an effect in delegitimising and undercutting a range of forms of activism. (This is exemplified by the idea of the National Security State as discussed in chapter 4.) As we have shown in previous chapters, some forms and focuses of activisms are being seen as threatening to the (neoliberal) state, and Australia is no exception with regard to this increasingly common perception. Environmental and animal welfare activisms, in particular, are being targeted as problematic, with recent and current attempts being made to criminalise a range of activities associated with these causes. Such a delegitimising of activism and protest is, however, problematic in the Australian context insofar as there are several significant points in Australia's public history which are underpinned by activist and public action. Here we might include the actions of protesting miners at the Eureka Stockade in Ballarat, Victoria, in 1854, which have been seen as emblematic of Australia's development as a democracy, as well as Prime Minister Billy Hughes's attempts to bring in conscription for the First World War, which were rejected twice by the Australian people in two public referenda in 1916 and 1917. Also for consideration here might be the significance of Indigenous Australian activists whose work was instrumental in the 1960s onwards in achieving for Indigenous Australians citizenship and equal pay, as well as (some) rights to their land and to the preservation of cultural heritage. On another issue, it was activism that halted the damming of the Franklin and Gordon rivers in Tasmania, work that was instrumental in the development of the Greens movement from an activist organisation to Australia's third most significant political party (Jackson, 2016). It is also worth noting that trade unions – along with friendly societies and mutual cooperatives – are arguably among Australia's earliest manifestations of 'activist' civil society; they are in many ways Australia's original non-governmental organisations and have played a highly significant role in the development of Australia's political history (Johns, 2002). In other words, the activist and civic voice has long been of import within this country, and attempts to problematise the legitimacy of this voice, to criminalise it, continue to be highly contested within the Australian public sphere.

DIGITAL CULTURES, PLATFORMS AND ACTIVISM

> In five years, the definition of what it means to be active and aware will be different. We've already started to push the space and say that a protester's not only somebody who goes into the street. A protester is not only somebody who disrupts a board meeting. An organizer is not only somebody who sits in the basement of a church every Wednesday. We have pushed the boundaries. When I think about what it means to protest, a protester is somebody who tells the truth in public and there are many ways to do that. (McKesson & Opam, 2016)

If the previous paragraphs have brought to the fore some of the contexts informing our examinations throughout this book of the different modes and focuses of Australian digital activism, what remains for us now is to return one last time to our key themes, arguments and achievements. In particular, as we noted earlier, we need to assess the affordances of digital culture to deliver productive mechanisms and spaces for the shaping and achievement of progressive social change and for shaping everyday consumer citizens into what we can call everyday activist citizens. This is our early point again that activists are focused not simply on achieving material changes in policy on their issues of concern but on actively changing beliefs and values in the broader community. (This is the point that legislative change needs to be preceded by changes in community attitudes.) And we need, as our final focus, to assess the future potential of digital culture to meet the key political, social and ethical challenges facing activists and advocacy groups in the twenty-first century. First, however, is to consider the current affordances of digital culture for activist and social change ends, in aim of which we wish to draw specific attention to several interlinked points.

To begin with, then, it is clearly inarguable that digital culture enables and facilitates the mass – potentially viral – circulation and recirculation of symbols, memes and trending topics. It is this viral potentiality that we see has first been so fundamental to activist campaigns, enabling them to stay at the top of newsfeeds and hence – given the increasing blurring between offline and online media topics – as visible topics within the public sphere. It is this viral potentiality that thus gives activist groups and causes the most chance of waking people up and having them join the chorus, to draw again on the analogies used in the beginning of this chapter, and of thereby creating and utilising tipping point moments. Alongside, and indeed informed by this viral potentiality, the private-to-public (and back again) networking models made possible through digital platforms such as Facebook, Twitter and YouTube, and even demonstrated in apps, as well as in email, have clearly vastly benefitted activist groups. In particular, the connective action networks (Bennett & Segerberg, 2012) such platforms facilitate have allowed for the building of weak social ties. As we have shown in our previous chapters, these can clearly facilitate forms of public mobilisation, which do not require participants to identify and develop a trusting relationship with the ongoing movement – that is, to explicitly label, commit or recognise themselves as part of a collective identity. This is important as we would consider weak ties – in being quick in establishment – as instrumental for topics going viral, for crowdfunding success and even app uptake and use and for the effectiveness of massive topical online petitions and campaigns such as Animals Australia's targeting of McDonald's via Facebook (see chapter 3). Certainly, weak ties may be as speedily broken as they are established – with individuals so tied tending perhaps to know more about what is trending rather than evincing any deep commitment to the activist cause – but the affordances of social media platforms do mean that such ties can also be easily re-established. Weak ties, thus, not only facilitate activist abilities to achieve and then harness enormous public outcries as one tactic towards achieving social change, but their use also importantly lessens the chances of activist activity being damaged by internal dissension about the group's collective identity or by individual burnout. Weak ties can allow the chorus to continue even as some breathe.

Certainly, as we have shown, not all Web 2.0 platforms serve the same function for activists. Even if all platforms – being so networked – facilitate issue visibility and virality, campaigns engaging different platforms do so differently; GetUp! after all does not work the same way as Chuffed, and the Make It Possible campaign is run differently from campaigns in AVAAZ. What is evident, however, is that platforms are most effective for digital activists when they are understood as best able to achieve fairly narrow purposes but en masse. That is, the more targeted the purpose – in both its scope and its fit with platform affordances – the more effective an action can be achieved at mass level. This, of course, is particularly the case within the domains of crowdfunding and app development (see chapters 4 and 6), but we would also stress that if activist actions are reliant in digital culture primarily on weak links – there are some counterpoints to this as we have previously noted – messages about campaigns and actions in any platform need to be specific and to the point to establish those links and facilitate their going viral. Here the works of AVAAZ and GetUp! but also of Animals Australia are pertinent examples, particularly with regard to their common awareness of the importance of timing for campaign releases.

What, of course, increases the potential efficacy of these weak links is the ubiquity, convenience and ease of use of the platforms and apps comprising digital culture throughout much contemporary life in a state such as Australia. This is their capacity to support, as one commentator has put this, a 'new kind of volunteering, giving one's name and money without leaving the house' (Coombs, 2016). Also important here is the special role that has been gained by the hardware vehicles of digital culture in everyday lives. As we noted in chapter 4, for instance, the devices which are now used by many users to access platforms and apps are intimate technologies (Goggin, 2011). Many of them are now highly mobile, and furthermore include geolocative capacities, meaning that they have become devices that users take with them to use wherever they go. They are typically carried or worn close to the body, and they tend to be kept nearby even when users are resting or sleeping. (They also require users to remain close to power stations so they can remain charged and ready for use.) It is also this device mobility that makes platforms such as Facebook, Twitter and YouTube, and apps such as CluckAR, so very effective in their capacity to link into and colonise everyday life, and to facilitate the weak links comprising much everyday activism. A user may, in other words, make only a weak connection with an app or its cause, but its convenience of use – and the strength of the user's connection with the app's mobile vehicle for use – can make that connection effective enough.

This reliance on weak links is also, we would suggest, informed by another of the affordances of digital culture, that of the support of digital culture for both the visual and the affective. Here the point is that activists, as we have shown, well know that campaign support is most easily gained through motivational frames such as moral shock and the evoking of various emotions, both negative and positive. This must be doubly so in the case of digital culture, if most actions are taken on the basis of weak links. It is also perhaps this recognition of reliance on weak links that is behind the digital activist's preference for evoking positive rather than negative emotions; as many guides to creating a successful campaign (whether activist or marketing oriented) note, a too-negative campaign will be passed over and has a substantially lower chance of going viral. It is with this need to create a positive affective response that the visual affordances of all platforms have been integral for digital activism insofar as images are peculiarly able to establish affective resonances towards the mobilising of action. This, of course, is a realisation at the heart of crowdfunding, for example, with guidelines towards achieving an effective campaign indeed typically stressing the significance of the visual (see chapter 6).

Digital campaigns are not only affectively sticky, however. We have also noted that the affordances of digital culture enable activists to effectively combine affective strategies with at least the capacity for some deliberative models of exchange (e.g., via the enabling of comments). Such combination is important because activists are desirous of participants gaining an understanding of their movement or organisation's claims and positions, given that such understanding is required for the building of longer-term member commitments from the basis of initial weak links. Indeed, it is this very desire that has arguably informed the development and roll-out of the Vegan Voices app (see chapter 4). What is important within this work, however, is that ideas of productive deliberative exchange are not constrained to those of some procedurally legitimated discussion. Deliberative practices, as we have stressed at several points in this book, rather need to foreground the importance of (a) actually mobilising participants to engage in debate over issues of public concern (they need some affective stickiness in other words), (b) including more than simply mainstream perspectives and arguments in debate, and providing spaces in which participants can (c) argue for preferred views, and (d) engage with differing viewpoints.

This is deliberative work, we consider, digital activists excel in and which is illustrated in a range of ways throughout the preceding chapters. The combination of the ubiquity of digital culture and the stress on affective mobilisation aimed at establishing only weak links – at least initially – has been, as we have shown, highly effective in engaging participants in issues of public concern. These, of course, are issues of concern that are already in dispute, and activist campaigns – insofar as they tend, by definition, to be engaging with issues either ignored by or inadequately tackled by the state (a situation, of course, exacerbated within a neoliberally inflected culture which tends to divest itself of the need to engage with social causes) – are constitutively striving to not just bring non-mainstream views and arguments into the public domain but gain traction for them. Digital culture too, by definition, is connective and social in a way that facilitates debate, and all platforms support interaction. More specifically, despite long-standing criticisms of factionalism and echo chambers – of digital domains tending to support like-minded people only talking to each other – we contend that digital platforms can clearly enable both communicative enclaves and shared nodes. It is these points we consider particularly essential for the deliberative aim of facilitating the inclusion and engagement of marginalised and excluded voices. Social media, for example, are clearly relied upon throughout the work of both Indigenous political bloggers and animal and environmental activists, all of whom are very explicitly using the varied affordances of digital platforms to build broader understandings of and connections with what are typically non-mainstream issues (see, e.g., chapters 2–4).

Another productive capacity of digital culture that is clearly being strongly utilised within activist campaigning is its capacity to be reshaped for specific interests. Certainly, as we have taken pains to show, current digital culture is intimately informed by neoliberalism, but it is also one of the important aspects of neoliberalism itself that has meant that digital culture remains so capable of being reshaped for multiple interests. That is, neoliberalism by its own definition always promotes and supports individual efforts in revisioning and refashioning its own products. It is this doubled capacity, then, that we would identify as enabling activists to both repurpose existing platforms and develop new platforms and apps for activist causes (an issue we have explored in chapter 4). Certainly, the development of completely new platforms is expensive and may well appear to require some kind of corporate investment, but development is nonetheless very much able to be – and is – carried out by activist groups. This is a point that Black Lives Matter activist DeRay McKesson takes pains to stress:

> There's no one way to use tech platforms. If we had used Twitter the way that all the articles say that you use Twitter, we wouldn't be here. We use it in a different way. We use Vine in a different way. You think about the beginning of the protests. It was before Periscope. It was before you could upload videos on Twitter. We were really patchworking platforms to make them work for us. (McKesson & Opam, 2016)

Activist capacities for such patchworking are given strength by two factors. First, of course, is the rise of digitally enabled crowdfunding, with platforms like Chuffed working in conjunction with social media platforms to facilitate easy connections for activists and their causes with broad public and private funding networks (an issue explored in chapter 6). Second, but also of importance for this kind of shaping work by activists, is the continued focus within digital cultures on the development of open source software. This refers to software in which the underlying source code is not only available to see but open for anyone to freely use, adapt and build upon. The affordances of open source software – including the broader point that software development can itself be carried out by a networked community – can thus mitigate many of the costs associated with activist-developed digital initiatives, allowing 'necessity and not resources' to be the 'greatest driving force behind innovation in e-democracy/e-activism' (Clift, 2004). As Clift (2004) stresses in what is his introduction to an article on open source tools that can be used by activists (see Bashaw & Gifford, 2004), the emergence of open source has been integral for what he calls the 'democratization of activism'.

A final affordance of digital culture for activism also arises from its ubiquity and colonisation of everyday life, but in this instance we are concerned with rejecting the idea – discussed at several points in the preceding chapters – that actions online are somehow intrinsically separable from those carried out in the so-called real world. This is the idea again that so-called clicktivism is not real activism, being too easy and not always needing much commitment or investment from participants. We would rather argue – and would see the campaigns and platforms we have examined as demonstrating – that if the overarching drive of all activist movements and organisations is to get individuals to participate in social cause debates, then, while this certainly occurs both online and offline, the digital models we have examined show clear success in facilitating such engagement. Indeed, they make such engagement easy through their own ubiquity – action can be carried out at the individual's convenience – and on the basis of their affective stickiness. We would certainly add that what drives and comprises participation and civic engagement is not – cannot be – limited to what happens online, a point verified by all of the activist work examined in this book where online campaigning and action is always entangled with offline campaigning and action. Indeed, while many of the activist campaigns we have examined here might have started online, in many cases they have also found their way into supermarkets, into and onto shopping bags, into print newspapers, into courtrooms and into physical demonstrations of various kinds. Many campaigns were also reported on television programs, and advertised on buses and billboards, and on people's t-shirts as they marched the streets or stood at polling booths. Overall, we would say that all participation matters in movements for social change, even participation at that least taxing level of liking a post in Facebook, a post about stopping animal cruelty. After all, all participation – even the changing of the colour or appearance of one's Facebook profile – marks a public declaration to others of that individual's support to change how we treat animals or how we can save the reef. All participation marks a joining of the chorus.

Finally, we need to turn back one last time to the issue of the interrelatedness of digital activism with neoliberalism and the state context. Previously we have explored the tendencies of these contexts towards foregrounding both commodification and securitisation, and some of the tensions – negative and positive – these can give rise to with regard to the activist context and remit. Our focus now, however, is to pick up again some of our earlier discussions regarding the positive affordances of this context for activism. Here we stress again that activist movements and organisations tackle the issues considered inadequately addressed or not at all addressed by the state. What is also clear is that many may have accepted (or resigned themselves to accept) new neoliberal norms which advocate that no matter an individual's circumstances, he or she is personally responsible for changing them for the better. This is the point where neoliberalism can be understood as framing a lot of activism as either incoherent or wrongheaded or indeed criminal. It is here in this same nexus, however, that we would suggest that digital activism can flourish. If neoliberalism assumes that individual decisions about injustice and inequality are of more import – and more trustworthy – than collective ones, then activists are being highly effective in using an individualised digital culture to call for and collate those individual decisions.

That is, all of the platforms we have investigated with regard to their possible support of activism target individual users – striving specifically to facilitate an individual's connection of his or her personal interests, beliefs and values with specific issues, causes and campaigns – but they also work to connect those individuals with each other. Connection might be via weak links, but these links are still clearly enough for information to be shared, for non-mainstream positions and arguments to be canvassed, for individuals to avow their (weak) alignment with a specific issue or campaign and for the shaping of this activity into a just-in-time public intervention of some kind. As we have already noted, after all, one of the most important affordances of digital culture for activism is its ability to make an issue highly visible and to maintain that visibility. Hence, it is arguable that digital activist movements perform a vital role as through their work in awareness raising and issue visibility they can and do mobilise citizens for a collective purpose and secure a common goal for publics and counterpublics (see Warner, 2002). Furthermore, although in many ways digital activist campaigns require only the weak interconnection of participants, the connective capacities of the platforms most utilised in digital activist campaigns also possess capacities supportive of the building of stronger, more tightly interlinked communities around issues. And indeed many activist groups are striving to achieve just this.

Is this enough for social change then? Certainly digital activism – given all of the points just considered – seems better able to tackle and achieve narrow purposes rather than broad systemic change. Indeed, many of the affordances of digital activism seem positively curtailed in their ability to address systemic issues – the narrower the cause, the better seems rather to be the case (see chapters 4 and 6 for clear exemplifications of this point). And yet, this criticism seems to miss the point with regard to activism as a whole. As Pagano (2014) and firecat (2006) stress, no substantial social change has ever been carried on the basis of an individual action – it always takes a chorus (and time). As far as the capacity of digital activism goes towards effecting social change, then, what we would say matters more than the fact that individual digital actions are narrow is that these individual narrow actions can be understood as aligning towards a broader cause. If we turn again to the achievements of crowdfunders using Chuffed as discussed in chapter 6, this is the point that the narrow causes for funding being profiled by the campaign founders also need to have a clear and coherent story as to how each specific fundable goal will contribute towards the achievement of the broader campaign issue. Certainly, not every contributor will be interested in understanding the fit of their action in response to a trending topic with broader campaign goals, but this is the case too for many offline actions such as participating in a demonstration or march or donating towards a specific cause when meeting a chugger. (This is that point about intentionality noted at the beginning of this chapter; a specifically activist intentionality is never necessary for an action to work for an activist cause.) Added to our earlier point that digital activism should not – indeed cannot – be separable from offline activism insofar as they inform each other, we stress again that digital activism, even while narrow in focus, can be extremely effective in bringing broader social causes to public attention and into public debate. Furthermore, in some cases it is doing this more effectively than direct offline actions can, which can be very easily framed as a threat to the state, although such negative framing too can be countered through the digital activist's presentation and dissemination of campaign materials. One clear example here is the way Animals Australia supports and undertakes direct action tactics which are disavowed by the state – such as clandestine surveillance of factory farming and live export practices – and then uses the material gathered to make high-impact multimedia digital campaigns that have a history of going viral and contributing towards the achievement of offline change.

It is these diverse capacities, then, that in our eyes stand for and demonstrate the overarching significance of digital activism. It is these capacities that we think in effect give activism its ability to engage participants in what seems to be becoming an increasingly individualised and mediated culture. Digital activism is thus not another kind of activism; it is simply activism's re-tuning of itself to be as effective as possible in a culture where digitalisation and a neoliberally inflected individualism are ubiquitous. Just as campaigns are changed to take account of changing social conditions, so too the medium of activism must change. To do otherwise, to not have activist movements and campaigns take full advantage of the affordances of digital culture, would be to let ideas of appropriateness of action (and motivation) override the importance of the cause. To do otherwise would be to pretend that forming a chorus is not important. To do otherwise is in fact counter to activism per se.

REFERENCES

Bashaw, D., & Gifford, M. (2004, January 7). Top 10 open source tools for eActivism. *Democracies Online Newswire*. Retrieved from http://partnerships.typepad.com/civic/images/OStools.txt.

Bennett, W. L., & Segerberg, A. (2012). The logic of connective action: Digital media and the personalization of contentious politics. *Information, Communication & Society*, *15*(5), 739–768.

Clift, S. (2004, January 7). Introduction to top 10 open source tools for eActivism. *Democracies Online Newswire*. Retrieved from http://partnerships.typepad.com/civic/images/OStools.txt.

Coombs, A. (2016, February 4). Turning clicktivists into real-world activists. *Australian Financial Review*. Retrieved from http://www.afr.com/.

firecat. (2006, August 8). A simile on community activism [Web log post]. Retrieved from http://firecat.dreamwidth.org/439257.html.

Goggin, G. (2011). Ubiquitous apps: Politics of openness in global mobile communities. *Digital Creativity*, *22*(3), 148–159.

Jackson, S. (2016). *The Australian Greens: From activism to Australia's third party*. Melbourne, Australia: Melbourne University Publishing.

Johns, G. (2002). Trade unions and civil society. Address to the HR Nicholls Society XXIII Conference: *The Changing Paradigm: Freedom, Jobs, Prosperity*. March 2002. Melbourne, Australia. Retrieved from http://archive.hrnicholls.com.au/archives/vol23/vol23-5.php.

Marres, N. (2015). Why map issues? On controversy analysis as a digital method. *Science, Technology & Human Values*, *40*(5), 655–686.

McKesson, D., & Opam, K. (2016, November 29). Building tools for digital activism. *The Verge*. Retrieved from http://www.theverge.com/a/verge-2021/deray-mckesson-interview-black-lives-matter-digital-activism.

Pagano, J. (2014, June 8). On fighting for marginalized people in tech [Web log post]. Retrieved from http://juliepagano.com/blog/2014/06/08/on-fighting-for-marginalized-people-in-tech/.

Warner, M. (2002). *Publics and counterpublics*. Brooklyn, NY: Zone Books.

Index

Note: Page references for figures are italicised.